MW01273779

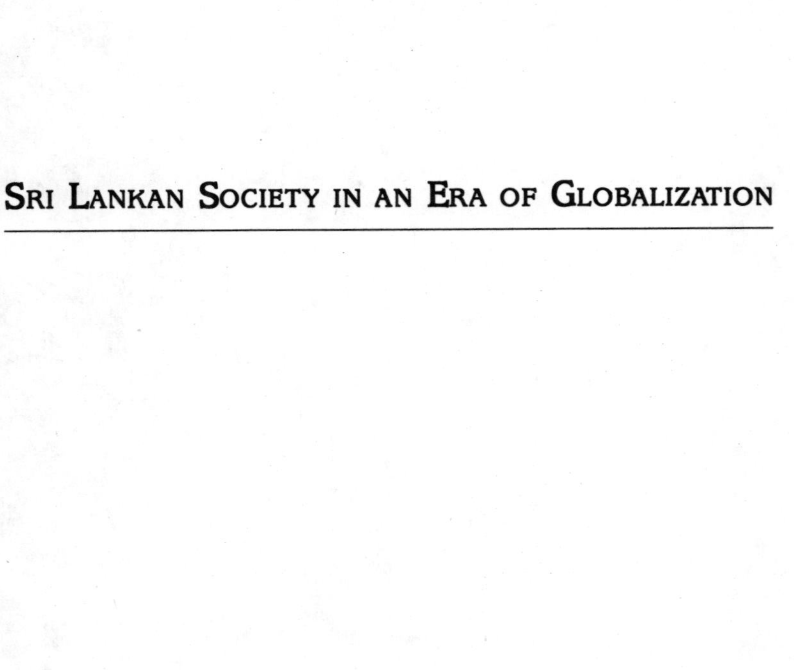

Sri Lankan Society in an Era of Globalization

SRI LANKAN SOCIETY IN AN ERA OF GLOBALIZATION

STRUGGLING TO CREATE A NEW SOCIAL ORDER

Editors

S.H. Hasbullah
Barrie M. Morrison

SAGE Publications
New Delhi • Thousand Oaks • London

First published in 2004 by

Sage Publications India Pvt Ltd
B-42, Panchsheel Enclave
New Delhi 110 017

Sage Publications Inc
2455 Teller Road
Thousand Oaks, California 91320

Sage Publications Ltd
1 Oliver's Yard, 55 City Road
London EC1Y 1SP

Published by Tejeshwar Singh for Sage Publications India Pvt Ltd, typeset in 10/12 Veljovic at S.R. Enterprises, New Delhi and printed at Chaman Enterprises, New Delhi.

Library of Congress Cataloging-in-Publication Data

Sri Lankan society in an era of globalization: struggling to create a new social order/edited by S.H. Hasbullah and Barrie M. Morrison.
p. cm.
Includes bibliographical references and index.
1. Sri Lanka—Social conditions. 2. Sri Lanka—Economic conditions. 3. Sri Lanka—Ethnic relations. 4. Social change—Sri Lanka. 5. Globalization. I. Hasbullah, S.H. II. Morrison, Barrie M.

HC424.S74 306'.095493—dc22 2004 2004009286

ISBN: 0-7619-3221-6 (US-Hb) 81-7829-350-1 (India-Hb)

Sage Production Team: Anamika Mukharji, Rajib Chatterjee and Santosh Rawat

Contents

III The Struggle to Build a Better Life, a Better Society

IV Building a Better Society? Large Problems with Weakened Capacity

Foreword

This book presents research findings concerning the effects of globalization on social cohesion in Sri Lanka. The research was conducted in connection with a project of the Institute of Asian Research (IAR) at the University of British Columbia, entitled 'Comparative International Studies of Social Cohesion and Globalization'. Supported by a strategic grant from the Social Sciences and Humanities Research Council of Canada, the project focused on research and knowledge-building on issues of globalization and social cohesion in five countries of Asia, namely China, Indonesia, Japan, Korea and Sri Lanka. This volume on Sri Lanka has been prepared under the direction of Professor Barrie Morrison of IAR and Dr S.H. Hasbullah of the University of Peradeniya. The context for this important work can be understood by reference to the broader dimensions of studies of globalization and social cohesion.

Perspectives on Globalization

Globalization has been a feature of the human condition for several centuries. In recent years, particularly in the aftermath of the Cold War, globalization conditions have accelerated with increasingly permeable national borders, easily penetrated by flows of capital, people and information. To a large extent, this process has been justified by ideologies of liberalism and concomitant support for free markets, free trade, and freedom of ideas. Globalization is not the same as internationalization, which presupposes cooperation and interaction among autonomous nation-states, but rather is a process by which the state itself is challenged.[1]

The phenomenon of globalization may be addressed in terms of material and ideological dimensions, recognizing that these are at once intersecting and yet possessed of distinct features. Material aspects of globalization extend to changing contents and processes of print and electronic media; diet and dress; economic, business and financial structures and processes; relationships between labour and capital; knowledge and technology; and many other operational elements of globalization. These material dimensions create new opportunities and expectations for exchange and communication. Also, the material dimensions of globalization encourage a self-supporting value system that privileges some and marginalizes others based on their access, familiarity, and facility with these material dimensions, which contribute to and derive from ideological dimensions.

These ideological dimensions include official and popular attitudes and rhetoric on social, political and economic organization and behaviour, and other expressions of norms, values and beliefs that both inform and derive from material elements. In particular, the discourse of globalization also describes the spread of liberal ideals of individualism, autonomy and capitalism around the world.[2] Globalization of private law, for example, is often juxtaposed against public law regimes aimed at a collectivist approach to social welfare;[3] it is also proposed as an antidote to 'crony capitalism' and other perceived ills in the economies of East and South-east Asia.[4] While the capacity of the liberal industrial economies to promote visions of globalization derives as much from political and economic power as from the inherent wisdom of the ideas themselves,[5] there is little doubt that the influence of liberal ideals of private property has spread dramatically in the past decade. The circumstances of the CISG Convention and the WTO agreements on intellectual property rights (TRIPS Agreement), trade-related investment measures (TRIMs Agreement), trade in services (GATS Agreement), dispute resolution (the Dispute Resolution Understanding) are particularly noteworthy examples of the globalization of private law and private property regimes.[6] The CISG convention establishes uniform default rules for international sales contracts that impose norms drawn from the liberal market systems. The WTO reflects, *inter alia*, the export of liberal notions of private property rights, particularly in the areas of intellectual property rights enforcement and protection of investment rights. The WTO's Dispute Resolution Understanding, particularly its provisions for binding decisions by dispute resolution panels, reflects liberal norms of legal institutionalism. The liberal legal norms associated with globalization constitute a belief system driven by changing historical conditions of socio-economic and political relations in Europe and North America. The essentially one-way dissemination of these norms around the world reflects imbalances in political and economic power between developed and developing economies that characterize the current dynamic of globalization.

In the face of these trends, state governments are challenged to devise policies to ensure protection of public good within their jurisdictions, despite their weakening level of control. Protection of labour and environmental conditions is threatened by the prospect of capital flight in the face of regulatory initiatives. The state's capacity to prevent the introduction of pornography and hate literature is undermined by the prospect of trade sanctions aimed at securing market access for media industries. Policies aimed at capital accumulation and development of indigenous technologies are challenged by a combination of private capital mobility and state action in pursuit of the free trade objectives of the private sector. While globalization has been linked to these and other issues of the political economy of markets, the linkage between globalization and local social cohesion is less well understood.

DIMENSIONS OF SOCIAL COHESION

Although the prerequisites and conditions for social cohesion are not well understood, its absence can be identified by reference to dimensions of conformity and diversity on political and socio-economic conditions, and by instances of social disorder.

CONFORMITY AND DIVERSITY

If the process of building social cohesion can be analyzed in light of the dimensions of belonging, inclusion, participation, recognition and legitimacy, these dimensions in turn can be assessed in light of the interplay between conformity and diversity. Conditions of conformity and diversity may be examined by reference to data on the extent of differentiation in patterns of social, economic and political relations.[7] Conformity and diversity in economic relations would be measured by reference to data on differentiation in patterns of income, employment, consumption, housing, transportation, and so on. In the area of social relations, conformity and diversity would be examined by reference to data on differentiation in patterns of religion, belief and ideology, norms of family relations, socio-economic dualism and pluralism, privilege and marginalization with respect to class and gender, ethnicity and so on. In the political area, the conformity and diversity would be examined by reference to data on differentiation in patterns of political participation, institutions and their operation and effect, political-legal culture, and other variables.

Social Disorder

While all states and their governments have a strong interest in maintaining social cohesion for the purpose of social welfare and good governance, the mechanisms by which social cohesion is achieved remain obscure. If social cohesion is taken to mean 'the ongoing process of developing a community of shared values, shared challenges and equal opportunity based on a sense of trust, hope and reciprocity',[8] then it falls to the state and the society to create the conditions by which this process can be achieved. Although the prerequisites and conditions for social cohesion are not well understood, its absence can be identified by reference to data on breakdowns in social order. Data on social disorder extend to conditions attendant on riots, political disturbances etc. in the selected countries prior to and during the globalization era. The analysis extends beyond simply the recording of events, to include content analysis of published reporting, so as to achieve an understanding of the contexts, origins, responses and aftermath of the reported breakdowns in social order.

By comparing conditions of conformity and diversity in social, political and economic relations with conditions of the breakdown of social order, the research builds on the work of Chandler, Sigelman and Tsai,[9] who looked strictly at the division of labour. Division of labour in economic relations is one, but by no means the only, measure of conformity and diversity. By separating social, economic and political relations, the study can examine the ways in which these relationships (which admittedly overlap to some degree) reflect conditions of conformity and diversity. This then permits the policy consequences to be seen in broader terms than simply as issues of economic performance.[10] The multifaceted approach would permit linkages to be drawn between conditions of social, economic or political conformity and diversity and instances of the breakdown of social cohesion, thus going beyond the existing work, which examines social diversity in the context of economic growth.[11] By examining the combined factors of social, economic and political relations and the extent to which conformity and diversity exist within this, the project addresses the more comprehensive issue of social capital. This in turn may be linked with conditions of cohesion, economic diversity and economic growth.[12]

By relying on various dimensions of social cohesion, the project builds on existing literature addressing social cohesion in general. However, rather than assume that diversity has the potential for social conflict or for contributing factors to social cohesion,[13] the project hopes to identify how complementarity between conformity and diversity can contribute to social cohesion under different conditions.[14] The complementary relationship between conformity and diversity may contribute to localized perceptions of and resolutions to issues of social cohesion by reference to the importance of building social capital. Approaches to complementarity may also help resolve the issue of perception, which is seen as a critical component in the feeling of belonging that is an important dynamic of cohesion.[15] This project examines these various factors in cross-national context to generate understanding of the global dimensions of social cohesion.

SRI LANKA COUNTRY STUDY

Understanding the relationships between globalization and social cohesion requires an international comparative approach that generates data and analysis on conditions in a diverse array of countries and societies. The experience of Western liberal states with globalization is mediated and eased significantly by the commonality of legal and political institutions. In Asia, by contrast, the governing legal and political institutions are either indigenous and relatively alien to the liberal tradition, or imposed through a process of colonialism and neo-colonialism and thus, also in conflict with the notion of the supremacy of liberalism. In addition, Asian states and societies embrace a wide variety of economic, social and political conditions. Besides this, partly due to their increased participation in the globalization process and also due to the phenomenon of rapid economic growth, the conditions of specialization of labour that Durkheim identified as an important factor in social cohesion are evident as conditions of transition.

The contents of this book on globalization and social cohesion in Sri Lanka include reports on such issues as displaced persons, the gem industry, nationalism and gender, work and family change, and collective mobilization. The Sri Lanka volume suggests that globalization's impact has been in stimulating the shift from agricultural toward manufacturing and service employment, the increase in job-related migration, and the international networking of civil society organizations. The Sri Lanka study suggests that the challenge posed for pre-existing norms and power relations is driven by a number of factors. Population growth in each of our societies, the competition for resources and status, and claims on the distributive benefits provided by the state all helped push along the questioning of existing societal arrangements. Necessity and widening horizons are working together to advance change. At the local level, people are collaborating much more frequently to seek improvements in their communities—agitating for a better school, questioning land use policies, and calling for accountability of local authorities. The number of civil society organizations has multiplied beyond any reliable accounting. At the national level new political parties, new social movements and new cultural mobilizations have emerged in unprecedented numbers in the last decades. In Sri Lanka, this is illustrated by the state-threatening challenges of the Liberation Tigers of Tamil Eelam and of the Sinhalese radicals in the Janatha Vimukthi Peramuna. The Sri Lanka volume also illustrates questions about social cohesion, providing evidence of ethno-nationalism promoted by the political and cultural leaders in both the majority Sinhalese community and among the minority Tamils. The 'reflexivity' in practices of social control and power relations that has been stimulated by globalization is both undercutting efforts to sustain existing forms of social cohesion and simultaneously creating ideological and social space for new forms of social control.

Pitman B. Potter
University of British Columbia

NOTES

1. Noam Chomsky, *World Orders Old and New*, New York: Columbia University Press, 1994; David Held, Anthony G. McGrew, David Goldblatt and Jonathan Perraton, *Global Transformations: Politics, Economics and Culture*, Stanford, CA: Stanford University Press, 1999; Saskia Sassen, *Losing Control? Sovereignty in an Age of Globalization*, New York: Columbia University Press, 1993.
2. For more details, see D. Barry and R.C. Keith, *Regionalism, Multilateralism and the Politics of Global Trade*, Vancouver: University of British Columbia Press, 1999; T. Ginsburg, 'Does Law Matter for Economic Development', *Law and Society Review*, Vol. 34, No. 3, 2000, pp. 829–56; F. Jameson and M. Miyoshi (Eds), *The Cultures of Globalization*, Durham N.C.: Duke University Press, 1998; K. Jayasuriya (Ed.), *Law, Capitalism and Power in Asia*, London: Routledge, 1999; F.J. Lechner and J. Boli (Eds), *The Globalization Reader*, Malden, MA: Blackwell, 2000; P.B. Potter, 'Property: Questioning Efficiency, Liberty and Imperialism', in N. Mercuro and W.J. Samuels (Eds), *The Fundamental Interrelationships between Government and Property*, Stamford, CN: JAI Press, 1999, pp. 177–90; F. Rajaee, *Globalization on Trial: The Human Condition and the Information Civilization*, Ottawa: International Development Research Centre, 2000; J. Tomlinson, *Globalization and Culture*, Chicago: University of Chicago Press, 1999; D. Trubek, Yves Dezalay, Ruth Buchanan and John Davis, 'Global Restructuring and the Law: The Internationalization of Legal Fields and the Creation of Transnational Arenas', *Case Western Reserve Law Review*, Vol. 44, No. 2, 1994, pp. 407–98; A. Woodiwiss, *Globalization, Human Rights and Labour Law in Pacific Asia*, Cambridge: Cambridge University Press, 1998.
3. D. Kennedy, 'Receiving the International', *Connecticut Journal of International Law*, Vol. 10, No. 1, 1994, p. 1.
4. For more details, read G.W. Noble and J. Ravenhill (Eds), *The Asian Financial Crisis and the Architecture of Global Finance*, Cambridge: Cambridge University Press, 2000; G. Segal and D.S.G. Goodman (Eds), *Towards Recovery in Pacific Asia*, London: Routledge, 2000.

   For discussion of the applicability of liberal models of financial regulation to developing economies, see S. Haggard and C.H. Lee, *Financial Systems and Economic Policy in Developing Countries*, Ithaca: Cornell University Press, 1995; and S. Haggard, C.H. Lee and S. Maxfield (Eds), *The Politics of Finance in Developing Countries*, Ithaca: Cornell University Press, 1993.
5. R.H. Wagner, 'Economic Interdependence, Bargaining Power and Political Influence', *International Organization*, Vol. 42, No. 3, 1988, p. 461.
6. Citations for all laws, regulations and treaties are provided in Appendix A: Table of Laws, Regulations and Treaties.
7. Emile Durkheim, *The Division of Labour in Society* (Tr. W.D. Halls), Basingstoke: Macmillan, 1984.
8. Jane Jenson, *Mapping Social Cohesion: The State of Canadian Research*, Canadian Policy Research Networks Study No. F03, Ottawa: Renouf Publishing, 1998.

9. Charles Chandler, Lee Sigelman and Yung-Mei Tsai, 'The Division of Labour and Social Disorder: A Cross-National Test of a Durkheimian Interpretation', *International Journal of Comparative Sociology,* Vol. 27, Nos. 3–4, 1986, pp. 161–71.
10. Dominique M.A. Haughton and Swati Mukerjee, 'The Economic Measurement and Determinants of Diversity', *Social Indicators Research,* Vol. 36, 1995, pp. 201–25.
11. Ajit Bhalla and Frédéric Lapeyre, 'Social Exclusion: Towards an Analytical and Operational Framework', *Development and Change,* Vol. 28, 1997, pp. 413–33.
12. John W. Wagner and Steven C. Deller, 'Measuring the effects of economic diversity on growth and stability', *Land Economics,* Vol. 74, No. 4, 1998, pp. 541–57.
13. Albert O. Hirschman, 'Social Conflicts as Pillars of Democratic Market Society', *Political Theory,* Vol. 22, No. 2, 1994, pp. 203–18.
14. Bert Useem, 'Solidarity Model, Breakdown Model, and the Boston Anti-Busing Movement', *American Sociological Review,* Vol. 45, No. 3, 1980, pp. 357–69.
15. Kenneth A. Bollen and Rick H. Hoyle, 'Perceived Cohesion: A Conceptual and Empirical Examination', *Social Forces,* Vol. 69, No. 2, 1990, pp. 479–504; J.C. Buckner, 'The development of an instrument and procedure to assess the cohesiveness of neighbourhoods', *Dissertation Abstracts International,* Vol. 47, 1986, pp. 2669B–2670B (University Microfilms No. 86–20. 752).

ACKNOWLEDGEMENTS

We wish to thank the contributors who have taken time from their varied responsibilities to respond to our request for help in putting this book together. Without them this book would not exist. And our thanks to Professor Pitman B. Potter, Director of the Institute of Asian Research at the University of British Columbia, whose conception, initiative and continuing support has carried forward the inclusive project entitled 'Comparative International Studies of Social Cohesion and Globalization' of which this book forms a part. Our colleagues in the project at the Institute of Asian Research and at the Asia Pacific Foundation kept asking helpful questions as we pursued our parallel country studies. The Social Sciences and Humanities Research Council of Canada provided financial support for the project, for which we are very grateful. In November 2001, the Shanghai Academy of Social Sciences provided us with an opportunity to share ideas with contributors to our edited volume at a workshop. The Academy staff's personal interest and the Academy's facilities helped to make it a successful workshop.

At a more personal level, we wish to thank Dagmar Hellmann-Rajanayagam for sending us the pictures and translating from Tamil the poems from the Heroes' Day pamphlet. We thank Dr Nawfhal of the University of Peradeniya for preparing the map. Donna Yeung coordinated the project, attended to the logistics of the Shanghai workshop and kept up everyone's flagging spirits. Cathy Lovering and Karen Jew helped attend to the paper work and took time to rescue us editors when we were mired in MS Word. Thank you all.

S.H. Hasbullah and Barrie M. Morrison

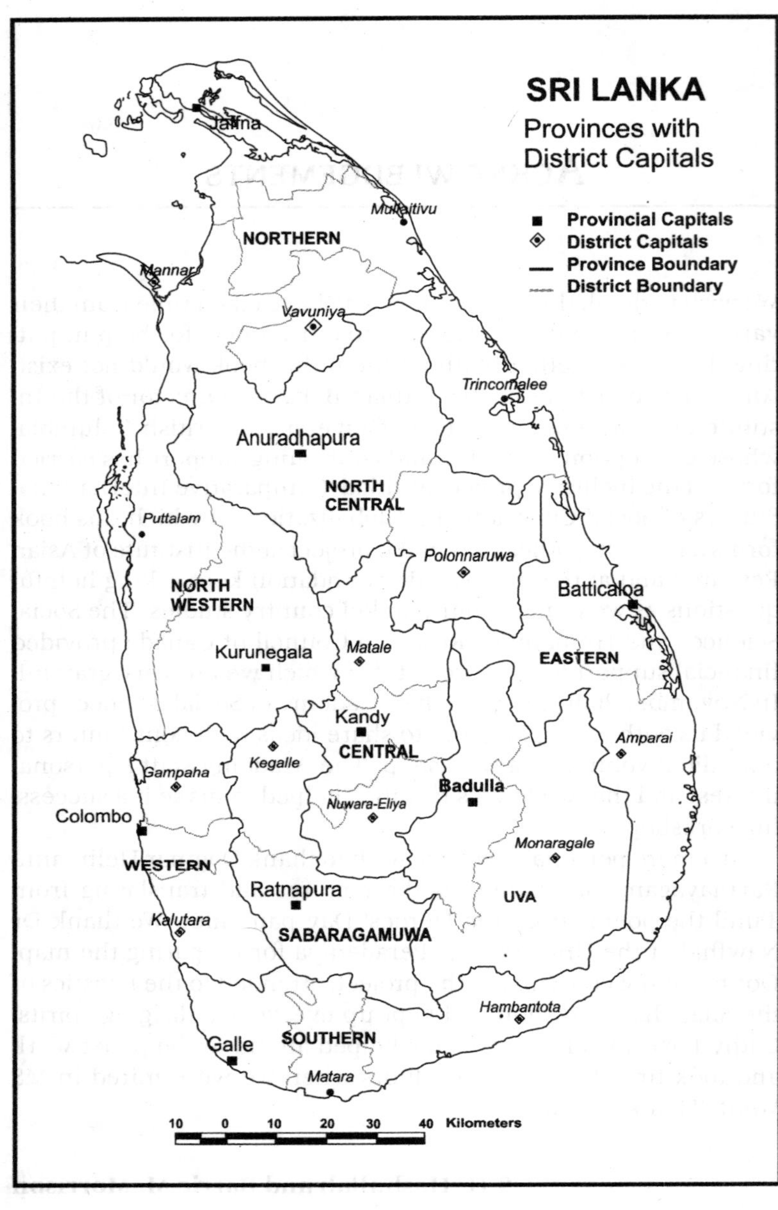

SRI LANKA
Provinces with
District Capitals
Provincial Capitals
District Capitals
Province Boundary
District Boundary
Jaffna
Mullaitivu
NORTHERN
Mannar
Vavuniya
Trincomalee
Anuradhapura
NORTH
CENTRAL
Puttalam
Polonnaruwa
NORTH
WESTERN
Batticaloa
Kurunegala
Matale
EASTERN
Kandy
CENTRAL
Kegalle
Ampara
Gampaha
Badulla
Nuwara-Eliya
Colombo
Monaragale
WESTERN
Ratnapura
UVA
Kalutara
SABARAGAMUWA
Hambantota
Galle
SOUTHERN
Matara
10
0
10
20
30
40
Kilometers

Introduction

S.H. HASBULLAH AND BARRIE M. MORRISON

The phrase 'Struggling to Create a New Social Order' is an important part of our book's title. It carries the message that the people of Sri Lanka will have to take up the task of consciously building a new society. Complex societies are not naturally occurring phenomena, but are dynamic social arrangements that require constant re-thinking, redefined purposes and renewed cooperation to flourish. When previous governing arrangements fail, when economies skew the distribution of benefits, when cultural traditions are invoked to divide people, when the individual's potential is truncated, then the time has come to think about alternative ways of organizing society. We believe that Sri Lanka has arrived at such a moment in its history.

There is no model that can be borrowed. For political organization the Westminster model of a post-colonial state was available, for better or for worse. For building support within a state there was and is the appeal of ethno-nationalism, which has been vigorously promoted and has contributed to many problems. For building an industrialized economy there is the currently fashionable, though severely criticized, prescription of the 'Washington Consensus'. But to scale up one's thinking to encompass the political system, the economy, the existing ethnic-cultural teachings and all the other interacting elements of a modern complex society, as in Sri Lanka, is to realize that there is unlikely to be any model anywhere in the world. To state the obvious, we think that Sri Lankans will have to undertake the rebuilding of society on their own.

But if there is no model available nor a prescription to follow, how should we proceed? Other societies in Asia, including those in our larger project—Japan, Korea, China, Indonesia, as well as elsewhere in the world are facing their own distinctive challenges to their societal organization. So far we can see that there are three recurring elements in the process of societal reconstruction. Giving them simple labels, they are the Problems, the Principles, and the Procedures.

A realistic assessment of the issues facing a society requires a careful and honest investigation, which includes a continuing role for those most directly affected. Fortunately Sri Lanka has a strong tradition of vigorous public debate and of local voluntary organization formed to address problems and give voice to grievances and concerns. It also has a strong tradition of socially informed empirical research kept alive at colleges, universities, and other research institutions. The chapters in our book fit into this last tradition and, we hope, contribute to the honest understanding of the Problems.

Among the Principles, the first and most important is that people are not helpless in the face of rapid change, globalization, the market economy or any of the other imagined impersonal 'forces' of the world. And second, that a proven method of dealing with change is democratic mobilization. We know that this involves creating opportunities for individuals to become more equal. It is not only equality before the law or in the exercise of an electoral franchise, but in gaining increased equality in competence to participate in society. When Tamil women or the Estate Tamils, as two examples, can analyze and articulate their concerns, when they can organize to seek improvement without jeopardizing their security, then they are gaining in the equality of a practising democracy. Obviously, the existing dominant practices and practitioners, patriarchy and the estate hierarchy, will have to make room for the previously voiceless and unorganized to contribute to society. Moving up from the familial and communal, the process of creating accountable, powerful forms of local government is beginning to contribute to the empowerment of more people and to political participation. Space for voluntary organizations to participate in policy making in the areas of their concern and experience is important, as the chapters by Sivamohan, Hasbullah, Ranjith and Caspersz suggest. Government policies in the various sectors of society will have to be rethought to ensure that they help open the way to participation and cooperation. So, for example, we doubt that foreign direct investment, the denial of rights of workers to unionize and to seek judicial redress for injury helps improve the democratic practices in Sri Lanka. And certainly, other principles besides democracy will have to be invented to sustain the long-term process of creating and sustaining a modern society.

The Procedures are the familiar accompaniments of the democratic theme. These include open communication, sharing of information in a form that is understandable by all participants, recognition that many different people have knowledge and, equally important, the capacity to stall the implementation of policies with which they disagree. Cooperation rather than coercion of any kind—social, economic, political—is probably the most effective way of gaining support for the long-term continuity of policies. Violence has torn the country apart. Something else has to be tried. Pinnawala writes about these issues in his chapter on stemming the flood of violence.

Turning from generalities about reconstructing society to our specific chapters, in the first part of our book we look at the failure to create an inclusive nation-state capable of managing the rush of changes. Morrison begins by identifying some of the major societal changes with their impact on families and communities. He reviews the over-expansion of government with some of the internal contradictions in security and development policies. The deficiencies of the state as perceived by the armed challengers are summarized. And the slow and halting process of building a more inclusive state for the plural society of Sri Lanka is outlined.

Then we turn to the development of the mutual exclusiveness of the two major communities in Sri Lanka and to their internal divisions, which further limit their social cohesion. Matthews and Rajanayagam begin by examining the creation of boundary markers differentiating the Sinhalese and Tamil communities. Religion and language have become the defining markers for the Sinhalese, largely due to the vigorous espousal and political mobilization led by the Buddhist monastic orders, which see their own status at stake. In contrast the Tamils, lacking an inclusive religious organization, have used language and the acceptance of the social hierarchy promoted by the landed castes as defining characteristics. But the Tamil definition has been challenged by the militant Karaiyar caste and rejected by the large Tamil-speaking Muslim community. The Muslims hold on to the conception of a community of believers, independent of language. The inadequacies of the conception of community and failures of both the community and national political leadership are brought out. Matthews and Rajanayagam continue with an examination of the internal divisions within the two major communities, which continue to impede a united approach to solving collective problems.

The emotional power of the Tigers' ideology is illustrated by a picture from the 2001 celebration of Heroes' Day and by a selection of the accompanying poetry. These poems contrast sharply with the contemporary poems translated by Sivamohan in the next chapter. One set glorifies death in service to the cause, in the fight for Tamil Eelam. The other is the pensive, sad and yet life-affirming poetry of Tamil women. With a courage equal to that of the warrior they confront death and affirm life and its continuation through their children.

Growing up into womanhood within the Tamil community, Sivamohan describes the pressures to fit into the role of obedient daughter, chaste wife and self-sacrificing mother that were generated by the patriarchal, land-centred, caste-stratified society of Jaffna. With the outbreak of violence and the enforcement of the authoritarian ideology of the Liberation Tigers of Tamil Eelam, the female image is recast into the mould of the avenging suicide bomber. The myth of the power of contained sexuality to redress injustice is used to once again confine young Tamil women, denying them the opportunity to find their own individual way. Their personal plight is sensitively brought out in a selection of poetry written by women.

In the third part, we turn to three local studies. Sri Ranjith examines the basis for social cohesion and cooperation in a Tamil working class urban neighbourhood that is under extreme pressure. The neighbourhood, wedged in between a cemetery and a main road, provides quarters for the lowest rank municipal employees of Kandy. Natural population growth and the migration of other Tamils seeking safety from ethnic violence have overwhelmed the infrastructure and housing of Mahaiyawa. The rapid commercial expansion of the city on three sides of the community has turned the land into some of the more valuable real estate in the urban core of the city. The municipal politicians want the land but the residents will not leave voluntarily. With variations, this is the story that confronts established residential neighbourhoods in many expanding cities.

Atukorala, drawing on his first-hand knowledge of gem-mining communities in Ratnapura, examines the recent transformation of mining as techniques improve and international markets expand. The government training programmes opened the door to lower-status groups to gain new skills and new wealth. The new rich seek to gain social standing by the right marriages and by rivalling the old rich in patronizing the Buddhist temples and supporting the schools. This industrial change is one with others that are transforming the Sri Lankan economy and society.

Sinnathamby writes about the situation of the most exploited community in Sri Lanka—the Tamil estate workers. Valued for their hard work and docility in the face of industrial and state repression, they are now finding a voice after 150 years of exploitation. Improving educational opportunities are beginning to open the gates on the estate roads for young people to leave the life of labouring that their parents have known. Many disabilities remain and the resentment of the younger people is reaching explosive levels.

Caspersz's chapter describes the creation of one of the earlier modern NGOs, Satyodaya, and its commitment to improve the lives of both the Tamil estate families and the poor Sinhalese villagers living around the estates. Satyodaya acted on the belief that ethnic violence by the impoverished against the exploited was a failure to recognize that both the Sinhalese and Tamils suffered under imperialist and capitalist exploitation. And that practical measures of training for new jobs, assisting with the construction of new homes, building sanitary water supply with joint teams of Tamils and Sinhalese, constructing community centres, and other such steps would help Tamil and Sinhalese to build cooperative relations. In the process they would gain competence and power and see how their local problems have been created, in part, by national policies.

In the fourth group of contributions, we examine some of the larger critical problems that presently trouble the society. One such problem is described by Hasbullah. What arrangements can be made for the displaced Muslims, over 100,000, who were driven out of their homes in 1990 by the LTTE and now live in camps and other temporary quarters elsewhere? They want to return home and rebuild their lives but continue to fear for their security and know that their homes and businesses have been taken over by others. How can they be restored to a productive life that is acceptable to them? Can their organizations gain the strength to deal with the LTTE and the government?

Waxler-Morrison explores the increased opportunities for work outside of the community of residence. In particular, women have been able to go abroad to work as maids and household servants in the Gulf and elsewhere. Quite often, they are married and leave children behind when they take up such jobs. In her field work and that of others, Waxler-Morrison learns that their absence can have a severe and negative impact on their families. The migration of educated men and women away from their parental community is aggravating the problem of care for the elderly. The combined impact of aging and migration places enormous strains on family relations and the cultural values that underpin family, community and society. These issues are not unique to Sri Lanka but are reported from the other Asian countries in the project as well.

Pinnawala tackles the difficult but central problem of growing violence in the society and how it is related to the growth of electoral and political party violence after 1970. He traces the two divergent forms: the southern one among the Sinhalese associated with the Janatha Vimukthi Peramuna; the northern and eastern led by the Tamil militants. He explores the reasons for successive regimes losing their legitimacy and the gaining of moral authority by the challengers to the government. The role of various elements of globalization—the NGOs, the media and the Tamil diaspora—in perpetuating the violence is examined. He then considers how the rise in the level of violence in society might be halted and reversed.

Finally, the editors offer their reflections on 'Globalization and Social Cohesion' in Sri Lanka.

I

The Challenge of Societal Reorganization

From the perspective of 2002, the need for social reorganization is clear. The changes, which Sri Lanka has experienced and continues to experience, cumulatively pose a unique challenge. There are no readymade models anywhere in the world to guide policy makers, stakeholders and citizens. Some of the values and traditions of the past can provide guidance for future development. But we can predict that the future will bring more changes, some anticipated, some unexpected. Many of these will require a collective response from an inclusive society with strong institutions. Barrie Morrison explores these issues in the following chapter.

1

Overwhelming Change and Faltering Institutions, 1948–2002

BARRIE M. MORRISON

Sri Lanka has experienced enormous societal changes in the last 60 years. These changes have forced the society and the government to confront issues which had never previously been encountered, or at least, never encountered on the same scale. A trebling of the population since independence in 1948, rapid urban growth, the diffusion of high quality education to those outside the political and cultural elite, challenges to authority, a shift from an agriculture-based society to one where most people are employed in manufacturing and the service sector—these and many other changes are forcing individuals and institutions to wrestle with new problems. The relative simplicity of the earlier public issues has been replaced by complexity. The old ways of thinking about social issues and government policies are no longer adequate. A new, relevant vocabulary and discourse is being fashioned slowly and through much conflict. Experimentation and flexibility seems to be the new approach for both people and policy makers but it is proving difficult to surrender the residual shell of the older certainties and values.

This chapter sets out some of the more important changes and briefly examines their implications. It calls attention to some of the tensions and conflicts and summarizes the steps towards one of the major changes in the government's organization: devolution.

Rapid Societal Change

Employment

The statistics on employment are useful and central indicators of change. At the time of independence, in 1948, most families provided for their own living from agriculture and fishing. The 1949 Statistical Abstract reports that 52.3 per cent of the employed population earned a living through agriculture or fishing. Behind the statistics, we have the particular details of life in some of these communities thanks to the unusual number and quality of local studies carried out since the 1950s. These local studies allow us to understand what life was like in the farming, fishing and plantation communities.[1] The plantation labourers, farmers and fishermen lived in stable communities with well understood conventions guiding reproduction and the socialization of children. Hierarchies of power and status, including caste rankings, were familiar even though resented, challenged, and sustained by threats of violence. The large tea estates were organized on a military model with the superintendent being the commander. But the Tamil labourers on the estates had stable sources of income, though it was miserably low. Even the latrine cleaner in the line rooms on the tea estate was assigned a room, had a wage and so could marry and raise a family. In the north and in the east some of the Tamil farming communities were dominated by higher caste landowners employing bonded labourers. But within the labourers' caste it was possible to find a spouse and to start a family. In the Sinhalese farming communities of the south, west, and central regions, the majority cultivated land in their own communities either under some ownership arrangement or as tenants. By and large the families controlled the productive resources and made arrangements for the marriage of their children. In 1976, when I asked the heads of various households about their marriage, the reply was that their parents had arranged their marriage. In these relatively more egalitarian communities, cooperation among independent producers was much more common. But no matter how reproduction or collective action was organized, these were stable communities compared to what was to follow.

Fifty years after independence, in 1998, only 38 per cent of the employed population worked in agriculture, down from 52 per cent in 1949.[2] The enlarged fraction of the population in manufacturing and services amounted to 45 per cent of the employed. In absolute terms, the number of persons in the service and manufacturing sectors grew from about 650,000 in 1949 to over 3 million by 1998—nearly a five-fold increase—while the total population grew only three-fold.

The structure of manufacturing moved decisively from diversified and dispersed small-scale workshops towards a more homogenized factory-type production heavily concentrated in or near Colombo. The service sector changed in the opposite direction, with the increasing diversification and dispersion of employment as new types of jobs opened up in the tourist industry, social services, and the information sector—in all, 30 per cent of the employed were in services, up from 20 per cent in 1946. In this sector there was a growing number of both men and women entering professional careers as architects, doctors, lawyers, engineers, teachers and others. By 1998, some 10 per cent of the employed were classified as 'professionals' or as 'technicians and associate professionals'.[3] Earlier, in 1946, the professionals had only constituted 3 per cent of the employed.

To ground the generalities of the statistics, I include some cases of social change from a farming village that I studied in 1976, again in 1984 and have visited from time to time since.[4] The multiplication of job opportunities outside of agriculture is clear. It is also clear that not everyone considered the changes an improvement over the circumstances of their parents.

- In a higher status, small, land-owning family, the couple's marriage had been arranged in 1946 and they lived in the wife's family home. The husband had been educated in a Buddhist school and had worked as a welfare officer in the Land Development Board. The family were strong supporters of the United National Party (UNP) and the wife was a secretary in the local branch of the party. They had seven children, all of whom had completed their senior high school examinations. The two boys were employed, one as a police constable and the other as a sergeant in the army. One daughter worked as a clerk in a government department and lived in Colombo with her husband. More remarkable was the third daughter, Indrani, who by 1984 had passed her London Guildhall examinations as a telephone engineer and was employed as telephone inspector. When I subsequently spoke to her, she was married to an engineer, whom she herself had chosen.

- In another case, the only daughter of a lower caste, illiterate farmer was able to attend university. The family had a small parcel of highland and cultivated paddy land as a tenant. The daughter was supported not only by her parents but by the cluster of close relatives living protectively in adjacent houses. It was understood that one member's success could be used to improve the situation of other relatives. She graduated with a Bachelor's degree and eventually obtained a salaried position as a teacher, married a teacher, secured land and built a substantial brick house serviced with electricity. Her uncle was an active supporter of the Sri Lanka Freedom Party (SLFP) and it was suggested that both her appointment as a teacher and the securing of land on an expropriated tea estate were due to his political connections. When I last visited her house she had two daughters and declared that 'two was enough'.
- In a poor, lower-status family, the marriage had been arranged in 1948. The family had a quarter of an acre of paddy land and about half-an-acre of highland planted with coconut and pepper vines. The couple had nine children. Only the youngest, a girl, had completed her senior high school certificate. Three boys worked as casual labourers in the Public Works Department, another as a night watchman, one as a clerk at a store in Colombo and another at a tourist hotel in Hikkaduwa. As they were identified as strong SLFP supporters, the little shop that they ran out of the back of their house had been looted and burnt by UNP supporters after the UNP election victory in 1977. The youngest girl, Jayanthi, had applied for admission to nursing school in 1984. She was not admitted and when I visited them in 1990, she was working in a foreign-owned garment factory outside Colombo. The pay was low with compulsory overtime of two hours a day. She had worked for four years and had been only able to save enough to purchase a gold chain. She lived

in a dormitory with other girls and was able to come home once a month, which is when I met her. She was planning to quit and start studying to be a Montessori teacher. She spoke to me of her difficulties in getting training and, urged on by her brother's comments, of the problems of finding a husband. Also participating in the conversation was her cousin, a trained Montessori teacher, in her mid-thirties and unmarried. With great embarrassment, the two women spoke about the possibility of remaining spinsters when Jayanthi's watchman brother (aged 44) spoke up about his own problems in finding a good job and a wife.

- Elsewhere, the old widow and adult children of a deceased Tamil tea estate foreman lived in a small house a mile-and-a-half from the nearest road. The estate where they had lived and worked had been abandoned by its English owner and it had been taken over by the government. It had gone out of business and the workers had been dispersed. The elder son, Maniwellu (aged 38 years in 1984), and his younger brother worked as casual workers at a small shop in a nearby town. The brothers were the only providers for a family of seven: the old mother, Maniwellu, his brother and his brother's wife and child, his unmarried sister and her child. Their job was to sort and package leftover tea which the owner purchased from nearby tea factories. Neither brother had worked in the past month as tea production was seasonal and provided only seasonal employment. They had been cutting firewood in the jungle to carry and sell by the roadside and had been forced to pawn their mother's gold ear-studs to buy food. Maniwellu had passed his junior secondary school examinations but could not find a job other than that in the shop run by a Tamil-speaking Muslim. While residing in Sri Lanka for three generations the family had been unable to establish citizenship under the discriminatory laws passed after 1948. They were not eligible for any form of social welfare support, though they had access to free medical care at the nearby rural clinic.

From these predominantly agricultural families in one village, there had been a dispersion of their daughters into a variety of new jobs: a telephone engineer, a graduate school teacher, a factory worker and an aspiring Montessori teacher. The sons from these households had ended up as a police constable, army sergeant, government clerks, Public Works Department labourers and casual shop workers in town. Most of the women thought their life chances had improved or had the prospect of improving. Among the men there was more uncertainty for some clearly saw that their fathers had been able to provide a living and form a family while they, at a comparable age, had not. The clearest case of a loss of position was that of the Tamil household whose situation had deteriorated.

The change in employment distribution is certainly associated with three other fundamental social changes: the increase in the years of education, the rapid growth of urban populations due to migration, and the increasing age of marriage for women, which has a major impact on the birth rate and the organization of societal reproduction.

Education

By the 1950s it was obvious that the children of farm families could not find enough land to set up independent households as farmers. New qualifications were needed to open off-farm jobs as government clerks, school teachers and so on. Education was the answer. Earlier, the government in a far-sighted policy had created a state system of free education all the way through to the university level. Educational change had a far-reaching effect.

Back in 1947, only 57.6 per cent of the children in the age group 5–14 were in school, though compulsory attendance was a legal requirement. Less than half (48.4 per cent) of the schools were government schools attended by less than half the pupils, the majority of schools were assisted or unaided ones run by religious organizations, private individuals, local groups, or individual estates. By 1998, virtually all schools were government-run and school attendance by children in the 5–14 age group was over 90 per cent.

Secondary education was streamed, starting in 1972, with separate curricula for Arts, Commerce and Science and with rigorous national examinations for the General Certificate of Education—Ordinary Level and Advanced Level. While various reforms and revisions have been carried out since 1972, the basic structure remains the same with nationally administered school-leaving examinations. These examinations have come to shape the teaching programme and study habits of the students for they are difficult to pass and are the gateway to employment and university admissions. In 1996, nearly half-a-million students sat the GCE (Ordinary Level) exams and 21.7 per cent qualified for admission to Advanced Level classes, and of the 170,000 who sat the Advanced Level exams only 12,500 or 7 per cent had the opportunity to enter the universities.[5]

Adding up enrolments in the university and in technical colleges in 1966, there were about 17,000 students following some programme of post-secondary education. Three decades later, in 1995, there were 50,000 students enrolled. And the gender distribution had changed. Women gained more than half the seats at the university, outnumbered men in law and were almost equal to them in number in commerce, management studies, medicine and other professions. They made up 54.1 per cent of those employed in 'professional, technical and related' fields by 1996/97.

Further, the cumulative effect of graduating successive generations of students was to gradually increase the number of well-educated people in the society. Higher education was no longer the preserve of the elite or of the clergy but was diffusing through the society. The trend is clear in the socio-economic surveys of the Central Bank: in 1953, 1.8 per cent of the household sample had a member with tertiary education; in 1978–79, 11.5 per cent; and in 1996–97, 20.7 per cent of households. The authority of the educated—whether Buddhist monk, Christian priest, lawyer or civil servant—dissipated as more and more people attained the same levels of education.

The spread of higher education helped encourage the expansion of what has elsewhere been called 'the public sphere'. More and more issues were now open to interrogation, discussion and criticism. And with the questioning of traditional practices and ideas came the rejection of many older values—of sexual mores at the personal level and of elite political authority at the more public level. This is discussed in greater detail later in the book.

URBANIZATION

Closely related to the shift away from agriculture was the enlargement of the cities and the associated impact on social conventions.

To hold a manufacturing or some service sector job the worker must usually leave the village or town and move to the city. The rural migrant living as an independent wage-earner in the city encountered a range of new experiences. Often the young adult found himself living in a freer environment where there were differing views on acceptable behaviour.

In the 1946 census, the urban population for the island was reported as 14.4 per cent of the population. By 2000, it was estimated to be 24 per cent of the much larger national population. For the primate city, Colombo, in 1946, the population was recorded as 345,000 living and working in a land area of approximately 5,000 hectares. Adding in the continuously built-up area around the city limits, there was a total of about 7,000 hectares which housed about 500,000 inhabitants. By 2000, the urbanized area had grown six times with much higher densities in the core area of the city. So the estimated population of the city and its extensions has also grown by a conservative five times to over 2.5 million people.[6]

Yet even the estimating of urban growth of the Colombo area has become increasingly meaningless. Not only are the urban boundaries drawn to meet outdated criteria, but the huge expansion of the low-cost transportation system has woven separate residential areas together—villages, towns and cities—so that what had been distinctive urban opportunities and services have become both dispersed and accessible to many more people. There is a great arc of people stretching from Puttalam in the north through Kurunegala, Kandy and Ratnapura to Matara in the south, sharing city-like access to information, jobs, schooling, medical care and other services.

Growth of cities by migration is far from the full story on the movement of people out of the countryside. A large number of Sri Lankans have left the country as short-term workers in the Gulf, as Tamil workers seeking an alternative to life on the estates by moving to India, as refugees from the fighting in the north, and as permanent migrants to other countries. The movement of some of these people is discussed in other chapters of this book.

MARRIAGE

The national statistics show very clearly that the age of first marriage of women has increased noticeably, and that of men very little. This statistic suggests a major change in the relations between genders and generations. Increasingly, women and men are accepted as self-directing individuals, capable of making their own decisions about marriage and child-bearing. The earlier concept of marriage as a contract between families is fading rapidly and with it the deference of child to parent. The data in Table 1.1 illustrates the extent of the change in the age of marriage.

TABLE 1.1
Singulate Mean Age at Marriage, 1946–81

Year	*Male*	*Female*	*Difference*
1946	27.0	20.7	6.3
1963	27.9	22.1	5.8
1981	27.9	24.4	3.5

Source: Bruce Caldwell, *Marriage in Sri Lanka: A Century of Change*, New Delhi: Hindustan Publishing, 1999, p. 41.

More recent information is reported by the periodic surveys of Central Bank of Sri Lanka, though they do not provide enough information to calculate the Singulate Mean Age of Marriage as used in Table 1.1. The 'proportion of women married under 20 years of age declined from 44 per cent in 1981/82 to 33 per cent in 1996/97 while the percentage of women married at above 25 years of age increased from 18 per cent in 1981/82 to 27 per cent in 1996/97.'[7] Clearly the female age of marriage continues to increase through 1996/97.

In our household surveys conducted in 12 communities in 1980 and in eight of the same communities in 1995, we learned something else. We were told that more women and men were not marrying. Household evidence supports this though the sample size is too small for it to be statistically demonstrated. The increase in women's age of marriage and in cases of both women and men remaining single is related to the change in the employment pattern in several ways.

Subordination to parental control gets eroded as the skills of a new type of work and the social expectations of city life are acquired. Children earning their own income start to assert their independence. Parents disengage from participation in marriage decisions, and young independent migrants are increasingly left to their own resources. Housing and household furnishing must be found and paid for—even living in an urban shanty requires resources. Thus, marriage is postponed until there are some savings and some prospect of a reliable income. A household in Galle City that we interviewed in 1995 illustrates the point.

> A 24 year-old woman from a village was admitted to medical school and found a boarding arrangement in the home of a spinster schoolteacher who was living alone with a servant. When she graduated in medicine, she married one of her fellow students. Both were then 28 years old. They could not afford to start a family until they had secure salaried positions and had made some arrangements for housing. She joined the pathology laboratory in the Galle Hospital while he enlisted in the air force as a medical officer. The schoolteacher, now retired, had helped by providing extra space for the married couple in her home where they shared her kitchen and facilities. When I spoke to them, they had both turned 32 and had just had a baby. They were in the process of negotiating the purchase of some land at the back of the schoolteacher's garden and were making arrangements to build a small house. I came away with the clear impression that there was also a benefit for the retired schoolteacher. The young couple had become her family and would provide help and support for her in her old age.

Also, as professional and semi-professional work grows to 10 per cent of the employed, these workers are more highly educated. And, as the education level goes up, young people look for a spouse with a comparable level of education. The data from other countries indicates that this is particularly true for women.[8]

The most obvious societal ramification of the changing age of marriage for women and the delay in child-bearing has been the very rapid decline in the Total Fertility Rate: from 5.3 in 1953 to 2.1 in 2000 (comparable to that of China). And with the decline in the birth rate and the parallel increase in life expectancy to 70 years for males and 75 for females (comparable to the Republic of Korea), the age pyramid of the population is reversing. The proportion of young people (0–14) in the total population is declining while the proportion of elderly (60 and above) is increasing. Some of the implications of these important changes in the age distribution are explored in Nancy Waxler Morrison's chapter. One of the more obvious implications was identified by the Prime Minister in 2002, when he announced that both the Employees Provident Fund and the Employees Trust Fund for private sector workers and the 'government employees' pensions plan did not have sufficient funds to pay claimants.

Organizations

With the growth of individual responsibility associated with education and displayed in the choices of work, residence and marriage, came a growth in the number of organizations. People saw that by collaborating with others they might improve or enrich some part of their lives. By the 1990s it was clear that people were organizing to help themselves and others at an unprecedented level—the 'organizational revolution' had come to Sri Lanka.

Our household surveys in Sri Lanka conducted in 1980 and again in 1995, reveal an increase in organizational participation in the intervening 15 years. Many more households had one or more members belonging to one or more organizations—in 1980 only half (158/316) of the households had members with a median of one membership, in 1995 three quarters (226/319) had members with a median of two memberships per household. Obviously, people understood that we were asking about the formal organizations in the community—the cooperative, sports club, political party and union and not the informal savings and loan circles. What we found at the local level was amply evident at the national level as well.[9]

In 1991, a directory was compiled of 293 development-related NGOs which responded to a questionnaire.[10] Tabulating the date at which these organizations were formed, the earliest were religious service bodies, which were established before 1900. Between 1900 and 1977, there were an additional 103 organized which still operated in 1991. But in the last 13 years of the tabulation (1977–90), there were over 180 NGOs created. By 1995, the newspapers were reporting that there were over 5,000 registered NGOs, which included all types and not just those focused on development.

A number of focal concerns for these new organizations are reported in both our household surveys and in the collected national data: women's rights, child and family well-being, consumer protection, environmental hazards and conservation, advocacy for the marginalized and poor, participation in public policy formation and democracy. In the 1991 directory, the two largest groups of NGOs were those which declared their principal objectives to be community development (25 per cent—74 NGOs), and social welfare (22 per cent—66 NGOs). Those who were concerned with education were also numerous (19 per cent—55 NGOs) as were those focused on the environment (11 per cent—31 NGOs).

The great increase in the number of organizations, whether state-sponsored, voluntary NGO, or commercial, tilts the locus of formal collective action away from Colombo. Many of the organizations' goals, resources or markets are local or provincial. As these organizations take on locally important projects and move away from Colombo, the government's control of their activity weakens.

Governments have been greatly concerned about the growth of these organizations beyond their immediate control. In 1980, the Voluntary Social Service Organization Act was passed. All of the defined organizations 'were compelled to register under the Act and, in so doing, submit themselves to direct government control. It empowered government officials to enter and inspect the premises of an organization, convene an executive or general meeting to take place at a venue and time of their choosing and give directions to the executive committee.'[11] However, this regulation proved to be unenforceable.

But in addition to such NGOs concerned with development and community relations are a number of more communally grounded and politically oriented organizations. Some of these organizations encourage and sustain a sectarian position which often spills over into violence. Matthews discusses some of these in his chapters.

These five indices of employment, education, urbanization, marriage, and organization provide strong evidence of both the extent and rapidity of societal change. There are other dramatic indicators which call attention to the stresses associated with change, such as the spread of insecurity marked by growth in the rate of suicides, by increasing electoral violence, or by the revolutionary conflict between classes and ethnic groups.[12]

But the rapid and, I suggest, 'overwhelming' social changes have not been matched by the spread of persuasive explanatory ideas about appropriate forms of social and political organization in such a society or by any accommodating formal institutional change. In a term used by social psychologists, there is a 'cognitive dissonance' between what is, how it is thought about and how it is acted upon. Societal stress increases and the coming of recent 'globalization' aggravates these stresses.

COMPETING AND CONFLICTING UNDERSTANDINGS

One of the companions of rapid social change has been the collapse of earlier interpretations of society and the growth of a jungle of competing and conflicting ideas about the nature of the changes, their consequences and interactions. If the image of the 'Tower of Babel' was ever applied to ideas rather than language, we must now be experiencing it worldwide.[13] Sri Lanka is no exception.

Ideas about two of the more important public concerns are those regarding security and economic development. Here all I can do is summarize some of the recent literature which identifies the tensions in and the limitations of the thinking.

SECURITY OF WHAT FOR WHOM?

On security, Nira Wickramasinghe starts with the premise that security, as such, does not exist. 'There are only "conceptions" of security—and hence of national security—that vary from agent to agent, from consciousness to consciousness, along lines of community, class, and gender and over time.'[14]

The newly independent government in 1948 was concerned about the position of India. India had used its military to establish control over Kashmir and to consolidate the mosaic of jurisdictions within its new boundaries. The Sri Lankans were very nervous about any expansive claims that the Indians might make to protect and, possibly, incorporate nearby Tamil-speaking peoples into their republic. The first understanding of 'security' was the security of the state. It was not 'the people' or 'the community' but the state whose security was paramount. The inviolability of its territories was an essential condition for this security. The government negotiated with the Indians the demarcation of the maritime boundary in the Palk Strait and the Gulf of Mannar. They pushed the idea that the Indian Ocean should be declared a zone of peace, trusting that this would restrain India.

The testing crisis came in 1984, when the Indian government in response to terrible attacks on Tamils by government supporters began to train Sri Lankan Tamil militants in Tamil Nadu and provide them with arms. As the violence grew in the north the Sri Lankan armed forces mounted an offensive in Jaffna in 1987, which led to civilian deaths and great shortages. Indian air force planes began to drop relief supplies and the Tamil Nadu state legislature voted $3.2 million to assist groups fighting for a separate Tamil state in Sri Lanka. In July 1987, on the same day that the Indo–Sri Lankan agreement was signed to pacify combatants, the Indian Peace Keeping Force (IPKF) began to land troops in the north. The security of the state and its supposedly inviolable boundaries had been breached. The breaching had been initiated by the deliberate discriminatory policy of the Sri Lankan government against its Tamil citizens and its related failure to provide protection to the person and property of the Tamils.

A second concept of security was articulated in 1971, with the Janatha Vimukthi Peramuna (JVP) insurrection. The turn to violence by alienated, unemployed/underemployed, Sinhalese youth challenged another tenet of Sri Lankan state ideology—creation of 'a just society'. In response, government officials spoke of security as being the equivalent of the maintenance of order and preservation of the status quo. The Public Security Act was invoked and the military joined the police together with some vigilantes in crushing the rising. Some 16,000 people who were suspected of undermining order and fomenting revolution were taken into detention, questioned and eventually released. Maintenance of public order and the status quo joined the security of the state and the integrity of its territory under the rubric of 'security'.

The contradictory tension between varying 'conceptions' of security emerged more clearly in the 1990s. With the escalation of attacks by the Liberation Tigers of Tamil Eelam (LTTE) in the south—blowing up of a refinery in 1995, bombing of the Central Bank building in the Colombo business district (1,200 people killed or wounded)—'security' came to mean security of the south. When the LTTE began to target Buddhist religious centres, probably in response to the armed forces attacks on Hindu temples in Jaffna and occupation of a Hindu shrine in Trincomalee, Buddhist sacred sites were added to the list of specially protected areas.

A corollary of the terrorist attacks in the south was heightened suspicion of all Tamil civilians living in the region. For the many thousands of Tamils living and working in the Colombo area, life came to be uncertain and intimidating. Interviews carried out in 1995 with 70 Sinhalese and 19 Tamils, revealed very different ideas about security. The Sinhalese were doubtful of the government's capacity to provide security for people and places in the south, yet clung to the idea that the government should defend the territorial integrity of the whole of Sri Lanka. For the Tamils, security of person was paramount and they believed that the greatest threat was posed by the government itself. 'Being a Tamil, my name, my birthplace is a source of suspicion. I am not accepted as a citizen of Sri Lanka. I don't have the same freedom as a man from the majority community.'[15] For the individual, the state either appeared unable to provide security or was held to be the source of insecurity.

An extension of this focus on Tamils as potential terrorists was the harassment of any organization that raised questions about the treatment of Tamil civilians after the army re-occupied Jaffna. In 1996, the thugs of the governing party (People's Alliance) repeatedly disrupted the meetings of the NGO Forum—a joint meeting with Europe-based agencies and Sri Lankan partners—which asked questions about civil rights and the treatment of prisoners. The concept of security was being extended, apparently, to include protection of the ruling party from legitimate comment on and criticism of its increasingly authoritarian practices.

By 2002, the conflicting views about the meaning of security underscored the need for the government to clearly declare and implement an inclusive policy. Neither the security of the state nor the preservation of the territorial integrity of the country can be assured when the security of individuals and cultural communities is not assured.

Economic Development

With independence, the Sri Lankan government took up the practice of economic development and careful of planning. There was little experience and no institutional structure to set priorities or to follow a consistent set of policies. An economist wrote in 1976:

> ... planning in Sri Lanka was in fact a series of disjointed and sporadic exercises with individual plans often failing to survive

> their formal life-spans. Secondly, the basic discontinuity in the planning process was further underlined by the failure to evolve a planning machinery armed with ... administrative and even political powers and imbued with the will to set about the tasks of actually implementing the various planning proposals.[16]

The one notable exception to the criticism lay in the planning and development of agriculture. D.S. Senanayake, who became the first Prime Minister of independent Sri Lanka, had come to the post after chairing the Committee on Agriculture and Lands in the earlier legislative council. He brought with him a conviction that the country should be self-sufficient in rice and had, in 1935, explained his views in a book titled *Agriculture and Patriotism*.[17] The growing national population and land shortages in the Wet Zone had drawn attention to the thinly settled Dry Zone. There, in earlier times, extensive irrigation systems had made possible higher-yielding wet rice cultivation. It was believed that many more people had lived in the area before the irrigation systems had fallen into disuse. The new government embarked on the restoration and extension of the irrigation systems and the re-establishment of wet rice production. Displacing existing land-owners was not a major problem, for the state claimed nearly 85 per cent of land as its own crown land. The government took upon itself the responsibility to construct the irrigation works and to set up agricultural colonies, recruited largely from Sinhalese short of land in the Wet Zone.

But the Dry Zone was not empty and, in parts, Tamils were cultivating rain-fed crops in a system of shifting cultivation as well as some locally irrigated lands. The expansion of irrigation and the settler colonies were largely instrumental in changing the ethnic composition in two of the three key districts, as seen in Table 1.2.

With the government's decision in 1977 to push forward an immense irrigation project in the Dry Zone—the Accelerated Mahaweli Project—it was estimated that 145,000 hectares would be brought under irrigation and thousands of settler families could be brought in as colonists.[18] How many Tamils were displaced and whether they were provided for in the new irrigation colonies has been the subject of heated argument.

TABLE 1.2
Changing Population Proportions from 1921 and 1981 Censuses

	Sinhalese		*Sri Lankan Tamil*	
	1921	*1981*	*1921*	*1981*
Trincomalee	4.5	33.6	53.2	33.8
Batticaloa	1.9	3.2	68.5	70.8
Ampara	8.2	37.6	30.5	20.1

Source: G.H. Pieris, 'An appraisal of the concept of a traditional Tamil homeland in Sri Lanka', *Ethnic Studies Report*, Vol. IX, No. 1, January, 1991. Quoted in *Sri Lanka: The Devolution Debate*, Colombo: International Centre for Ethnic Studies, 1998, p. 7.

What is very clear is that the Tamil political parties regarded the movement of Sinhalese settlers into areas where Tamils had been the majority as a threat to their hopes of having a cultural homeland, whether as a federated province or as an independent state. The elected Provincial Council of the Tamil-majority North-east, which briefly functioned from November 1988 to March 1990, severely criticized the Colombo government for failing to transfer control over land settlement to the province and continuing to settle Sinhalese in their jurisdiction.[19] Control over land has been and continues to be the most important issue in the fight for a Tamil homeland—Tamil Eelam. In an unprecedented press conference on 10 April 2002, Prabhakaran, the head of the LTTE, said: 'We have made a statement saying that the formula or framework for a final settlement has to be worked out based on the Tamil demand for a **homeland** (emphasis added), nationality and self-determination.'[20]

At the same time, after 1977, the government was vigorously pushing an industrial development policy that was dependent on foreign investment. In its early years, the programme of creating a congenial environment for private firms to set up export manufacturing plants was a great success. Taking 1977 as a base, the contribution of factory industry to GNP was 9.1 per cent (Rs 6,338 mn at 1982 factor costs) by 1996 and factories were contributing 17.3 per cent (Rs 30,216 mn at 1982 factor costs).[21] Driving this 20-year record of growth was direct foreign investment, which grew rapidly in the first years following 1977. However, political instability and ethnic conflict exacerbated by tension over land began to alarm foreign investors. 'FDI (foreign direct investment) inflows, which recorded an impressive expansion in the immediate pre-reform period, continued to decline from 1984, reaching a mere 10 per cent of the 1980–83 average by 1989.'[22] Two large multinationals which had set up electronic manufacturing plants pulled out because of the political instability. Investment flows subsequently improved but the published data by the Central Bank of Sri Lanka reveal huge fluctuations year-by-year as both the investment environment was assessed and external markets changed. In 2001, two Korean-owned garment factories closed their doors, whether due to political instability or better opportunities elsewhere is not known.

The costs of the ethnic conflict mounted though I have found no recent estimate that attempts to sum up the costs of lower growth rate of GDP, the infrastructure and property damage, and the migration of skilled and professional people. An earlier estimate made in 1993, which only considered the opportunity costs of the high level of military expenditure, was that 'the cost of the war in terms of lost output from 1983 to 1988 is estimated at over 1.5 billion 1988 US dollars. This is the equivalent to 22 per cent of Sri Lanka's 1988 Gross Domestic Product.'[23]

A major unresolved tension in economic development was between the expansion of irrigation with the planting of predominantly Sinhalese colonies in the Dry Zone and the creation of a stable political environment for foreign and domestic investment in export manufacturing. The internal war, provoked in part by the government's agricultural development policies, was undercutting the government's industrialization policies.

THE AUTHORITARIAN AND CENTRALIZING STATE AND ITS CRITICS, 1948–80

As the society became more varied and fluid, the political elite at first intensified its commitment to a centralized, authoritarian form of government. Jayadeva Uyangoda describes the state as follows:

> The centrality of the state in regulating our social existence became particularly prominent with the postcolonial welfare state. Consequently, ours has become an intensely paternalistic and interventionist state where for education,

employment, food and clothing, health, transport and even for taking revenge on an adversary, the state was expected to step in as the supreme regulatory agency. In short, the state is not merely the institution of class domination and exploitation as Marxists would want to see it, but also the prime facilitator of material existence, social mobility and group interests.[24]

THE STATE

The definition of the state's role as 'the supreme regulatory agency' carried with it a persistent policy of co-opting other political, religious and social authorities and the expansion of bureaucratic controls.[25] For the government to set up organizations to regulate the society and develop the economy was costly. The proliferation of government, quasi-government bodies and state corporations led to a ballooning of government expenditures. This growth was marked by growing deficits and an accumulating debt.

The growing size of the population and the improving educational level created an enlarging pool of claimants for white-collar jobs. The opportunity to become an agricultural colonist in the Dry Zone was not appealing to these young adults. The government extended the practice of using government agencies and corporations as job provision centres. Professor K.M. de Silva, the doyen of Sri Lankan historians, commented critically on this overstaffing.

> All the corporations were overstaffed especially at the lower levels, and because of the political influence wielded by some of the appointees, the financial viability of the corporations received very low priority. Subsidies provided by the state concealed losses and gross inefficiency. But the corporations served a very useful purpose in generating employment, and on a scale that no efficient private organization could have done and survived.[26]

As indicators of the expansion of government functions, the statistics on government employment and expenditure summarize the trend. At the time of independence in 1948, the number of government and semi-government employees numbered 155,320, constituting about 6 per cent of the gainfully employed. By 1981, the numbers of government employees had grown until they constituted over 30 per cent of the employed. This number includes the workers on the recently nationalized plantations. In 1948–49, government expenditures were 19.8 per cent of GNP and the government was effectively debt-free. By 1989, expenditures had risen to 34 per cent of the GNP while the public debt, domestic and foreign, exceeded the GNP.

But while the government expanded its functions, it faced two insurrections by disaffected Sinhalese mobilized by the JVP (1971 and 1988–89). Both were serious and had a major impact on society. The number of deaths in the second JVP insurrection ran into thousands. Then in the north, the government lost control of nearly 10 per cent of its territory by 1986 to the LTTE and other militant Tamil groups. Clearly, there was something profoundly wrong with the government's policies and the practices within the political elite. Among the more consequential criticisms were those by the JVP and the militant Tamil groups.

The Critics

Janatha Vimukthi Peramuna: By 1968, the JVP had developed a critique of the government and society which was embodied in the Five Lectures. These were presented in varying forms depending on the audience and were developed and modified over the years to meet changing conditions.[27] As of 1983, these lectures were entitled 'The Crisis of the Capitalist System', 'There is No Solution in the Old Leftist and Capitalist Systems', 'How Can We Solve This Crisis', 'The History of the JVP', and 'The Path to Socialism in Sri Lanka'. When the Indian Peace Keeping Force (IPKF) landed with the consent of the government in 1987, an additional lecture was added: 'Save the Motherland from Indian Imperialism.'[28]

The JVP's support came principally from the densely populated districts of the South-west. Its appeal was to the educated Sinhalese-speaking young people who aspired to but saw little prospect of a secure job, marriage and respected place in their society. (Earlier, I described the situation of Jayanthi and her brothers working as labourers and as a night watchman. They had been supporters of the JVP in the 1971 insurrection.) The appealing critique was based on the assumption that it was the state's responsibility to look after the people—more jobs, better housing, cheaper food, free medical care. Their argument was not for a minimal state but, as mentioned earlier, for 'an intensely paternalistic and interventionist state'. And the first concern of the paternalistic state should be for the well-being of the people believed to be at the centre of Sinhalese culture—the rice-farming Buddhist villagers.

The distribution of resources and benefits should be determined by the state and not left to the market. Thus, central to the JVP was a criticism of capitalism and of the beneficiaries of capitalism—the rich, the large landowners, the successful business people. Those who had the advantage of a superior education, were fluent in English, possessed expensive consumer goods, lived in fine houses and who failed to identify with the poor Sinhalese were the enemy. The political elite based in Colombo who possessed these advantages, as well as their agents in the political parties and police must be replaced by persons responding to the needs of the true people of Sri Lanka. The 'status quo' was not acceptable, nor were the governmental institutions, used by the political elite to control society. The class society had to be overturned by violent revolution, if need be.

The argument that Sri Lanka was a multi-cultural society, that other groups had cultural rights and that the benefits provided by the state should be fairly distributed among the different cultural groups, was rejected. The JVP held that the island of Sri Lanka was the only home of the Sinhalese in the world and its integrity must be protected. Discussions by Bruce Matthews later in this book document these points. And the greatest threat to the future of the Sinhalese came from the Tamils, not just the Tamils of Sri Lanka but from the 60 million living across the narrow Palk Straits in Tamil Nadu.

The JVP shifted back and forth between these two objectives. At one time, senior JVP cadres had conversations with various Tamil militant groups to challenge the Sri Lankan political elite. At other times they regarded the Tamils as the greatest threat and were willing to forgo revolutionary action, enter the political arena, and campaign against any compromise with the Tamils that would endanger the supremacy of the Sinhalese. In April 2002, the JVP was organizing demonstrations and strikes to protest against the peace negotiations which the government had entered into with the LTTE. They feared that the negotiations would lead to the formation of an independent Tamil Eelam and so jeopardize both the position of the 'Sinhala race' and the position of the Buddhist religion.

THE TAMIL MILITANTS: In addition to the LTTE there were other militant Tamil groups who shared the general goal of Tamil Eelam but who analyzed the situation very differently, which led to different political strategies and to different views of the government. The Eelam People's Revolutionary Liberation Front (EPRLF) and the Eelam Revolutionary Organization of Students (EROS) were among the more important of such groups.[29]

As Rajanayagam makes clear in her contributions to this volume and as may be seen in the illustration and poetry, the LTTE based their claim to Tamil Eelam on being a separate nation and therefore being entitled to their own territory. The symbols that they used to define themselves looked back to the imperial glories of the Chola dynasty of Tamil Nadu. They adopted the symbol of the Cholas—the tiger. They emphasized loyalty to the ruler (Prabhakaran) and obedience to his commands as though he were a dynastic ruler. They demanded that other Tamil groups subordinate themselves to their direction or face elimination. This is illustrated by their killing of the followers of the Tamil Eelam Liberation Organization (TELO) and the EPRLF, both of which had tried to follow an independent line. No rivals were tolerated. The most heroic act was to sacrifice one's life for the nation. Any fraternization with the Sinhalese was a betrayal of the Tamil people's struggle. They shot the headmaster of St. John's College for organizing a cricket match between his students and the Sinhalese army. Tamil women as keepers of racial purity were instructed to stay away from outsiders: 'If you are born in our ethnic group and then destroy our ethnicity by consorting with outsiders, you commit treason and cannot call yourself a Tamil any more.'[30] Preservation of a homeland, of the language and the culture of Tamils could not be compromised. Groups occupying a culturally ambiguous position, such as Tamil-speaking Muslims, who would not subordinate themselves to the LTTE, were driven out of their homes and out of the Tamil 'homeland'. (See the chapters by Rajanayagam and Hasbullah in this volume.) This core position based on the existence of a cultural nation gave the LTTE great strength, justified their ruthlessness in dealing with traitors and made political compromise difficult.

In contrast to the LTTE, the EPRLF's position was grounded in a class analysis. They did not fight for a people or a language but for all suppressed groups. In the context of Sri Lanka in the 1980s, one of the suppressed groups consisted of the Tamils. The EPRLF focused their attention on the instruments and agencies of oppression—the Sri Lankan governmental administration, the police and armed forces. They did not specifically target poor Sinhalese workers or villagers as did the LTTE. Of course, they opposed the expansion of Sinhalese colonies into what had been Tamil-majority areas. But when they contested the election for the North and East Provincial Councils in 1988, their election manifesto emphasized equal rights for all ethnic groups living within the boundaries of the Tamil areas. They came out against religious bigotry and fundamentalism and for a multi-ethnic culture.[31] Beyond the election, where they won a majority of the seats in both provinces and where the LTTE had ordered a boycott, they looked to the liberation of all of Sri Lanka from class oppression.

The leader of the EPRLF, Annamalai Varadaraja Perumal, former lecturer in Economics at Jaffna University, became Chief Minister in the combined provincial councils on 10 December 1988. The LTTE refused to recognize the legitimacy of the elected Provincial Government. In its short life it was starved of funds by the central government. The Indian government undertook to support Perumal's government and helped train a Tamil police force for the provinces—mainly made up of former PLOTE (People's Liberation Organization of Tamil Eelam) and TELO militants. Then in March 1990 when the negotiated withdrawal of the IPKF began, Perumal declared the Eelam Democratic Republic and called for a constituent assembly to unilaterally draft a new constitution for an independent Tamil state based in the North and East with its capital at Trincomalee. The attempt failed and Perumal fled with the last of the Indian troops.

The EPRLF's view of government was more akin to other Marxist and left-wing parties that contested elections in Sri Lanka since before independence. They hoped to mobilize the poor and oppressed into a formidable electoral base which would challenge the existing political elite. Class position rather than ethnicity was held to be the decisive element in building and cementing group solidarity.

Yet, the criticism of the government both by the JVP and by Tamil militants was being overtaken by the changes in society. Certainly the role of the state as a distributor of benefits continued to be a fundamental concern as did the balance between individual and group rights. But the JVP remained centralist and did not come to terms with the diversity of group rights and regional differences. They clung to the increasingly anachronistic belief that all power came from the centre. The LTTE organized their alternative to government policies around the idea of protecting Tamil culture through the creation of an autonomous homeland. By the 1980s, if not before, the actual behaviour of the Tamil speakers was becoming increasingly diverse. They were much more mobile, with some family members living and working in Colombo and others overseas. The prospect of forming a homeland that would be culturally homogeneous and that could preserve the Tamil way was increasingly illusory. (See the vigorous discussion on this subject by someone who has lived under the LTTE in Sivamohan's chapter.)

It appeared that the government and these two major critics of government were still drawing on a set of older and increasingly irrelevant concepts.

'BUILDING A TRULY PLURALIST NATION STATE' AFTER 1980

By the late 1980s it was recognized that the old style of government could not be sustained and that a change was needed. The President, Chandrika Bandaranaike Kumaratunga said while delivering the first Madhavrao Scindia Memorial Lecture in April 2002, 'In Sri Lanka, we have faltered in the essential task of nation-building since independence ... we have failed to address the issue of building a truly pluralist nation state.'[32] Earlier governments had created this problem and now it was up to the current and future governments to rectify the mistake. If this was not enough, there were the other issues which all modern states have to address—stable employment, urban growth, aging population and the breakdown of authority and social control. These were not issues which any other sector of the society could address—not the institutions of the economy, not the civil society organizations.

Only the government had the constitutional mandate and the administrative reach.

DEVOLUTION AND THE PLURAL SOCIETY

The decisive beginning of the building of a pluralist state came with the signing of the Indo–Sri Lanka Agreement on 29 July 1987, by the Prime Minister of India, Rajiv Gandhi, and the President of Sri Lanka, J.R. Jayawardene. The agreement provided for the sending of the IPKF to act as a third-party buffer between the Sri Lankan forces and the Tamil militants. The Indian intervention had been brought about by the Sri Lankan army and air force attacks in Jaffna, which were killing civilians and causing much suffering. The agreement provided for the following changes: the north and east Provinces to merge but a referendum at the end of one year in the east about continuance of the merger; limited autonomy for Tamil areas; ceasefire in the north and east; and the surrender of arms by Tamil militants. The agreement led directly to the Thirteenth Amendment to the Constitution, dated 14 November 1987. This was characterized by a leading legal scholar as 'an attempt at formulating a new social contract for sharing of power between the majority and a minority community and for sharing power between the centre and periphery'.[33] But since the terms of the initial agreement and also the Thirteenth Amendment were arrived at without any public consultation, no political constituency had been enlisted in support.

In spite of the absence of support, the Provincial Councils Act was passed in 1988, under which elections were held throughout the island. There was little interest in the strange new Provincial Councils and the government was slow in transferring resources and functions as provided by the act. The short life of the joint North-east Council under the leader of the EPRLF, Perumal, demonstrated the inadequacy of the government's response.

A new parliamentary election in 1989, after the ruthless suppression of the second JVP insurrection, returned the UNP as the largest party, though still a minority. It sought to rectify the lack of consultation and to build a supportive constituency for devolution by striking an all-party Select Committee of Parliament. After 40 meetings, all the Committee could agree upon were some rudimentary interim recommendations: '(*a*) on the establishment of two separate units of administration for the Northern and Eastern Provinces; (*b*) to adopt a scheme of devolution on lines similar to those obtaining in the Indian Constitution; and (*c*) to devolve more subjects that are in List III (Concurrent List) or to dispense with the List.'[34]

The People's Alliance (PA) headed by Chandrika Bandaranaike Kumaratunga won the next national election in 1994 with the promise that they would bring peace to the country. This was understood to mean a serious policy of devolution of resources and power to the provinces/regions and, probably, introducing a constitutional revision which required both a two-thirds majority in parliament and winning a national referendum. Both hurdles were nearly insuperable given that the PA only had 94 of the 225 seats in the legislature and was dependent on the support of other minority parties. There were two devolution proposals issued by the government (August 1995 and January 1996) which were criticized and ultimately rejected by the UNP-led parliamentary opposition. In October 1997, the Parliamentary Select Committee on devolution reported that it could not reach an agreement on the unit of devolution and whether the Sri Lankan state should be a unitary state or a union of regions.

The government delayed holding any further provincial elections until its hand was forced by a suit brought into the Supreme Court of Sri Lanka. In January 1999, the court declared that voting was a fundamental right within the ambit of freedom of expression and ordered the Elections Commissioner to hold elections for five provincial councils within three months. (The elections could not be held in the Northern and Eastern Provinces because of the fighting and the elections in the Western Province had been held earlier.) The court said that the suspension of elections was arbitrary and unreasonable and that the rights of speech and expression were violated.[35] The provincial elections that were held in April and June 1999 were vigorously contested, with 12 parties campaigning and over 2,400 nominees. Voter turnout was 70 per cent. It appeared that the idea of provincial government was widely accepted, after the slow start 10 years earlier. How well the delegation of powers and resources to the provinces could be used to protect and advance group rights remained unclear.

But the war had to be settled before there could be a realistic devolution to the Tamil majority areas in the north and east. The most promising prospect for peace came when the newly elected UNP government (October 2001) signed a Memorandum of Understanding with the LTTE to put in place a ceasefire, pending a negotiated peace. The Memorandum of Understanding, which was signed on 22 February 2002, provided for an international team, known as the Sri Lanka Monitoring Mission, led by a retired Norwegian army officer to monitor the ceasefire. The Memorandum was severely criticized by President Kumaratunga in a letter to Prime Minister Wickremasinghe. Then the Buddhist establishment mounted a major political challenge to the Memorandum. On 23 April 2002 a propagandistic letter was sent to the Prime Minister and the President. It said in part:

> For the first time in our history, ominous signs threatening the break up of the 2,500 year long unitary character of our motherland are already visible ... it appears to us that the so-called peace process initiated with the MOU now in place is primarily aimed at the establishment of Eelam rather than achieving real peace ... the LTTE is not interested in peace but in the establishment of a powerful Tamil state within the territory of Sri Lanka. This will be inevitable unless we resist it with all our might. And the failure to prevent it with result in the subjugation of the majority race by the minority Tamils and the extermination of the Sinhala race and the Buddha Sasana from this island. It is therefore the bounden duty of every member of the Maha Sangha and lay people to do their utmost to prevent the designs of the Tamil terrorists from becoming Eelam a reality. [sic][36]

The letter continued by itemizing seven non-negotiable conditions 'from the point of view of the Sinhalese people' for the peace negotiations. Among them was the maintenance of the unitary character of the constitution and a rejection of any 'federal or quasi federal or a confederacy' reform. The letter was signed by the heads of the various chapters of the Siam Nikaya, the Amarapura Nikaya, and the Rammana Nikaya. Officers in various Buddhist lay organizations also signed. The same day, protest rallies against the peace negotiations were mounted in Colombo led by the JVP.

Twenty years earlier such formidable opposition might have proved insurmountable. By 2002, with a much more educated public and with many more experienced outside of the village and the country, these exhortations to political action by the religious leaders had lost some of their commanding force. When ending the conflict is so important to the society, such archaic fulminations are not likely to halt the process.

Also a Fair Basic Structure for Sri Lanka

The environment for devolution and a pluralist state, as well as the many other issues faced by a modern society, would require an expanding tax base and the employment generation of a growing economy as well as the social activism and political participation of civil organizations to rebuild confidence in the future. There would be many actors, each with a fragment of power. Yet, to avoid deepening confusion and contradictory policies some stabilizing vision of the value of Sri Lanka to its residents and a stabilizing practice of a just system of cooperation among the main social and political institutions are needed.[37] The state as the only all-island institution recognized both internationally and, barring some of the Tamil militants, domestically as well, carries the double responsibility of maintaining its capacity to decide and act and also to create an environment for the fair use of its power. Obviously, if the state's power is eroded too far, whether by political devolution or through the loss of its capacity to control its own economy, then it is in danger of losing the capacity to lead in the fashioning of a more peaceful and tolerant society.

Notes

1. Partial bibliographies of these studies can be found in Claire M. Lambert (Ed.), *Village Studies: Data Analysis and Bibliography*, Volume Two, London: Mansell Information Services for the Institute of Development Studies, University of Sussex, 1978; and in S.W.R. de A. Samarasinghe and Vidyamali Samarasinghe, *Historical Dictionary of Sri Lanka*, Lanham, Md.: The Scarecrow Press, 1998.
2. *Statistical Abstract of the Democratic Socialist Republic of Sri Lanka, 1999*, Colombo: Department of Census and Statistics 1999, Table 4.2.
3. *Economic and Social Statistics of Sri Lanka, 1999*, p. 16, Colombo: Central Bank of Sri Lanka.

4. The 1976 research is reported in 'Meegama: Seeking Livelihoods in a Kandyan Village', in Barrie M. Morrison et al. (Eds), *The Disintegrating Village: Social Change in Rural Sri Lanka*, Colombo: Lake House, 1979, pp. 71–113.
5. *Pravada*, 1997:2.
6. This circuitous route to a justifiable estimate of urbanized population of the Colombo area was necessary because of the badly out-of-date definitions of an urban area in the Sri Lanka census and the lack of published data for Colombo in the 2001 census. The estimates were generated from data in Malik Majeed, 'Urbanization Trend in the Greater Colombo Area from 1956 to 1994', *Economic Review*, Vol. 21, No. 12, March 1996, pp. 26–28.
7. *Report on Consumer Finance and Socio Economic Survey, Sri Lanka, 1996/97*, Colombo: Central Bank of Sri Lanka, 1999, p. 29.
8. Richard Leete, *Malaysia's Demographic Transition: Rapid Development, Culture, and Politics*, Kuala Lumpur: Oxford University Press, 1996, p. 162.
9. Barrie M. Morrison, 'The Transcendence of Locality and the Persistence of Community in Sri Lanka, 1980–1995', *Journal of Asian and African Studies*, Vol. 33, No. 2, May, pp. 205–22.
10. *Development NGOs of Sri Lanka, A Directory*, Colombo: IRED Partners in Asia, 1991.
11. Quoted in Paikiasothy Saravanamuttu, 'Sri Lanka: Civil Society, The Nation and the State-Building Challenge', in Alison Van Rooey (Ed.), *Civil Society and the Aid Industry*, London: Earthscan/North South Institute, 1998, p. 119.
12. Karunatissa Atukorala, *Suicide, Problem and Prevention*, Kandy: Integrated Development Association, 1998.
13. Two discussions of political and policy confusions aggravated by conflicting ideas are: Zygmunt Bauman, *In Search of Politics*, Stanford: Stanford University Press, 1999; and David Garland, *The Culture of Control: Crime and Social Order in Contemporary Society*, Oxford: Oxford University Press, 2001.
14. Nira Wickramasinghe, *Civil Society in Sri Lanka: New Circles of Power*, New Delhi: Sage Publications, 2001, p. 17.
15. Ibid., p. 31.
16. L.A. Wickremeratne, 'Planning and Economic Development', in K.M. De Silva (Ed.), *Sri Lanka: A Survey*, London: C. Hurst, 1977, p. 144.
17. Robert S. Anderson, Edwin Levy and Barrie M. Morrison, *Rice Science and Development Politics: IRRI's Strategies and Asian Diversity 1950–1980*, Oxford: Clarendon Press, 1991, pp. 161–62.
18. 'Mahaweli Ganga Development Project', *Economic Review*, Vol. 4, Nos 8–9, November/December 1978; and H.P. Muller and S.T. Hettige (Eds), *The Blurring of a Vision—The Mahaweli: Its Social, Economic and Political Implications*, Ratmalana: Sarvodaya, 1995.
19. Sunil Bastian (Ed.), *Devolution and Development in Sri Lanka*, Colombo: International Centre for Ethnic Studies, 1994, p. 171.
20. *http://www.theacademic.org*, accessed on 11 April 2002.
21. Calculated from Prema-chandra Athukorala and Sarath Rajapathirana, *Liberalization and Industrial Transformation: Sri Lanka in International Perspective*, New Delhi: Oxford University Press, 2000, Table A1.
22. Ibid. p. 41.

23. L.M. Grobar and S. Gnanaselvam, 'The Economic Effects of the Sri Lankan Civil War', *Economic Development and Cultural Change*, Vol. 41, No. 2, p. 403. Quoted in Gnaneshan Wignaraja, *Trade Liberalization in Sri Lanka: Exports, Technology and Industrial Policy*, London: Macmillan, 1998, p. 246, note 8.
24. Jayadeva Uyangoda, 'Political Dimensions of Youth "Unrest" in Sri Lanka', in S.T. Hettige (Ed.), *Unrest or Revolt: Aspects of Youth Unrest in Sri Lanka*, Colombo: Goethe Institute and American Studies Association, 1992, p. 43.
25. A fuller discussion of the expansion of state functions can be found in my paper, 'The Transformation of Sri Lankan Society, 1948–1999: The Fragmentation of Centralism', *Journal of Asian and African Studies*. Vol. 36, No. 2, 2001, pp. 181–202.
26. K.M. de Silva (Ed.), *Sri Lanka: Problems of Governance*, Colombo: International Centre for Ethnic Studies, 1993, pp. 95–96.
27. As of 2002, the JVP was no longer proscribed and had successfully contested elections, holding 16 out of 225 seats in the national legislature.
28. Rohan Gunaratna, *Sri Lanka a Lost Revolution? The Inside Story of the JVP*, Kandy: Institute of Fundamental Studies, 1990, p. 61.
29. An excellent discussion may be found in Dagmar Hellmann-Rajanayagam, *The Tamil Tigers: Armed Struggle for Identity*, Stuttgart: Franz Steiner Verlag, 1994, pp. 54–85.
30. *Cutantirap Paravani*, January–February 1991, p. 2. Quoted in Rajanayagam, n. 29, p. 70. See also Sivamohan's chapter.
31. Rajanayagam, n. 29, p. 76.
32. LacNet News Update, 23 April 2002.
33. Radhika Coomaraswamy, 'Devolution, the Law, and Judicial Construction', in Sunil Bastian (Ed.), *Devolution and Development in Sri Lanka*, Colombo: International Centre for Ethnic Studies, 1994, p. 121.
34. Quoted in *Sri Lanka: The Devolution Debate*, Colombo: International Centre for Ethnic Studies, 1998, p. 219.
35. *The Sri Lanka Monitor*, January 1999.
36. Translation of letter as reported on LacNet News Update, 23 April 2002.
37. The term 'basic structure' was used to describe such a public understanding and practice of justice by John Rawls in his final work, edited by Erim Kelly. See *Justice as Fairness: A Restatement*, Cambridge, Mass.: Belknap Press, 2001, pp. 8–12.

II

Tensions of Class and Caste, Group Rights and Individual Freedoms

Cultural categories, social divisions and hierarchies of power have been transformed in Sri Lanka since independence. The shift from an agriculture-based society—with its caste divisions justified by occupational functions and customary practice—towards an urban-oriented society has undermined one set of social certainties. The earlier determination of large farmers, whether Sinhalese or Tamil, 'to keep those fellows (tenants and labourers) in their place', has been undercut by new employment and residential opportunities for all castes.

Similarly, with the decline in the significance of land and of power alliances in village society, the deep concern with female chastity, marriage and inheritance waned. Education and the new urban economy opened the doors for women to gain greater independence. Parents lost control of their daughters. The international women's movements and the multiplying NGOs concerned with women's rights helped create a 'warmer climate' for women in the work place and for the individual woman to find an independent voice.

But while some shaping ideas and practices were losing their force, others were gaining new power. Definitions of what it meant to be Sri Lankan came to be the subject of bitter conflict. The leaders of the Buddhist clergy used their respected status to demand primacy for the Sinhala 'race'. Marginalized and alienated Tamils mobilized around equality for their language and culture. Sinhalese-dominated governments overrode the claims of cultural minorities to equality. The struggle tended to force the citizens of the island into one narrow social mould or another. The values of cultural pluralism were overwhelmed by the new narrow fundamentalisms. The individual's freedom to find alternate lifestyles was regarded with suspicion and sometimes labelled disloyal.

Something of the emotional intensity of these conflicts within the Tamil community is illustrated by the picture from the Heroes' memorial pamphlet of 2001 and by the contrast between the poetry glorifying death in service of the Tamil liberation cause and that of the individual Tamil women's life-affirming poetry found in Sivamohan's chapter.

2

Religious and Ideological Intransigence among the Sinhalese

BRUCE MATTHEWS

Religion and cultural ideology are the most important factors delaying the development of *vishvasaya* (Sinhala for 'trust') in Sri Lanka's complex society. In this chapter, we shall examine these topics from the perspective of the Sinhala and Ceylon Tamil communities. Both have deep cultural timelines, centuries of ethnocentric allegiance expressed through the language and religion, and claims to a traditional homeland. By way of method, the chapter first examines religion, specifically Buddhism, among the Sinhalese and shows how the faith has been unable to contribute to the development of a pluralist society and an urgently needed federal-style polity. Tragically and ironically, Buddhism stands in the way of any political transition that might bring stability to the island nation. The following chapter then turns to Ceylon Tamil society, which has found its historic civilization and self-understanding radically altered, if not subverted, by the ideological dominance of the Liberation Tigers of Tamil Eelam (LTTE). The latter brooks no opposition among the million or so people under its direct authority.

The Sinhalese comprise 74 per cent of Sri Lanka's population of 20 million. Of the Sinhalese, 70 per cent are Theravada Buddhists, and the remainder of non-Buddhist Sinhalese are usually Christians. It is important to point out, however, that Sinhala Christians share with Sinhala Buddhists many of the same cultural sensitivities and customs. There are times when the devotees of the two religions act together in the name of a single Sinhala culture (*samskrutiya*). For example, many Christians identify with a traditional Sinhala caste (*kulaya*) or, in the perceived cause of protecting Sinhala culture, express reservations about adopting any other political model than the present so-called 'unitary state' (which denies ethnic minorities any real political autonomy). At the same time, Sinhala Christians are seriously disadvantaged as members of the armed forces or as politicians in search of high office. Thus, Buddhism remains absolutely essential to any definition of Sinhala culture. Some aver that it is not so much Buddhism (*dhamma*) as it is Buddhists and their political attitudes that have had such a vexing role to play in the modern history of Sri Lanka. There is some truth to this, and when reference is made to 'Buddhism' being a problematic feature of political life, this distinction should be kept in mind.

Much has been written by both Lankan and foreign scholars about the contemporary Sinhala Buddhist world-view and the culture that sustains it. Indeed, it could be argued that no other modern Buddhist country has had its religion so minutely examined. One reason for this is that the faith, so often militant and even bellicose in the name of a culture, appears wildly at odds with the humane, logical teaching of Gotama Sakyamuni, or with the gentle version of Buddhism expressed in textbooks on world religions. What has emerged over the last half-century in particular is a religion attached to what Scott Newton once described as antirational political sentiments entrenched in a widespread Sinhala Buddhist attitude and world-view.[1] These sentiments continue to make a primary appeal to raw emotion. They have been fuelled by the LTTE's many violent attacks on some of Sri Lankan Buddhism's holiest sites. These have left a deep, lasting bitterness among the Sinhalese.[2] Long before these depredations occurred, however, there had emerged in Sri Lanka a Buddhism that was absolutist, ethnically totalitarian, receptive to violence, yet deceptively assuming the guise of a rational argument.[3] Many Buddhist monks, politicians and a vast sector of Sinhala society apparently continue to accept this world-view (*arkalpa*), thus preventing the development of intra-ethnic trust. There is certainly no widespread desire to restructure the state to accommodate the new political needs of the aggrieved Ceylon Tamils. On the contrary, a stepping back into an idyllic past, to a notion of state as *rata, jatiya, agama* (homeland, nation, religion) is frequently encountered. As Steven Kemper writes: 'When contemporary

Sinhalas speak of the past, they do so as if yesterday's actors were moved by today's motives.'[4]

Buddhism is not a monolithic organization in Sri Lanka. The Sri Lankan monastic order (*sangha*) is made up of approximately 30,000 monks (*bhikkhus*) and novices (*samaneras*) belonging to three principal *nikayas*, Siam, Ramanna and Amarapura.[5] The fact that these fraternities are in turn divided into many smaller groups (*parshava*) is important, as is the fact that each monastery (*vihara*) is virtually an autonomous unit. It means that the *nikayas* are somewhat nominal entities and that centralized authority over the conduct of *sangha* members is almost non-existent. Splintering of the *sangha* continues.[6] Its many nuances, structural and ideological, make it impossible to propose any one sweeping commentary on its participation in the political destiny of the country.

Some historical background is necessary to understand the current role of Buddhism in national life. H.L. Seneviratne and others show how the patriot Anagarika Dharmapala (1864–1933) may be seen as the architect of modern Sri Lankan Buddhism, including a much more socially engaged *sangha*.[7] Despite the rise of new *nikayas* and an opening up of professional religious life to the lower castes, Buddhist monks in colonial nineteenth and early twentieth century Ceylon were still locked in a paralyzing time-warp. Few monks had the education or vision to see that new models of ministry and social outreach were necessary in an era of accelerated change. A monastic vocation that focused on reciting *pirith* (sacred verses to ward off evil), receiving *dana* (foods and gifts) in order for the laity to make merit (*punna*), and on long sermons (*dharmadasena*) delivered at a time inconvenient for working people, was increasingly irrelevant to a society that instead needed directions on how to co-exist with the educational, political and economic realities of colonialism and modernization. Perhaps most importantly, the *sangha* had lost contact with the Sinhala elite, who increasingly had access to the English language, using it for educational, commercial and even everyday social purposes. Dharmapala challenged these insufficiencies, and urged reforms based partly on grudgingly admired aspects of Christian missionary work, including punctuality, short religious services, emphasis on secular education and involvement in the social concerns of the people. For Dharmapala, monks had become lazy, pampered, given to expectations of public deference, and completely divorced from serious social, economic and political problems. His response to this has left a legacy that is still potent in the *sangha* today.

Dharmapala's efforts were commendable, but through a series of unpredictable events, his awakening of the 'sleeping monkhood' had what some would argue were bad results in the long run. His 'Protestant Buddhism', based in part on the hallmarks of Christian missionary discipline, work habits and enthusiasm, was re-expressed in such a way that many Buddhists came to believe they were there all along in the Theravada tradition. This was in contrast to the traditional ritual role of the monk. Protestant Buddhism advocated direct *sangha* participation in such 'economic' ventures as village and urban development. Unfortunately, the economic aspect was soon pervaded by politics and ideology. Within a decade of independence, a highly politicized *sangha* emerged—'paving the way', as Seneviratne has argued, 'for a national tragedy on a scale previously unknown'.[8] There were serious attempts to bring elements of the powerful *sangha* into meaningful contact with the Westernized Sinhala elite who would have a political role to play when Ceylon gained independence. As far back as 1873, when the Vidyodaya Pirivena (a famous Buddhist seminary) was established, it aimed to meet the emerging middle and upper classes with a 'new scripturalism' or way of adapting Buddhism to the economic and political opportunities of the time.[9] However, although this mission met with some success, the *sangha* never took advantage of an opportunity that could have had an enormous positive influence—modern education for young monks. Possibly some could have attended the great schools so important to twentieth century Ceylonese national life (though admittedly many of these were associated with Christianity). The monks might have been connected with, rather than divided from the society that was newly emerging.[10]

By the end of the colonial era, the *sangha* exhibited many signs of tension and disagreement over the role of the clergy in society and politics. Most factions claimed interest in social issues (*dhammakathika*), but from very different perspectives. An increasingly ethnocentric and politicized Buddhist *sangha* gained momentum and authority. Nowhere was the motivation for an activist role more clearly articulated than in Ven. Walpola Rahula's 1946 ground-breaking publication *The Heritage of the Bhikkhu* (*Bhiksuvage*

Urumaya).[11] Rahula (1910–97) is a figure of vital importance to modern Sinhala Buddhism. His shadow lies across the *sangha* to this day, and his rallying cry ('the nation and religion have to move together') is still pertinent. A brilliant, multi-lingual scholar of immense erudition, Rahula maintained that the contemporary monk, alert to the decline of Buddhist influence in cultural, educational and national or political affairs, should see it as his personal responsibility to prevent further deterioration. He encouraged the development of a monk who was educated, open to Western languages and secular learning, one in whom religion blended with a new sense of social service. But it was not to be. Instead, a tougher, uncompromising, anti-Western and ethnocentric Buddhism developed from *The Heritage*, and from two 'declarations' of the same period (Vidyalankara, 1946, and Kelaniya, 1947).[12] Vidyalankara (Vidyodaya's rival seminary) already had a reputation for championing Sinhala Buddhist cultural nationalism, claiming that monks were justified in engaging in political activism and even militancy. A number of societies arose to safeguard Buddhist interests (*sasanaraksala samiti*) over the next half-century. The 1950s and 1960s saw an outpouring of raw Sinhala cultural emotion, which populist politicians quickly seized upon to further their control of the emerging independent state. These included an unofficial but still influential 1952 Buddhist Commission of Inquiry (which finally published its report in 1956 as *The Betrayal of Buddhism*), and the 1954 formation of the Eksath Bhikkhu Peramuna (a frank attempt to organize the *sangha* politically in order to implement the findings of the Commission of Inquiry).[13] The 2,500th anniversary (*jayanti*) of the Buddha's enlightenment in 1954 furthered enthusiasm for playing up the traditional link between Sinhala 'race' (*jati*) and Buddhist religion (*sasana*). An appeal to neo-traditionalism, rather than a much-needed reappraisal of the role of *sangha* and religion in public life, became commonplace. This also focused on emphasizing the much touted 'fear of extinction' of both Theravada Buddhism and the Sinhala language. These were threatened, Sinhala patriots maintained, by a hegemonic Hindu Indian (and specifically Tamil) *enosis* agenda for Lanka. From such sentiments as these emerged a new Buddhist orthodoxy, a martial Buddhism that has replaced the concept of peace and non-violence.[14] Sinhala was promoted as the official language of the country, and political efforts made to support the general principle of 'according to Buddhism its rightful place in the country' (even though Buddhism did not receive special Constitutional status until 1972).[15]

As Lanka's ethnic communalism became increasingly heated, and moderate Ceylon Tamils were excluded from parliamentary participation (they were effectively locked out of the democratic system by the Sixth Constitutional Amendment of August 1983), Buddhism was frequently evoked to prevent a negotiated federal-style polity.[16] This is best seen in the sudden promotion of Buddhist ultranationalist patriotic (*deshapremi*) associations. A glance at the names of these organizations reveals their intent: to appeal to Buddhism as a justification for aggressive political action. A narrow, religiously-focused patriotism is just beneath the surface of the more radical *deshapremi tharuna peramunas*.[17] To what extent they meet widespread public favour and support is questionable, for they have generally not done well in local or national elections. On the other hand, there can be little doubt that a *deshapremi* spirit is kept alive by monks, some of whom are powerful preachers with significant public appeal, and by lay patrons whose political ideology is enhanced by an association with the faith. Among the more important organizations or ideologies are the Sri Lanka Sinhala Bauddha Sammelanaya, the Mawbima Surekeemy Viyaparaya, the Bauddha Sasanika ha Bauddha Katayuthu Adikshana ha Karya Sadhaka Mandalaya, and Jathika Chintanaya, all still to some degree active in the twenty-first century.

The Sinhala Bauddha Sammelanaya was established in 1985 by Gamini Iriyagolle, an articulate and renowned lawyer. A member of the English-speaking upper middle class (and with a record of distinguished service in the one-time highly regarded Ceylon Civil Service), Iriyagolle had a wide outreach to all levels of Sinhala society in the 1980s and early 1990s. The Bauddha Sammelanaya is open to monks and laity and, until his death in 1999, was supported by the powerful prelate of the Asgiriya chapter of the Siam Nikaya (the acme of the Sinhala Buddhist fraternities), Ven. Palipanne Chandananda. Both Iriyagolle and Palipanne subsequently founded the Mawbima Surekeemy (Movement for the Defence of the Motherland) in 1986, which brought together monks and politicians to protest against any concessions concerning the 'national question' resulting from discussions between Colombo, the LTTE and the government of India. The Mawbima claimed it had no specific Sinhala Buddhist identity, and to some degree this was correct—from time to time there were a few Christian and Muslim members. But within a year the organization fragmented, with the most significant wing coming under the influence of the eloquent and dynamic monk Ven. Sobitha Mahathera and the arch-Sinhala lay nationalist Dinesh Gunawardene, and returning to a specifically hard-line Sinhala Buddhist focus.[18] Finally, the Bauddha Sasanika ha Bauddha Adikshana (Task Force to Supervise Buddhist Religious Activities and Affairs), established with the specific purpose of preventing a merger between the Northern and Eastern provinces (a central Tamil political demand), was supported by the prelates of all three major *nikayas* and many lay Buddhist organizations. The pressure on the major Sinhala political parties to embrace the views of these cultural organizations for the 'protection' or 'fostering' of Buddhism was intense.

On the other hand, the Jathika Chintanaya ('national ideology' or 'way of thinking') movement first surfaced in 1984. Not an organization so much as an ideology (there is no 'membership'), Jathika Chintanaya nonetheless identifies with cultural exclusivism and nationalism. Though somewhat diminished in the public attention it receives, Jathika Chintanaya is still a force to be reckoned with. It reflects a concern, not so much about the civil war, or even the place of Buddhism in the destiny of the state, as about the effects of globalization on Sinhala culture. The nomenclature was initially adopted by Nalin de Silva, a Colombo University mathematics professor, and Gunadasa Amarasekera, a dental surgeon, to define the need for a specifically Sinhala educational strategy and methodology.[19] At its height in the late 1990s, Jathikha Chintanaya was popular on university campuses and among some elements of the urban elite and the *sangha*. Nalin de Silva claimed its 'philosophy' could be found in every Buddhist village temple.[20] Though this is an exaggeration, for it never became a 'grass-roots' peasant movement, Jathikha Chintanaya has certainly been influential, a unique expression of concern over the destiny of Sinhala culture. By rejecting the adequacy of Western 'extreme rationalism', de Silva and Amarasekera aim to reinvigorate a specifically Sinhalese way of understanding and learning, a 'revolution by way of thinking' (*chintanaya viplavaya*). Monks associated with this endeavour urge universities to raise 'indigenousness' (*desiyatvaya*) and 'nationalness' (*jati kativaga*). A chief target is the primacy of the English language, particularly in education, but also in business and politics. Knowledge of English is seen as the sword (*kaduwa*) that divides those with privileged backgrounds from the disadvantaged. This emphasis on rejecting English at a time when its educational and commercial importance is widespread and in demand is a return to the *swabasha* ideology that surrounded S.W.R.D. Bandaranaike in 1955 when, under pressure from Sinhalese Buddhist militants, he claimed that 'if returned to office, he would effect the switchover from English in twenty-four hours'. He did, with catastrophic results.[21] *Swabasha* is consistent with the nostalgic vision Jathika Chintanaya has of Sri Lankan history, the idyllic pastoralism of the '*stupa*, tank and paddy'. But de Silva insists they are not trying to turn the clock back and are not 'mythologically fundamentalist'. Inter-cultural experience may be unavoidable, he claims, but the 'native people should decide what to absorb'.[22]

In sum, although Jathika Chintanaya ideology might appear naïve in the context of Sri Lanka's ensconced free-enterprise economy and reasonably successful experience with democracy, what it represents—a pride in Sinhala cultural accomplishments, resentment of Western ideological, financial and technological domination—is an understandable collective emotion fraught with political significance. More than any other Sinhala institution, the Jathika Chintanaya movement responds to the concern that the old, stable agrarian society, with its clearly defined social roles, is in the process of being swept aside by the forces of globalization, which have touched every corner of the country. Jathika Chintanaya is no longer the force that it once was. It represented a trend in the 1990s, but was too closely associated with Nalin de Silva, who in due course lost his position and forum at the university. But the ideological issues are still kept very alive in newer organizations and political ventures.[23]

This leads to a second issue: whether the *sangha* appreciates the importance of adjusting the Sinhalese Buddhist world-view to the new political, economic and social realities confronting society and state in Sri Lanka today. One recent commentator suggests that 'what is most urgently needed is not a reinforcement of Buddhist religious identity or government policy that gives "pride of place" to Buddhism ... but monks and nuns of intelligence, insight and sensitivity'.[24] At the heart of the matter is a *sangha* that cannot adequately provide this without considerable reform. Many of those who take holy orders do not evidently possess these desirable qualities, and some appear unduly materialistic. Today, we can see monks who frequent restaurants, handle money and insist on the right to have an income-generating occupation. Other maverick behaviour, including overt renegade political involvement, is not infrequent and usually beyond *sangha* control.[25]

Monastic education is another controversial subject. Spiritual growth and self-transformation are the *sangha's* appropriate aims.[26] Seminaries (*pirivenas*) train monks (nuns are still completely excluded) to be village pastors, but the curriculum is arguably too traditional and dated to be of much use beyond a ministry carrying out the ritual responsibilities. It is an education, as one monk has put it, 'capable of preserving a religious culture not very different from that of the 16th century'.[27] Traditional subjects such as Pali, Sanskrit, Buddhist cosmology, scripture and Sinhala history are rarely complemented by what some monks call 'modern subjects', such as elementary physical sciences, geography, politics, world history, comparative religion, economics and Western philosophy and languages. Monks may set themselves up as experts in these areas, but few have any substantive knowledge about such key contemporary topics as jurisprudence, human rights, multiculturalism, or the geopolitical consequences of the civil war. In this regard, Seneviratne writes, 'it is one of the stark and unbelievable facts of contemporary Sri Lankan Theravada that there is not one single monk who can truly be described as an urbane intellectual who has imbibed contemporary knowledge and has developed a contemporary outlook and sensibility'. Others, such as Ananda Wickremeratne, take Seneviratne to task for this kind of sweeping statement, but probably most scholars would agree that the Lankan *sangha* lacks good thinkers or theologians, and is ill-prepared to guide the nation, as it is sometimes wont to do, on Sri Lanka's compounded ethnic and geopolitical problems.[28] In a similar vein, Regi Siriwardene has asked where all the socially radical Buddhists are, as well as a *sangha* that can express in religious terms the ideology and problems of the working class?[29] Any 'liberation theology' in Sinhala Buddhism is couched in heavy nationalist and ethnic language with not much concern for the politically and economically oppressed in class- and caste-dominated Sinhala society.

A third concern is that the *sangha* and Buddhist spokespersons, in the name of the faith, are using religion to foster war spirit against the LTTE. It is true that they have not succeeded in persuading the middle and upper classes of Sinhala society to commit themselves to an all-out war, but it is alarming and paradoxical that the *sangha* should be involved in war propaganda.[30] They have been consistently opposed to peaceful solutions. Not a single attempt (and there have been many) by Colombo to secure a memorandum of understanding on some kind of federal solution to the 'national question' has been supported by the *sangha*, though the ultimate alternative to negotiations is war.[31] For example, on explaining a *sangha* plan of action to derail an agreement between the state, India and the LTTE in 1985, the distinguished but hawkish Ven. Walpola Rahula announced that although all possible peaceful avenues would be used to prevent an agreement, if they failed, 'there is a weapon that the *sangha* has. Using that weapon will wage a battle all over the country. The police, the armed forces or any other force will not stop us because the *sangha* is willing to lay down their lives'.[32] It can be argued that if the monks had taken a stand for peace, the main political problems could have been solved.[33] It is one thing for the clergy of any religion to extend its patronage to the armed forces in a time of crisis, but the Lankan *sangha* appears to have gone much further than mere patronage and has lost the chance to bring resolution and healing to a shattered people.[34] It is, however, to Buddhism's credit that it has not been involved in any violence against the Ceylon Tamils in the south after the infamous pogrom of July 1983, and that is a huge advance.

In this chapter religious intransigence among the Sinhalese majority has been reviewed largely from the perspective of Buddhism. This is not to ignore the fact that religious identity in Sri Lanka is as variegated as in any in Asian country, but the other religions have only incidental roles to play in the historical conflict between the Sinhalese majority and the Ceylon Tamil community. Interestingly, Sinhala Buddhism rarely exhibits overt disrespect for other faiths. Even Hinduism is acknowledged as profoundly sacred, and is usually divorced from the opprobrium associated with the Tamil enemy.[35] Rightly or wrongly, Christianity is to a degree perceived by Buddhists to be empathetic to, if not in support of, the Ceylon Tamil cause for political autonomy, but this has not resulted in overt Buddhist hostility against Christians. Because of the presence of many Muslims in the Eastern Province, and the fact that the Muslims ('Ceylon Moors', one million strong) use Tamil as their mother tongue, Muslims have had to respond to the war question—but always on the side of the state, with communal support never couched in theological language. Strangely, Sinhala Buddhism will not tolerate any form of Buddhism other than Theravada on the island, despite its attempts to 'internationalize' itself.[36] In particular, Mahayana is invited for its wealthy Oriental patrons, but, on the argument that Sinhala Buddhism is 'vulnerable', is not permitted to set up any physical presence (temples, schools, seminaries). Some Sinhala Buddhists go so far as to label Mahayana a 'parasite growth'. For example, when the Sinhala monk Ven. Pelpola Vipassi returned from Japan as a convert to Mahayana in 1990 and attempted to set up a centre, he was attacked and prevented from doing so. Addressing the All Ceylon Buddhist Council at the time, Professor M.B. Ariyapala announced that 'though we accuse Buddhists for embracing Christianity, the worst thing that could befall the Buddhists is to embrace Mahayana'.[37]

The picture that emerges, then, is of a Sinhala Buddhism that is protective of its 'foremost place' in society, but not able to adjust in key ways to the vast changes underway that will continue to challenge its relevance. The *sangha* in particular appears sclerotic, unable to produce new commentary or to support new strategies that might help the Sinhala majority recognize the seriousness of their social and political predicament. Tradition and culture are indispensable to human society.[38] Monks of stature like the chief incumbents of the Siam Nikaya's famous chapters, Malwatte and Asgiriya, seem complacent and not self-critical at all, unable to see the political rights of the Ceylon Tamils or even how the present situation came about. Buddhism remains a potent conservative force in Sinhala society; it protects and ennobles the past and provides stability for the present but rarely shows signs of a reforming instinct. The challenge here is to bring to life an inclusivist nationalist discourse, which acknowledges the significance of the Sinhala Buddhist past but allows Lanka's substantial minorities, with their many skills and talents, to have a place in society, economy and polity.

NOTES

1. S. Newton, 'Sinhala Buddhist Nationalism and the Politics of the Anti-Rational', *Thatched Patio*, Vol. 15, August 1987, Colombo: International Centre for Ethnic Studies.
2. Sri Mahabodhi at Anuradhapura, the sprig of the tree under which Gotama is said to have received enlightenment, was sprayed by machine gun fire in a devastating raid in May 1985. Ten years later, in January 1998, some portion of the Dalada Maligawa (Temple of the Tooth) in Kandy was blown up by LTTE suicide cadres. These events have, not unexpectedly, hardened the *sangha*, much reducing its collective pity for the Ceylon Tamil victims of the civil war. They remain the most serious tactical blunders of the LTTE's campaign to bring the civil war to the south.
3. Sometimes this exclusivist attitude is associated with a Buddhist fundamentalism, though historians are divided on the appropriateness of that theological term in this context. See Tessa J. Bartholomeusz and Chandra R. de Silva (Eds), *Buddhist Fundamentalism and Minority Identities in Sri Lanka*, Albany: State University of New York Press, 1998, p. 4. The term 'fundamentalist' is rarely used in Sri Lanka. K.M. de Silva rejects it as too ambiguous, carrying with it associations of the Islamic Middle East or such features as 'missionary zeal', which are absent in Sinhala Buddhism. See K.M. de Silva, 'Buddhist Revivalism, Nationalism and Politics in Modern Sri Lanka', in J.W. Björkman, *Fundamentalism, Revivalists and Violence in South Asia*, New Delhi: Manohar, 1988, p. 107.
4. S. Kemper, *The Presence of the Past: Chronicles, Politics, and Culture in Sinhala Life*, Ithaca: Cornell University Press, 1991, p. 12.
5. Complex customs associated with caste kept all but the highest caste (Goigama) from access to the *sangha* until the nineteenth century, when the Amarapura Nikaya (1802) and its offshoot the Ramanna Nikaya (1875) opened opportunities for Salagama, Karava and Durava caste ordination. See K.M. de Silva, *A History of Sri Lanka*, New Delhi: Oxford University Press, 1981, pp. 249–341.
6. An example is Rev. Inamaluve Sumangala, who broke off from the Asgirya chapter of the Siam Nikaya in 1980, ostensibly over the hierarchy's lack of support for his initiatives to thwart the construction of a resort hotel at Kandalama, near the Dambulla shrine. Inamaluve's new fraternity became 'caste-free'.
7. H.L. Seneviratne, *The Work of Kings: The New Buddhism in Sri Lanka*, Chicago: University of Chicago Press, 1999, p. 25; George Bond, *The Buddhist Revival in Sri Lanka*, Columbia: University of South Carolina Press, 1988, p. 53. Kumari Jayawardene provides the fullest account of Dharmapala's biography, with his *durava* caste roots in the wealthy Hewavitarne Don Carolis family. See Kumari Jayawardene, *Nobodies to Somebodies: The Rise of the Colonial Bourgeoisie in Sri Lanka*, Colombo: Social Scientists' Association, 2000, p. 267.
8. Seneviratne, n. 7, p. 96. The term 'Protestant Buddhism' is associated with Richard Gombrich and Gananath Obeyesekere's *Buddhism Transformed:*

Religious Change in Sri Lanka, Princeton: Princeton University Press, 1988, Part 3. But note that 'the extreme Protestant Buddhist (like his Christian forebear) is anticlerical, holding that the clergy's corruption is so deep as to be irremedial and their function probably obsolete' (p. 231).

9. Seneviratne, n. 7, p. 125. Seneviratne shows how Vidyodaya continued to produce outstanding, broad-minded, tolerant and far-thinking monks. Three mid-twentieth century examples are Kalukondayave Pannesekhara (influenced by John Calvin's 'work ethic'); Hinatiyana Dhammaloka (who urged the spread of the 'sanitized, moralistic and ethical Buddhism of the urban elites' in rural areas); and Hendiyagala Silaratana (who supported more opportunities for women and argued that 'development involves respect towards other religions').
10. Ibid., p. 176.
11. *The Heritage of the Bhikkhu*, New York: Grove Press, 1974. Walpola has indicated that in many ways he preferred the English translation of the original Sinhalese (published in Colombo by Swastika Press, 1946). Interview, March 1989.
12. The latter was held on 6 January 1947, at the Raja Maha Vihara, Kelaniya Temple.
13. The Eksath Bhikkhu Peramuna had as one of its foremost aims advising and directing the people on political matters. It stood behind S.W.R.D. Bandaranaike and brought him to political victory in 1956. The price was steep for Bandaranaike, obliged to make the claim that Sinhala was the language of the state, and to increasingly edge out ethnic minorities from prominent or fruitful positions in politics. A federal alternative to the strictly centralized polity was close at hand, but sabotaged by Sinhala Buddhist political and *sangha* opposition. See R.N. Kearney, *The Politics of Ceylon (Sri Lanka)*, Ithaca: Cornell University Press, 1973, p. 176. Mention should be made as well of the impact of D.C. Vijayavardhana's *Dharma Vijaya (Triumph of Righteousness* or *Revolt in the Temple)*, 1953, a curious mixture of Buddhism, cultural nationalism and socialism.
14. *Pravada*, Colombo, November 1993.
15. See *Buddhasasana Komision Varta Samalochanaya* (Buddha Sasana Commission of February 1957), Havanapola Ratnasara Sthavira (Ed.), Colombo: M.D. Gunasena, 1961; and K.M. de Silva, *A History of Sri Lanka*, n. 5, p. 516.
16. The Sixth Amendment to the Constitution followed one month after the disastrous pogrom of July 1983 (which is commonly used to mark the beginning of the civil war). The Amendment required all Members of Parliament and government officials to swear an oath to the unitary state of Sri Lanka, which, of course, honourable Ceylon Tamil parliamentarians like Appapillai Amirthalingam could not in conscience do. A.J. Wilson, *The Break-up of Sri Lanka: The Sinhalese–Tamil Conflict*, Honolulu: University of Hawaii Press, 1988, p. 218; and *Sri Lankan Tamil Nationalism: Its Origins and Development in the 19th and 20th Centuries*, London: Hurst, 2000, p. 138.
17. There were exceptions. The Deshapremi Tharuna Bhikksu Peramuna was initially not confined to just Sinhala membership (a Ceylon Tamil Buddhist monk was involved), and the founders did not look down upon ethnic minorities (*para wambhana*). Interview with Rev. Lewela Sumangala, founding member, July 1988. Similarly, the Sinhala Arakshaya Sanvidhanaya

(Sinhala Defence League), founded in 1987 by the respected cabinet minister Gamini Jayasuriya, claimed that cultural diversity 'is one of the glories of our country and should at all times be protected and fostered'. *Sunday Times*, Colombo, 21 February 1993.

18. Bruce Matthews, 'Sinhala Cultural and Buddhist Patriotic Organizations in Contemporary Sri Lanka', *Pacific Affairs*, Vol. 61, No. 4, 1989, p. 629.
19. The central work of Nalin de Silva is *Mage Loke* (*My World*), 1992. Gunadasa Amarasekera's expression of a similar ideology is set down in *Ganaduwa Madiyama Dakinemi Arunala* (I See a Streak of Light in the Thick Darkness), 1987.
20. Interview, Colombo, 13 June 1991.
21. A.J. Wilson, *Politics in Sri Lanka 1947–1973*, London: Macmillan, 1974, p. 142.
22. Interview, Colombo, 13 June 1991.
23. For example, the Janatha Mithuro ('Friends of the People') and Chinthana Parshadaya ('Group to discuss ideology', not necessarily extremist). Much more left-of-centre is the Sri Lanka Pragatishili Peramuna (Sri Lanka Progressive Front), associated with the JVP.
24. Bhikkhu Bodhi (pseudonym), 'Sangha at the Crossroads', *The Island*, Colombo, 28 March 2001.
25. Obeyesekere and Gombrich point out that the 'average state' of monks today 'is close to the worldly life', and that many of them 'go bad' at the universities when they get 'mixed up' with politics. See *Buddhism Transformed,* n. 8, p. 300. Some monks (e.g., Piyadasi Thera) argue that although 'social' and 'hospital' work might be perceived as 'worldly', they are nonetheless important aspects of their ministry. Others maintain that there is a new sort of monk, a *nagavasin* (as apart from the traditional forest and village monk, the *arannyavasin* and the *gamavasin*) who aim to engage in various professions and not rely on the traditional charity of others.
26. Rev. Kannimahara Sumangala notes that 'the Sangha becomes a strong institution to the extent that it is a haven to which lay society, caught up in the intricacies of day-to-day life can hope to turn when its own tensions become too hard a burden to bear ... life in the Sangha is fulfilling in many different ways: one can be a thinker, an experimenter with ideas, a helper to fellow men in distress—and yet one is also not isolated. One feels that among good fellow monks one is in the company of the best of men.' 'The Tradition Needs Review: An Examination of Possibilities of Refining Theravada Interpretation', in John Ross Carter, *Religiousness in Sri Lanka*, Colombo: Marga, 1979, p. 126.
27. Bhikkhu Bodhi, 'Sangha at the Crossroads', n. 24. Similarly, Michael Carrithers writes, 'The *sangha* is so conservative and the conditions of its agrarian environment so enduring, that this structure is discernible throughout its 2,500 year history.' *Man*, Vol. 14, 1979, p. 296.
28. Seneviratne, *The Work of Kings*, n. 7, p. 203. Seneviratne's book, with its frank assessment of Lanka's intellectually impoverished *sangha*, is obviously controversial and wounding to some readers. Perhaps not unexpectedly the book was severely criticized by Ananda Wickremeratne. In a long

review article ('O Ye Buddhist Monks in Sri Lanka: A Plague upon Thy House', *The Journal of Religion*, University of Chicago Press, July 2001, Vol. 81, No. 3), Wickremeratne writes: 'One is never sure how much of the text reflects Seneviratne's opinions or is based on solid evidence' (p. 446). But Seneviratne's 'evidence' is corroborated by the expert analyses of many other social and political scientists who have experienced or witnessed the grim reality of a politicized *sangha* in Lanka's post-independence history.

29. *Lanka Guardian*, Colombo, 1979, 15 March 1979, p. 17. This is not to suggest monks have entirely avoided such issues as the perceived rights of workers. For example, the government of J.R. Jayewardene had many challenges dealing with the militant head of the nurses' union, Ven. Murultuwe Ananda, a strident activist on the part of a largely female profession that needed the kind of political pressure a powerful monk could render.
30. *Pravada*, Colombo, May 1992, p. 1.
31. 'Four Mahanayakes Reject Package' shout the headlines of *The Sunday Times* (Colombo, 1 February 1998), typical of more than a dozen other such banner press announcements since the failed talks of July 1985 in Thimpu, Bhutan.
32. *Lanka Guardian*, 1 January 1985.
33. Seneviratne, *The Work of Kings*, n. 7, p. 324.
34. Gombrich and Obeyesekere, *Buddhism Transformed*, n. 8, p. 1.
35. Writing about the celebrated religious shrine at Kataragama, Gombrich and Obeyesekere note: 'While the formal control of the (Kataragama) ceremonies has always been in Buddhist hands, the substance of what goes on at the shrine has for the most part been Tamil Hindu in culture.' *Buddhism Transformed*, n. 8, p. 184. There are exceptions to this respectful attitude. When the civil war spread to Amparai in the Eastern Province in the early 1990s, Sinhalese troops desecrated Hindu kovils. Eyewitness account of Her Excellency Nancy Stiles, Canadian High Commissioner to Colombo, and Professor Bruce Matthews, July 1992.
36. The most self-evident example of this is Ven. Galeboda Gnanissara of Colombo's Gangarmaya Vihara, ironically built and sustained largely by Japanese donations.
37. *Lanka Guardian*, 1 June 1990. Pelpola was Director General of the Japan-Sri Lanka Friendship Association who claimed that the main idea of his move to Mahayana was 'to serve the poor who are suffering'. He was fiercely opposed by Ven. Madihe Panaseeha and Panditha Labbugama Lankananada, senior *nikaya mahanayakes*.
38. Edward Shils, *Tradition*, Berkeley: University of California Press, 1982, p. 1.

3

Religious Ideology among the Tamils

DAGMAR HELLMANN-RAJANAYAGAM

Whereas social exclusion is practised in Jaffna in multiple subtle and unsubtle forms, religious exclusion is a much rarer phenomenon and nowadays virtually non-existent. Religious syncretism has traditionally been a feature of Jaffna society, but has become pronounced and is being explicitly demonstrated by the militants. The struggle of the LTTE is not religiously informed, in contrast to the claims of the Sinhalese that they fight for the survival of Buddhism against the Tamil Hindus. The Tamils do not principally exclude or fight for or against any one religion and thus they do not target Buddhism either.

In South India and in Jaffna—the area of predominantly Tamil culture—religion traditionally was not or was only a very minor criterion of (ethnic) exclusion. The term *Sramana*, which is often translated as 'Buddhist' and used as such in Jaffna Tamil, originally applied to virtually all beliefs which did not follow classical Brahmin tradition. These comprise Buddhists as well as Jains, but also sects that reject Brahmin tradition, such as some types of Bhakti or the Virasaivas, which are nowadays subsumed under the term 'Hindu'.

The Role of Religion in Jaffna

Religion earlier played an important role for Tamil identity, which was only trumped by language in the early twentieth century. Without religion, religious renewal and religious controversies, language could not have attained the predominance it has today.

Language and religion united in a complementary and yet contradictory relationship. But religion never became as important an instrument of exclusion as caste.

This does not mean that religious antagonism did not occur or was negligible in Jaffna. Examples of religious riots at the end of the nineteenth and at the beginning of the twentieth centuries are numerous. These antagonisms were less severe than among the Sinhalese and nearly always occurred in a social and/or political context. Conversion to Christianity could be and was used by the low castes, particularly the Pallar and Nalavar, to claim higher status, and conflicts often arose over attempts by the low castes to appropriate status symbols of the Vellalar or to deny them customary services with the argument that after conversion the old constraints no longer applied. Caste allegiances often worked against religious ones. This applied particularly to the Vellalar Protestants who often allied with Vellalar Saivites rather than with Karaiyar Catholics where political questions were concerned.[1] This caste-denomination rivalry overrode that of the Hindus and Christians.

After the British had reintroduced religious freedom in 1813, many nominal Christians reverted openly to Saivism, though a residue of Christians, both Catholic and Protestant, endured and remained at a steady 15 per cent (among the Sinhalese it is 7 per cent). When we argue that Christians were not excluded from Tamil society on the basis of religion, we must remember that Christians did not want to be excluded either. They made every effort to prove that they belonged in Tamil society and to demonstrate their Tamil identity. They felt part of their society, in ethnicity and culture, and they were accepted and acknowledged by society as long as they complied with the way of life and the social structure, viz., the caste system.

The question arises as to why the integration of the Christians into the Tamil cultural realm did not work with the Muslims. Muslims and Christians found completely different answers to the question of whether there were greater advantages in being defined as Tamil or in being defined by religion. Muslim self-exclusion did not occur because the Tamil Saivites refused them inclusion, but rather in spite of this offer. Tamil-speaking Muslims had lived in the East in the region around Sammanturai and Akkaraipattu for at least three centuries. Dutch reports show these areas to be inhabited by a Muslim majority, and they are frequently mentioned in the various Tamil chronicles.[2] Though on the whole the coexistence between Muslims and Hindus had been peaceful, we do find instances where Hindus objected to certain practices of the Muslims or their establishing places of worship and settlement. These conflicts are not solved by open attacks or riots, but by more cunning and subtle means: such as throwing pork into the wells and mosques of the Muslims, whereupon the latter leave the areas where their presence is resented and settle elsewhere.[3] For the Tamils generally, religion played a comparatively minor role, but the Muslims made it into an important distinction. For Saivites, religion in the sense of religious dogma and doctrine is less important than ritual and caste discipline, in other words, they emphasize a certain lifestyle, the 'Tamil way of life'. The actual convictions and beliefs of individuals are comparatively unimportant, since in the last instance everybody is supposed to believe in the same god or the same ultimate principles. For Muslims, in contrast, the religious dogma and doctrine, the 'truth', is of overriding importance. These differing perceptions hamper dialogue and so it resembles one between blind men and deaf mutes. Tamils cannot understand what the Muslims fear losing by identifying themselves as Tamils, because this—in their eyes—does not at all concern or harm their religion. The Muslims, on the other hand, do not understand why language and culture should be privileged over religion.[4]

Yet, Christianity in its more extreme forms insists as much on the sole possession of the 'truth' as Islam. So why did Christians *want* to be Tamil? And why did they not, like many Sinhalese, adopt western culture and lifestyles on conversion? Tamils had been converted to Christianity for three-and-a-half centuries. The converts were Tamils, whereas the Muslims considered themselves immigrants who could have come from the Malabar Coast or from Arabia, but were not often local converts. Christianity in Ceylon was the religion of converts, not that of an originally immigrant minority from India and Arabia. Moreover, the Christian claim of to being Tamil occurred in a totally different context from the Muslim claim of not being Tamil. Christians wanted to be included in the prestigious group, they never were a class apart. Muslims wanted separate political representation. Muslims always felt, and strove to be, a group beyond and apart.

SINHALESE BUDDHISM AND ATTEMPTS TO PROTECT RELIGION

In the subsequent chapter on social exclusion we describe attempts by the Tamils to subsume the Sinhalese under the racial/cultural category of Dravidians. A similar attempt at inclusion was undertaken with regard to religion—Hindu origins of Buddhism were emphasized, the common gods of both religions named, and the common tradition highlighted. Besides, the Buddhist rituals in Ceylon were described as characterized by strong Hindu elements. The outcome resembled the result of the Tamil attempt to define the Sinhalese as Dravidians—an even stronger endeavour by the Sinhalese to differentiate themselves from Hinduism and to erase 'Hindu' influences from religion and ritual as 'un-Buddhist'.[5] Even today, this need not mean a perception of the Sinhalese as religious enemies. In fact, this is very rare, but the endeavours on both sides to clean and purify their faiths by rejecting 'alien' elements led them to drift apart. Moreover, like the attempt to subsume the Sinhalese under Dravidians, the latter attempt suffered from ambivalence and ambiguity: it is nowadays acknowledged that Buddhism to a large extent was brought to Ceylon by Tamil Buddhists and that many Tamils in the early times were probably Buddhists. Neither side is prepared to concede this fact. Sinhalese are equated with Buddhists; Tamils, if at all, with Hindus. Implicitly, religion is defined ethnically.

THE FIGHT FOR A SECULAR SRI LANKA

One point in nearly all Tamil party programmes of the Federal Party (FP) and the Tamil United Liberation Front (TULF) was—besides the abolition of caste—secular status for Sri Lanka. It was also one of the six points included in the party programme of the TULF in 1976.[6] But secular status for Sri Lanka was not included in any constitution of Sri Lanka. Instead Buddhism was made into the foremost religion, which had to be protected. This was the point the Tamils, both Hindus and Christians, opposed most vehemently. Though Hinduism and Islam were also denoted as protected, they were considered secondary to Buddhism. As the Sinhalese created a hierarchy of religions, the Tamils demanded equality of all religions, that is, equal protection by the state.

Christians did not even want, as Peter Schalk demonstrates, to be made into a protected religion, because that would mean state supervision and control.[7]

The protection of established religions had been demanded by Tamils and Sinhalese equally during colonial times, even if this meant a constraint of individual freedom of religion. In the Report of the Special Committee on Education (1943), the question arose whether non-Christian children could be forced to attend the only school in a location if it happened to be a Christian school. The answer, in a rider by one of the Committee members, Shivapadasundaram, was a vehement 'no'. He said that even if the Hindu parents agreed to let their children attend Christian schools, it should not be permitted. They must, on the contrary, be forced to send their children to Hindu schools.[8] Many Hindu parents who sent their children to Christian schools were illiterate (and of a low caste) and could not provide religious instruction for their offspring themselves. These children therefore either got no religious education at all or they got a Christian one.[9] The danger of conversion was thus everpresent. The problem here was not the lack of religious instruction, but the desire of poor and/or low caste parents to provide better chances for their children in a Christian school. This incident highlights another particularity of the religious tolerance in Jaffna: any established religion is accepted, as long as it does not try to proselytize and to gain converts (especially low-caste converts). Established religion must remain just that—established. The point is important, because it explains the ferocious opposition of the Tamils to the attempts by the government in the 1960s to convert low-caste Tamils in Jaffna to Buddhism (which met with a certain degree of success). The resentment was based on two principles—first, on the assumption that Tamils must not be Buddhists, and second, on the fear that this conversion was aimed at more than that, namely social mobility of the lower castes. Social mobility through either education and/or conversion has to be prevented with all the means at the Vellalars' disposal. The opposition again was directed less at the religious than at the social effects of this step and the Sinhalese knew this very well. They tried to change the social set-up with religious arguments. Religious and social (and ethnic) considerations thus became intertwined.

We see this again during the controversy about the nationalization of schools in 1961, which followed the 'Sinhala only' law of 1956. After 1956 the Tamil Christians considered this law and the subsequent school nationalization even a greater threat than violent Saivism. They therefore cooperated with the Tamils rather than with their brothers in faith among the Sinhalese. The nationalization hit (and was intended to hit) particularly the Hindu- and Christian-led schools: they were no longer allowed to charge fees and now new regulations about entry rules, language of instruction and religious instruction had to be complied with. Many Christian and Hindu schools simply had to give up and agree to nationalization; the few that remained private financed themselves through donations by the parents and charity.

The Problem of the 'Sacred Sites'

The controversies surrounding the government's land colonization programme were enhanced by a religious factor: the problem of the sacred sites.[10] The favoured status of Buddhism and its protection led to the application of the designation of 'sacred sites' in regions where former Buddhist settlements were said to have existed or in locations pronounced sacred to Buddhism. Only Sinhalese were allowed to settle here 'within the reach of the temple bell' as the saying goes.[11] Influential members of the clergy, moreover, demanded increased Sinhalese settlement in the East, in order to reclaim assumed Buddhist sacred sites located there and protect them from alleged 'Hindu vandalism'.[12] This was part of a campaign endeavouring to 'prove' ancient Buddhist settlement in the North and East to support Sinhalese claims to these regions. Archaeology became an instrument of policy. Neither Tamils nor Sinhalese acknowledged the possibility of a Tamil Buddhist presence in these regions in earlier centuries.

In 1955, Federal Party President Vanniyasingam had called Trincomalee an ancient Tamil bulwark, whose temple was founded by the Chola dynasty of Tamil Nadu and had been praised by the Tamil poets.[13] This motif appears again and again in the literature, particularly that of the militants. For them, the town had not so much religious as historical significance, because it was considered a Chola foundation.[14] This indicates the emotional significance of Trincomalee. The conflict surrounding the temple had flared up in the 1960s and turned into one of the most poignant examples of the combination of religious, political and ethnic interests. The controversy erupting in 1968 caused M. Tiruchelvam to resign as Minister of Local Development.

In his resignation speech Tiruchelvam retraced the development of the controversy. The demand for and establishment of 'sacred sites' was not new, it dated back to the 1920s. Anagarika Dharmapala had demanded the protection of Buddhist monuments and had particularly mentioned Anuradhapura in the Central Zone and Seruvavila near Trincomalee. He even accused the Hindu trustees of the alleged Buddhist monument in Seruvavila of neglecting the site.[15] The British had then initiated the protection of 'sacred sites' of all religions. Anuradhapura had been a particular concern of theirs, but they had rejected Dharmapala's claims to Seruvavila. No protection was granted to the Hindu temple in Trincomalee either. Since 1954 therefore, the Tamils had tried to designate the temple in Fort Frederick a Hindu 'sacred site'.[16] As minister for local development, Tiruchelvam therefore took up this cause and even obtained Prime Minister Senanayake's tacit consent to appoint a temple committee. A few months later the plan became public and was fiercely criticized. Suddenly, Senanayake termed the region a military security site, which could not be declared a 'sacred site'. He further stated he had not been informed about the whole plan, statements which Tiruchelvam said were pretexts and untrue. Some monks had voiced their criticism of the declaration of Trincomalee as a sacred site and had even claimed to have found Buddhist relics in Trincomalee and Seruvavila. Hindus, they said, had desecrated and defaced them. They claimed to have found foundations of a Buddhist temple even under the temple. Tiruchelvam claimed that Senanayake withdrew his consent to his plans because he had been told that 'a Buddhist sanctuary must not be administered by Hindus.'[17] Tiruchelvam was particularly bitter about the personal attacks on him by Senanayake and the totally unfounded accusation of having started the whole scheme without the latter's knowledge. This conflict forced him to resign.[18]

What worried the Tamils was not so much how to exclude the Sinhalese, but the fear that they themselves were to be excluded and driven to the brink by the Sinhalese. They felt their religion threatened along with their language and territory. This was worse than anything before, the sacred sites of the Tamils were being corrupted by Buddhist claims to their possession. This had never happened to the Hindus before. The Christian colonial powers had destroyed and desecrated their temples, but never the Buddhists, even during the rule of Sapumal. Religions had always coexisted more or less peacefully in Jaffna. In Anuradhapura Tamils and Muslims had complied with restrictions on their places of domicile (they were excluded from the centre and the inner town for religious reasons). In Kataragama, at the shrine of Murugan, protests had already been voiced when the Sinhalese had monopolized the site. Kataragama, however, lay far to the South, and the restrictions on this religious site did not hit the Tamils as hard as those in Trincomalee, which was connected to their religion and their religious literature far longer and much more existentially. And the dispossession went further: not only was the temple denied the status of sacred site for 'security reasons', Buddhists even claimed parts of the temple premises as theirs, and the Hindu parts became increasingly smaller. Nowadays, just a tiny yard surrounding the temple on the peak belongs to the temple property. The Tamils saw this as just one element of a larger plan to suppress them politically, economically, culturally, and now also religiously, to turn them into 'non-persons'. The fears were vastly enhanced during the civil war, when the Sinhala army attacked and destroyed both Hindu temples and churches regardless of whether they were full of refugees or not.

Religion in the Perception of the Militants

Religion is essential even for the militants, but it has an entirely new definition and weighting, which has far distanced it from the original equation between religion and Saivism. We could say religion has now taken the place of caste in defending the 'way of life'. At the same time, a secular state is clearly envisaged by the LTTE, with protection, but no supervision, for all recognized religions.[19] In LTTE political propaganda, religion does not play an obvious part.

The marker of 'religion' is understood in a vague and undetermined way and is not tied to one particular religion. Hindus, Christians, even Muslims can be Tamils, provided they accept the Tamil 'way of life'. The FP used the term 'Tamil-speaking population' instead of talking merely about Tamils as did the Tamil Congress (TC). From the beginning they included the Muslims, particularly those of the East, in their programme. The FP even promised to make Amparai, a district with Muslim majority, into an autonomous unit in a federal scheme, in order to decrease the Muslim fear of being dominated by the Tamils.[20] It also vehemently opposed colonization in Amparai, because that would have rendered the Muslims a minority in the one region where they were in a majority.[21] Similarly the LTTE, in a blueprint for the state of Tamil Eelam, promises certain safeguards for the Muslim population. Among these were a guaranteed 33 per cent of the electorates in the east and 18 per cent in the combined north-east, a guaranteed 30 per cent of all seats in parliament, 35 per cent of all newly developed land in the east, 5 per cent in the north and 30 per cent in Mannar.[22] They refute the claim that the Muslims are descendants of Arabs, and call them Tamils. All this was to no avail because, soon after, 50,000 Muslims were expelled from Jaffna and their property confiscated, which exposed the precarious relationship between the two groups.[23]

Buddhism has never been singled out as a means of separation and exclusion by the militants, but in the course of the militant struggle, a subtle change has occurred regarding the Sinhalese and their religion: the enemy is nowadays increasingly designated as the Sinhala-speaking Buddhist. Religion and language now mutually enhance each other, religion increasingly follows linguistic and territorial borders. Buddhism has become an ethnic, not a religious, category. The militant attacks on religious buildings and institutions are not so much attacks on the religion, but reactions to similar attacks on the part of the Buddhists. When the LTTE attacked a bus carrying 150 monks in Anuradhapura in 1985, they justified this attack by claiming that the Buddhist clergy were the most radical and hostile regarding the demands of the Tamils and even instigated attacks on them. The LTTE claim that it is the Buddhist clergy who consider Sri Lanka a unitary state belonging exclusively to the Sinhalese Buddhists, where Tamils find no place. The 1988 attack on the Dalada Maligawa, the most sacred shrine of the Buddhists, came after a large number of similar attacks on Hindu temples and Christian churches in Jaffna, such as the Navali Church, where over 100 refugees had sought shelter, and many of whom died.[24] The linking of Buddhism and Sinhalese can thus be seen as a reaction to exclusion from the Sinhalese.

While the militants draw on the Tamil tradition, it is not a religious tradition they have in mind—neither the Bhakti nor the Saiva Siddhanta find a place in their ideology. Rather, it is the martial traditions of the Purananuru and the Mahabharata as well as the glory of the imperial Cholas.[25] The choice is selective, and Saivism hardly finds a place in it. But there is ambiguity here: the imperial Cholas are crucial for the self-understanding of the LTTE, who even adopted their symbol, the Tiger. But it was this dynasty that conquered Lanka and at one stage persecuted non-Saivite religions.

Whether Saivism informs LTTE ideology or not, religiously informed symbolism is, on the other hand, extremely important, and we have here a clear instance of the secularization of religion.[26] It shows most clearly in the treatment of their fallen heroes. They are called martyrs, and a complete cult has risen around them.[27] Every year on or around 27 November (Prabhakaran's birthday), Heroes' Day is celebrated among Tamils worldwide. The ceremony is syncretistic and not traceable to any one religion—Hindus cremate their dead, but the martyrs are buried, which points to Catholic models as does the English term 'martyr' itself. In Tamil, 'martyr' is represented by several terms, which are partly borrowed from Saivite and Hindu tradition. We must remember that the leadership and some of the membership of the LTTE are Karaiyar, and they contain a high percentage of Catholics. For the fallen soldiers, hero stones (*virarkkal*) are erected, which resemble the tombstones or headstones of a Christian cemetery. On the other hand, hero stones go very far back in Tamil and Indian tradition: victims of war and sacrifice, and *satis* were honoured thus. But in the parlance of the LTTE, the cult of the martyrs is not religiously informed, but 'secular', i.e., neither superstitious nor interfering in religious life. The martyrs and their monuments become public property.

As an illustration let me give a short description of the annual Heroes' Day as celebrated in Dortmund, Germany, in late 2001. On a stylised sand-covered cemetery dotted with flowerpots three graves are arranged, triangular sarcophagi with headstones bearing the title '*Mavirar*'. In reality the name of the departed would be engraved. While the headstones resemble a lotus, they cannot quite be identified with any particular religion. The walls around the graveyard are plastered with the photos of the dead heroes and their date of death. If no photos are available, the picture of a red rose is substituted. The participants file past the photos and donate flower buds; some are weeping. In the sand the map of Tamil Eelam is picked out with tomb lamps (left over, one suspects, from All Souls Day) to which everybody adds one, and in the middle the *kuttu vilakku* or the eternal light (as one wishes to call it) burns steadily. What strikes a chord in the observer is the strongly Christian concept of the martyr (witness) who gives his life his faith and his community. The hero, venerated with the erection of a *virarkkal*, will with time probably turn into a minor god or a saint.

CONCLUSION

The premise that nationalism began in the colonized countries with the rejection of a foreign faith and only proceeded to resistance against foreign rule by using the methods, principles and values of this very rule does not really apply to the Tamils.[28] For the Tamils, the acceptance of a foreign faith did not hamper the retention or emergence of an indigenous identity and an indigenous national consciousness. Religion, therefore, could not really become a means of exclusion. The equation of religious antagonism with colonial antagonism did not apply to the Tamils. Tamil nationalism referred consciously to its own indigenous criteria and components, which simultaneously completely changed the contents of the term nationalism. It is this changed content which the militants nowadays refer to and which could be said to make Tamil nationalism into the new religion of Tamil Eelam. In fact, the new secular religion can be said to have strong integrative power precisely because it syncretistically uses religious symbolism and quasi-religious terms to unite Sri Lankan Tamils into a Tamil nationalism based on its very own concept of culture and tradition.

NOTES

1. Society for the Propagation of the Gospel, Ceylon Letters Received Series, Bodleian Library, Rhodes House, Oxford: Correspondence of 6 July 1894; also, Journal of the Bishop of Colombo's First Visitation to the Northern

and Eastern Province of his Diocese, 7 July till 18 August 1846, p. 48 (Unpublished).

2. J. Burnand, Memoir on the district of Batticaloa, 1794 (Translation), pp. 128ff; also see, memoir of the late Mr Burnand explaining all the improvements made in the province of Batticaloa while he was chief of that province, dated 22.9.1796, in Commissioners of Eastern Inquiry 1829–30, Mr Burnand's Papers, CO 416/24, p. 146 (Unpublished).
3. D. Hellmann-Rajanayagam, *Ursprünge und Entwicklung ethnischer Konflikte in Sri Lanka seit dem 19. Jh. - Wechselwirkungen religiös-nationaler Erneuerungsbewegungen und britischer Verwaltungs- und Verfassungspolitik*, Heidelberg: Unpublished thesis, 1998, p. 199.
4. P. Ramanathan, 'The Ethnology of the "Moors" of Ceylon', *Journal of the Royal Asiatic Society (CB)*, Vol. X, No. 36, 1890, pp. 247–50. Ramanathan's article was well written and thoroughly researched. But the controversy turned on the assumption of the Muslims (probably quite correct), that Ramanathan pursued political, not academic aims with this article. He would have liked a Tamil to have represented the Muslims in the Legislative Council, too, by reason of common language and culture. He was unsuccessful, because the British followed the arguments of the Muslims.
5. Heinz Bechert, *Buddhismus, Staat und Gesellschaft in den Ländern des Theravada-Buddhismus*, Vol. 1, Allgemein und Ceylon: Wiesbaden, 1966, p. 124. See also Gananath Obeyesekere, 'The Vicissitudes of the Sinhalese Buddhist Identity through Time and Change', in Michael Roberts (Ed.), *Collective Identities, Nationalisms and Protest in Modern Sri Lanka*, Colombo: Marga, 1979, pp. 279–313.
6. A. Amirthalingam, 'The Path of Principle, Part II', in the *Commemoration Volume for the Silver Anniversary of the Ceylon Tamil Government Party*, Jaffna, 1974, pp. 54–55 (in Tamil; henceforth 'Commemoration Volume').
7. Peter Schalk, 'Present Concepts of Secularism among Ilavars and Lankans', in Peter Schalk and Max Deeg (Eds), *Zwischen Sakularismus and Hierokratie, Studien Zum Vehaltnis von Religion und Staat in Sud- und Ostasien*, Uppsala: Acta Universitatis Uppsaliensis, Historia Religiorum 17, 2001, p. 51.
8. Sessional Paper XXIV, 1943, Report of the Special Committee on Education, 24 September 1943, PRO CO 57/273, 'Rider' by Shivapadasundaram, pp. 135–36.
9. Ibid.
10. This scheme was intended to reclaim the ancient irrigation works and farmland in the North-Central Dry Zone, the so-called Vanni. Originally planned as a scheme to provide land to all landless Ceylonese, after independence it quickly turned into a scheme exclusively for the Sinhalese to reclaim the 'rajarata', the ancient royal land.
11. ITAK Extraordinary Congress 1972, in Commemoration Volume, Jaffna, 1974, pp. 94, 114.
12. Ibid., p. 103.
13. FP–President Vanniyasingam: 'We have decided that we Tamils unitedly will achieve Tamil self-government and nobody can detract us from our goal,' at the Party Congress on 17 April 1955 in Trincomalee, quoted in 'Talks by the Leadership', Commemoration Volume, Part I, Appendix A, p. 9.

14. Today, another change of argument has occurred. While for nearly a decade Trincomalee was designated as the future capital of the envisaged Tamil state, nowadays this honour has reverted to Jaffna, which is called the cultural capital of the Tamils. Trincomalee and Batticaloa might have been equally eligible for that status.
15. A.W.P. Guruge (Ed.), *Dharmapala's Writings: His Writings in Sinhalese*, Colombo, 1965, pp. 159–60.
16. Hansard, 16 September 1968, p. 789. See also A.J. Wilson, *S.J.V. Chelvanayakam and the Crisis of Sri Lankan Tamil Nationalism, 1947–1977*, London: Hurst and Co., 1994, pp. 109–10.
17. The opposite case, viz., a Hindu sanctuary being administered by Buddhists, seems to be acceptable to the Buddhists.
18. Hansard, June 1968, p. 786 and November 1968, p. 802.
19. The model of the future Eelam is set out in 'Towards a Socialist Tamil Eelam', n.p. (probably Madras), 1980. For a detailed discussion see Dagmar Hellmann-Rajanayagam, *The Tamil Tigers—Armed Struggle for Identity*, Heidelberg, 1994. More information in Chapter 5, n. 15, p. 87.
20. Model Constitution 1972, in Commemoration Volume, Part I, Annex I, p. 15.
21. Chelvanayakam, 'The Muslims have to fight together with us, if we hesitate we will become homeless!', in Commemoration Volume, Part I, Annex I, pp. 75–76 (in Tamil).
22. *Tamil Eelam*, April 1988, pp. 26–27 (in Tamil).
23. In an interview Sathasivan Krishnakumar (Kittu)—the LTTE spokesperson in London—claimed that this was done for their own protection and they would be allowed to return in more peaceful times. Conversations of the author with Kittu, London, October 1990. See also *Tamil Times*, 15 November 1990, pp. 3, 9.
24. S.J. Emmanuel, *Let my people go*, London: Tamil Catholic Chaplaincy, 1996.
25. The examples cited are often extremely gruesome, e.g., that of the mother who finds her son cut to pieces on the battlefield and weeps with joy, or the mother who sends her small son (who cannot even hold the spear), into battle because all other male relatives are dead. For more examples see A.K. Ramanujan, *Poems of Love and War. From the Eight Anthologies and the Ten Long Poems of Classical Tamil*, New Delhi: Oxford University Press, 1985.
26. Peter Schalk, on the other hand, calls it the sacralization of politics. Peter Schalk, 'The Revival of Martyr Cults among Ilavar', *Temenos*, 33, 1997, pp. 151–90.
27. Ibid. Schalk describes in great detail the emergence and development of this cult, which he terms traditionalistic.
28. The premise can, however, be accepted in the context of Sinhalese nationalism.

4

Tightening Social Cohesion and Excluding 'Others' among the Sinhalese

BRUCE MATTHEWS

The question of social ranking in Sri Lanka, in particular the exclusion of certain major components of society from economic, educational and political opportunities, is an old story in the history of the nation. It continues as a feature of both urban and rural life almost everywhere on the island, sometimes subtle, often explosive. The residual impact of the Janatha Vimukthi Peramuna (People's Liberation Front) uprisings in 1971 and 1988, as well as the recent civil war in the north and east, are two important examples in Sri Lanka. A multi-cultural and religiously pluralist society, its population of 20 million (as of 2001) has long been fragmented into distinct ethnic communities: the majority Sinhalese, the Ceylon Tamils, Indian Tamils, Ceylon Moors and various smaller ethnic groups.[1] This chapter reviews the issues of caste-class polarity, ethnic discrimination and struggle among the Sinhalese.[2] It considers how these distinctions still manage to hold a place in the social order, and to what extent they compromise community trust (in Sinhala, *vishvasaya*) in government, in political policy, in public institutions and even in traditional religious bodies (notably the Buddhist *sangha* or monastic order). While caste and class among the Sinhalese are the focus of this chapter, the next chapter turns to the Ceylon Tamil community as described by Hellmann-Rajanayagam, where an often overlooked inter-caste rivalry continues to have crucial effects on the political and cultural destiny of these people.

It can be argued that although caste continues to be a pervasive presence among the Sinhalese (notably in marriage alliances), it has long been challenged by class (defined largely by material wealth) as the leading social hierarchical indicator. Both caste and class divide Sinhala society into privileged and not privileged, haves and have-nots. Racial or cultural fear-mongering further fragments Sri Lankan society, especially when other ethnic communities are identified as interlopers or undesirable competitors. An analysis of Sri Lanka's universities in the mid-1990s found that they seethed with all kinds of resentment, envy and conflict based on caste, class and ethnicity. It concluded that a double tragedy was unfolding: the country was quite possibly breaking into two, and meanwhile the Sinhalese majority had not been able to address its own internal problems of class division and revolt against the status quo.[3] This situation has continued into the new millennium, and it will be very difficult for the nation to build social cohesion. How it continues to thwart the development of trust, however defined, is a vital collateral factor. We will first outline briefly some of the features that identify what caste (*kulaya*) is in the contemporary Sinhala context, and then reflect on class (*pantaya*) as a competing hierarchical factor.

Although the topic of caste is subject to strict social taboo in everyday conversation, and is often said to be of no significance in modern Sri Lanka, the fact remains that commitment to the caste doctrine is still widespread.[4] Historically, caste was associated with usufructuary rights and other privileges received in return for service to the Sinhala royal court. This occupational and feudal system was abolished by the British colonial authorities in 1833, but remnants of the traditional arrangement still persisted in aristocratic lineages, lifestyles and political leadership. Indeed, caste distinctions were so implacable in the nineteenth century that they provoked the formation of two major Buddhist sections (*nikayas*) of the *sangha* in order to allow those from lower castes access to holy orders.[5] One might argue that caste institutionalizes inequalities and prevents social mobility, although importantly, Sinhala caste has none of the features of social purity and pollution (e.g., commensality) found in Indian caste traditions. On the other hand, some aver that caste provides its own sense of social order and security in some South Asian contexts.[6]

A feature of Sinhala caste is its 'inverted pyramid' structure, with the Goigama (Goyigama) agriculturalist and land-owning sector on top (over 50 per cent of the population). This did not, and does not necessarily indicate a life of economic privilege. Some 50 years ago, Bryce Ryan observed that 'generally the Ceylonese are peasants and the bulk of the (upper caste) Goigama peasants live much as do their low caste peasant neighbours'.[7] This is still the case: most Goigama are commoners, though some claim to be 'farmer-aristocrats'. It is further useful to distinguish between caste in up-country traditional Kandy, and caste in the so-called 'low country'. Up-country caste designations once associated with aristocracy and with 'service' to the court no longer have the import of pre-colonial times, but are nonetheless still used to identify one's birth status and background. The Goigama are dominant. It comprises a cluster of sub-castes, which take on class-like distinctions as aristocracy or non-aristocracy (the Radala being the highest). The one-time 'service' castes follow the Goigama, and, at the very bottom, are the depressed castes, so low that until recently they had near untouchable status (e.g., the Rodi).[8] Low country caste designation and structure also centre on the Goigama, followed by the Karava (traditionally, the fisher caste), Salagama (cinnamon peelers), Durava (toddy tappers)—the KSD triumvirate—and Wahumpura (raw sugar makers).[9] These occupations have long ceased to characterize these castes.

In a recent study, Kumari Jayewardene shows how a privileged sector of Sinhala society arose in British times, based in part on hereditary caste but also on economic opportunism associated with geographic location. Certain great Goigama families, both up-country and low country, found it expedient to cooperate with colonial rule, achieving honours as 'gate keepers' (Mudaliyars), and replacing the really old aristocracy that faded away after British suzerainty was secured in 1815. Because economic prosperity was initially more accessible in the low country, and up-country pedigree considered the most refined, alliances between low country, newly rich Goigama ('arrivistes', whom Jayawardene lightly identifies as 'nobodies') and up-country Goigama aristocracy ('somebodies') were much sought after.[10] This was to have massive political significance, as illustrious names such as Obeyesekere, Dias, Senanayake, Attygalle, Kotelawala, Ilangakoon, Siriwardena, Wijewardene, Corea, Ratwatte and perhaps above all Bandaranaike, became associated with rich extended families—the founders of Sri Lanka's later 'dynastic democracy'.

On the other hand, for the KSD castes, different opportunities to prosper became available largely through their access to coastal trade and entrepreneurial initiative. The Karavas in particular were exposed to Westernization and commercialization. Michael Roberts notes that the rich Karavas 'never abjured their caste origins but saw themselves as community leaders and sought to raise the status of their caste as a whole'.[11] The KSD competed with the Goigama newly rich (as apart from the older, English-speaking Goigama elites), leading to a marked escalation in inter-caste rivalry. Successful and wealthy Karavas and Duravas began to question their caste's position in the traditional hierarchy. In the nineteenth century, certain members of these castes made fortunes as agents or 'rentiers' of franchises from the crown for the distribution of arrack and other spirits.[12] Some have argued that access to prosperity resulted in decisive changes in the caste system during the colonial period, with the KSD 'succeeding in rising to near top levels' of influence and prestige.[13] Caste rivalry and competition among the Sinhalese predated ethnic rivalry, which only became a major factor in national life with elections to the Legislative Council in 1921. Under the political reforms suggested by the 1931 constitutional report of the Earl of Donoughmore, however, KSD and minority representation was greatly reduced—universal suffrage, with Goigama dominance, saw to that.

The significance of caste among the Sinhalese today is a vital question. If one enquires about its role in an urban, English-speaking setting, the response will usually be that caste is fading away. There is some truth to this, as caste is being slowly replaced by class in key social, economic and political ways. But if one asks the question elsewhere, in Sinhala *swabasha*, and particularly among representatives of underprivileged castes (in families, villages, even in universities), the response will be more guarded. Tamara Gunasekera, for example, shows how Kandyan Sinhalese society remains permeated by caste, sanctioned as the correct order of society. It continues to be inextricably linked with power and class, especially in rural peasant communities. The advent of schools, modern communication, the Westminster parliamentary system and democracy have all made some difference, but higher castes remain dominant in everyday life.[14]

Nineteenth century casteism perhaps survives most notably in the continuation of the same upper-caste, politically powerful families.

There are few places left in the quasi-democratic world—to which Sri Lanka belongs—where President and Prime Minister have been daughter and mother, or, a little later, where the Speaker of the House was a brother and son of the above.[15] The cachet of the elite, Radala, Bandaranaike name continues to have a powerful political resonance. It still inspires trust, perhaps excited by nostalgia, for rule by a privileged family. There may then be a few positive ways in which caste becomes involved in public life, as part of a system some still trust will bring order and equilibrium to society. But most, if not all, of the old vehicles ensuring wide caste representation in cabinet, parliament and public life are gone. The introduction of proportional representation in 1978 effectively did away with electorates whose candidates were largely elected on the basis of caste. Sri Lankan national elections still regularly produce representatives from all castes, but it is of interest to note that since independence in 1948, virtually every government, and every major political party, has had (and continues to have) a Goigama leader. The exceptions are the brief and freakish interim leadership of the Sri Lanka Freedom Party by C.P. de Silva of the Salagama caste (March–May 1960), and the United National Party administration of Ranasinghe Premadasa (1989–93).[16] The latter came from a caste so low (Hinna or Dhobhis to the Salagama) that it did not threaten the delicate caste status quo between the two or three upper castes. The fact that Premadasa was the first non-Goigama head of state is an anomaly that does not indicate a significant or lasting change in Sinhalese caste attitudes. Yet it does show that caste is no longer the rigorous impediment to public office it would have been in earlier times. And caste has become much less of a barrier to the accumulation of wealth and social status.

Notwithstanding these observations, caste stratification was a major issue in the serious trouble associated with the radical movement, the Janatha Vimukthi Peramuna. It is worth briefly tracing the motivation for this 'people's front', as the issues it confronted in two violent attempted insurrections in 1971 and 1988–89 are still by no means resolved. Established in the late 1960s by Rohana Wijeweera, the JVP's 'Che Guevarist' revolutionary programme appealed mostly to the widening sector of disaffected rural youth. A Sinhalese Anglican priest very close to the movement has noted that it was in every way a 'deep movement of liberation ... though the JVP lacked widespread mass support, they nonetheless arose from the mass of the people.'[17] In the March 1971 insurgency, no clear caste pattern emerged, but the rebellion definitely gained support among those from economically and socially deprived castes, from the lowest social strata. Janice Jiggins sums it up:

> For my own part, I was sure that a major impulse had been provided by the social dynamic between the castes. The continuing depressed status of two of the largest up-country castes, combined with the political frustrations of the south and west coast fishing caste (denied adjustment with the existing political parties) formed a core of disaffection to be exploited by insurgent leaders.[18]

Large groups of depressed caste youth were heavily involved in the 1971 uprising. Rebel sectors from the lowest castes were seriously mauled (e.g., among the Batgama in the Pelmadulla area near Ratnapura and throughout the Kegalle region), partly because these groups were clustered in areas where they could be easily surrounded. For strategic reasons, although low-caste stigma fuelled JVP enlistment, Wijeweera never made capital of caste inequality to gain as wide a base of support as possible. His celebrated 'Five Lectures' avoided the issue entirely, just as they offered no criticism of Buddhism.

Despite the horrendous human loss associated with the failed 1971 uprising, the JVP quickly regained its strength. For the most part it was proscribed by the state (a brief window of political legitimacy was closed in 1983), surfacing in 1988 to conduct a masterly and nearly successful campaign. Although much had changed in Sri Lanka since the insurrection of 1971, one observer present for both the first and second insurrections noted that in 1988 'most of the social and economic causes of the 1971 trauma remain—notably widespread poverty, unemployment, lack of social and economic mobility, landlessness, village isolation and alienation from a political system found by many to be dishonest and opportunistic. To these must be added several new factors, such as the secessionist war in the north and east, and the negative effects of the UNP's "open economy".'[19] This time, the leading collective JVP refrain was, 'Whom can I tell?' (*kaata kiannada*?), a reference to the fact that their woes were not being heard by the government or by a rapidly changing society increasingly affected by a capitalist economy and globalization. Once again, the JVP showed itself to be exceptionally skilful at exploiting vulnerable sectors of society, in particular the six Sinhala universities. Although perhaps as few as 10 to 20 per cent of the 20,000 undergraduates were active JVP supporters, the institutions were effectively shut down by the JVP for two years under the slogan 'First the Motherland, then a university degree' (*palaweni mawbima, deweni upadhiya*). It was a period of grave national tension, and Ranasinghe Premadasa proved to be a wily and capable leader through this parlous time. Only brutal and uncompromising resistance by the state, with abuse of human rights, kept the JVP from victory.[20]

The one-time anarchist movement and its ideology appear moribund, but it has the potential to reassert its revolutionary agenda. Although the summary execution of Wijeweera in November 1989 marked the end of the actual rebellion, the JVP survived as a party by breaking up into smaller units (e.g., the Deshapremi Janatha Viyaparaya). Later, the JVP was returned to Parliamentary status by the then Prime Minister Chandrika Kumaratunge's People's Alliance government. The JVP exists now as a bona fide political party led by Tilvam Silva (a coastal Karava). With 10 seats in Parliament (proportional representation gave most of these), the party is in key ways very different from the one that backed the youth and depressed caste and sector revolts of recent years. Its likely appeal today is to those alienated by Colombo's monopoly of power and economic opportunity (responsible for the not uncommonly heard phrase that 'there's milk in Colombo but not elsewhere'—*kolambata kiri apata kekiri*), and, still, to those whose low caste status is an economic impediment or painful insult to human dignity. Caste may not be as stigmatic as it once was, but it would be simply wrong to ignore the fact that caste customs are firmly entrenched in all sectors of Sinhalese society, and that it may well be a factor in any future extra-parliamentary political activity. Victor Ivan, editor of the leftist newspaper *Ravaya* (Echo) and one-time JVP activist, remarking on Sri Lanka's unpredictable political environment, suggests that about once a decade the lowest sectors of society 'will come out onto the streets'.[21] It is not uncommon to hear from local folk of all walks of life that Sri

Lanka is due for just such a response to the widening gap between privileged and not so privileged, and sooner rather than later.

Is caste stigma likely to be a feature of such agitation? Perhaps not by itself, though attached to the increasingly self-evident polarity between poor and rich (*duppat-pohosat*), caste will continue to be something that exacerbates exclusion rather than heals it. In a 1994 series of remarkably frank and informative articles entitled 'Inequality and the Hierarchy' in the Sinhala publication *Yuktia*, the celebrated social scientist Jayadeva Uyangoda reveals how he, even as a senior *acharya* or professor, continues to feel the stigma of low birth caste. He cites several examples of grave insult, sometimes by the lips or pens of colleagues. His *Yuktia* pieces generated all sorts of vitriolic responses to *Yuktia* and other newspapers as well. 'We know who your parents are,' wrote an angry critic in one of many letters published by the English language newspaper, *The Island*. Uyangoda suggests that these attacks were deliberately made widespread in order to publicly humiliate and silence him by identifying his caste.

Humiliation in public through posters, notices and the media is not uncommon. Humiliation is, indeed, part of the dark side of Sinhala culture, which has its own rich vocabulary (e.g., *lajjawa*, *samajana* or public shame; *lajja-baya*, fear of ridicule; *baldu*, loss of status; *ninda*, insult). The phenomenon has been carefully analyzed by Gananath Obeysekere in his fine anthropological study, *The Cult of the Goddess Pattini*. Obeyesekere uses the example of an ancient village ritual, the *ankeliya* (horn), 'as a reflection of, and a mechanism for venting, a deep-seated need or drive in the Sinhala personality to humiliate others and glorify oneself. These needs arise from the socialization of shame status in Sinhala childhood and culture and have consequences for the individual's "self" ....'[22] Obeyesekere argues that although the *ankeliya* ritual has practically disappeared, the *ankeliya* model of public vilification and abuse, of literally crushing the opposition (e.g., in politics, even in sports) is still dominant. More to the point, this translates into such things as the inability of schoolteachers from low caste backgrounds to hold order in their classes, as the parents of a child disciplined by a teacher of low caste take it as an insult to their own caste. But there are also examples where the low castes return the insult, particularly in the ragging of university students. Matthews has shown how a geographically-focused quota system ('affirmative action') associated with university admissions has brought to the varsity many underprivileged youth, giving them a chance to 'initiate' new students (especially young women and those from the great schools). This is often a sadistic and humiliating scenario, the prospect of which has been known to deter some qualified students from accepting a place at a university.[23] To sum up, *kuliya* or caste is still a critical exclusionary factor in Sinhala society (e.g., a quick review of the marriage proposal columns in the newspapers almost always indicates caste preferences). The caste system tends to be antiquated and anti-egalitarian. It works against the kind of 'trust' that would deliver order in life and society. Yet it is seldom acknowledged by analysts of Lanka's political and social turmoil as a serious factor.

A second feature of Sinhala sociology pertinent to the issue of 'exclusion' from national prosperity and opportunity is class (*pantaya*). It is reasonable to use such classic terminology as 'aristocracy' (still best defined by the highest Goigama sub-caste, the *Radala*), bourgeoisie, proletariat and peasantry to describe Sinhala classes, though today these may seem somewhat dated. Other class designations might be upper class (recognized, powerful, rich families, usually but not always higher caste), middle class (professional, reasonably wealth: all castes), lower middle class (including most school teachers, *bhikkhus* and ayurvedic practitioners: all castes) and lower class (peasants: all castes, particularly lower agricultural and old 'service' castes).[24] These class models are nonetheless riddled with caste distinctions. Thus Kumari Jayewardene states, in her study of re-casting caste in a class society, a reassessment of the power and authority of caste. Early in the twentieth century, social status became subject to a complex interplay between caste and class wealth.[25] The impact of colonialism, free enterprise and education all made some change in the existing social status quo at least a possibility. Colonialism provided a need for 'non-caste' professions such as clerks, translators and an emerging class of capitalists (the 'rentiers' referred to above, as well as those involved with coastal trade in a time of rapid economic expansion).

The Kandyan Goigama lacked the mobility and initiative to engage much in new economic ventures. They rarely took advantage of the economic, professional and educational opportunities created by the colonial presence, strongest in Colombo and on the west coast. Forming a completely new bourgeoisie class, by 1920 the non-agriculturalist elements of the KSD castes all became 'higher' than the Goigama from the perspective of mercantile prosperity. Access to training in such professions as law, medicine and engineering made possible a shift from petite to haute bourgeoisie, in some instances very quickly.[26] There were social tensions, to be sure, marked by caste claims and caste language. Importantly, however (as Jayawardene rightly notes), 'the fact ... that many of the new rich were Karava has led to the interpretation of the conflict as being primarily based on caste. But a closer analysis of the forces at work shows the conflict was basically intra-class controversy expressed in caste terms rather than caste controversy per se.'[27]

The new bourgeoisie class of Sinhala rentiers, indigenous capitalists, traders, entrepreneurs and plantation investors became a major feature of the colonial economy and polity. However, it was a capitalism dependent on state protection, and it provided limited space for real entrepreneurial talent and opportunism, compared, for example, to India. Acculturation to British customs was a commonplace collateral feature, sometimes partial, such as a tweed sarong over trousers, sometimes much more, as in conversion to Protestant Christianity, particularly Anglicanism.[28] A remarkable feature of these momentous sociological shifts was that the wealthy of all Sinhala castes found themselves politically in accord, even to the point of opposing social reforms suggested by the 1931 Donoughmore constitution which might have compromised their prosperity.[29] For a time, upper class collegiality even transcended ethnicity. A.J. Wilson points out how the post-independence government of D.S. Senanayake had the support of 'conservative-minded political notables' from the 'big families', the landed interests, the Sinhala Maha Sabha (Great Council of the Sinhalese), Ceylon Muslim League and important sections of the Ceylon and Indian Tamils. This was consociationalism at its best.[30] But it was not to survive the 1956 victory of S.W.R.D. Bandaranaike's ethnocentric, pro-Sinhala populist political strategy, the first of several tragedies that ultimately sentenced Lanka to civil war, fratricide and near-collapse.

The Sinhalese class structure remains an important feature in Sri Lanka's present context. Although class is to a degree indicated by such features as education and profession, as argued earlier, in Sri Lanka its chief association is with economic well-being. Prosperity has in crucial ways become more significant than birth status as a social indicator. It would be fair to say that for some groups at least, class has become more important than caste. Notwithstanding this, the upper castes resist class attempts by moneyed or nouvean riche classes to transform the importance of the traditional hierarchical system.

Three points can be made here. First, the gap between 'haves' and 'have-nots' is widening. A UN report of 2001 indicates significantly different levels of development in the provinces in the south and west, with stagnant economic conditions still in place where the JVP first found cause for revolution.[31] Rural poverty has not diminished, and the cities exhibit spiraling economic polarity. Colombo in particular shows all the signs of class privilege based on money: expensive foreign automobiles, ostentatious homes and a generally lavish lifestyle (among high-ranking politicians and the nouveau riche). But beyond the exclusive neighborhoods and the moneyed class (of whatever caste), the standard of living falls precipitously. Estimates of income distribution suggest the richest 10 per cent hold between 45 to 50 per cent of the country's wealth. In 2001, the percentage of those below the poverty line was 44.5 per cent (4,305,276 families in 19 out of 25 districts).[32] With average wage earnings of Rupees (Rs) 5,000 per month (Rs 80 = US $1), and with cost of living continually accelerating (in 2001, a family of four needed Rs 30,000 per month to maintain a basic standard of living by local standards), such straitened circumstances are politically destabilizing. A welfare programme (*samurdhi*) provides minimum assistance for some of the poorest, but critics claim the programme is politicized and insufficient.[33] It is questionable whether Sri Lanka is anywhere near becoming what is sometimes referred to as a 'lower middle income country', as some analysts aver.[34]

A second issue that continues to affect class place and role among the Sinhalese is the recent civil war, now on hold, between the armed forces of the state and the Liberation Tigers of Tamil Eelam. The expense of this conflict has drained the public treasury (military expenditure in 2000 was US $880 million, constituting 30 per cent of overall government revenue).[35] An additional 'war defence levy' has brought the general sales tax to 20 per cent—a further burden for the poor. A major consequence is insufficient monetary support from the government for training programmes to help create jobs, or to improve the much deteriorated condition of the country's universities. Attempts to establish private tertiary-level educational institutions that would regain international standards have all failed. The prospect of student activism, resentful of the putative privilege these schools might bring, guarantees that no government will have the political will to risk their introduction. Information technology remains seriously undeveloped when compared to the initiative taken in this matter in neighbouring India.[36] Unemployment, and lack of employment mobility, has led to an estimated 1 million Sri Lankans finding work in the Middle East, sometimes as professionals such as nurses, accountants, or engineers, but more often as drivers, maids and menial labourers.[37] The social critic, Victor Ivan calls this a 'prosperous slave trade'. From what he can determine, next to revenue from the tea industry, expatriate labour remains the second highest source of the nation's foreign income.[38] Ivan also suggests that the real danger is that it permits the government of Sri Lanka to shy away from its responsibility to provide adequate employment at home.

The civil war has also had an important effect on the class composition of the armed forces. Much of the evidence for this is anecdotal, but it is well known that few affluent upper- or middle-class young men join the services. Not many graduates from the great old schools loosely associated with class privilege (St. Thomas's, Trinity, Ananda, even the top state school, Royal College) choose to proceed to the defence college or take a commission. The other ranks are not unexpectedly comprised entirely of village recruits (*mee api kolow*—literally, 'these are our boys'). But the fact that the village is now the chief source of the officer corps, many of whom come from the rural poor, is new. Some claim this is in part a result of the extreme danger of the battlefront. A recently retired major-general has reiterated that the upper classes just will not participate in combat risk, and by default have surrendered key armed forces positions to individuals from very different sectors of society.[39] Opportunities to train at distinguished overseas staff colleges (Camberley, Wellington, etc.) though still available, are now diminished, and so are truly professional general staff operating with the highest standards. There have been calls for national conscription in order to field a much bigger army that can operate on several fronts, but public support is not forthcoming, apart from a certain amount of public bravado ('if you want war, we'll have war; if you want peace, we're prepared for peace', *yudhaya nam yudhaya samaya nam samaya*) there is no national 'war-spirit' (*yudha manasikatya*). But there is a 'war industry', directly responsible for at least 150,000 jobs, and lucrative profits to be made for suppliers. Those who join the forces often do so for employment. There is, for example, the opportunity to make a considerable salary on the front lines. Even a private can earn Rs 30,000 per month in the war zone, the pay of a brigadier behind the lines, and if killed in action, a soldier's family will be well compensated by the state.

Clearly, however, there are dangers in having an unbalanced class dimension in the forces. The burden of the state's defence at a time of extreme crisis is borne largely by villagers and the underprivileged. The armed forces are not representative of a national commitment, and, perhaps not unexpectedly, the forces experience frequent desertions and low morale. Much of this must result from the truly punishing confrontations with highly committed LTTE cadres (some recent battles have seen up to a thousand troops killed in action on a single day).[40] The forces have also been politicized and open to cronyism, a feature that arguably affects every promotion above the rank of major. This in part goes back to a 1962 attempted putsch, which unfortunately provoked then Prime Minister Sirimavo Bandaranaike to purge the officer corps along religio-ethnic lines. Within a few years, virtually all Christian and Ceylon Tamil officers were fired, on the basis of promoting and protecting a specifically Sinhalese Buddhist identity for the army, pointing to a dangerous psychological and social twist in the road.[41] The urban Sinhalese have never been much infused with enthusiasm for the military during this struggle, but in the villages a 'war hero' (*rana viriya*) cult has appeared, marked by frequently garish statues to the war dead and the spread of an uncompromising, aggressive, pro-military attitude towards the civil war. To sum up: Sri Lanka's armed forces have been largely abandoned by the Sinhala upper and middle classes. The educated and affluent sector of society has no inclination to share the discomfitures of war with village troops who have joined for decent salaries and possible career advancement.

There is clearly danger in having an army that is not representative of the whole people. Further, in the long term, as the conflict is resolved, there will be a serious challenge in disbanding an armed force of 150,000 troops, who have, in a sense, a vested interest in the conflict. They will want a say in how the civil war is brought to its conclusion, and in the political destiny of the country.

A third aspect of the class phenomenon is the Buddhist monastic order (*sangha*). In this matter, caste is still an issue, denying as it does non-Goigama entrance into the oldest and arguably most influential *nikaya* (Siam). But the issue of possible class mobility probably lies behind many young monks' decision to enter the *sangha*. Although no statistical base exists to support this claim, the *sangha* has long been recognized as a stepping-stone for those from underprivileged backgrounds to gain an education and place in the social order. Those from lower class backgrounds are thought to comprise the largest element of the estimated 32,000 strong order of *samaneras* (novices) and *bhikkhus* (monks). Even in the caste-privileged Siam Nikaya, many members, though Goigama, are from poor rural families. Not a few monks, then, will stay in the *sangha* for a few years, perhaps to attain a university degree, and then suddenly give up orders. This is a sign of changing times, seen by many lay devotees as frank opportunism in a tradition whereby *bhikkhu* ordination is for life.

Three conclusions may be drawn. First, the divisions of caste and class among the Sinhala majority compromise public trust and foster inequality and discrimination. The present caste-class combination is probably as rigid and divisive as the old caste system. Caste, though slowly diminishing in authority, is still crucial. There is some blurring of caste-class distinctions but, especially in matters of marriage, caste by itself still has wide social acceptance—even with the younger generations. Second, from a class perspective, the poorest Sinhalese are dependent on the armed forces or on the Middle East for employment, and this does not bode well for the future. If either opportunity suddenly collapses, the resulting strain on society and polity will be very serious. Third, there will be a heavy price to pay for the fact that the lower class has become the dominant component of two important public institutions, the armed forces and the *sangha* (albeit for different reasons). What remains to be seen is what the price will be.

NOTES

1. The ethnic distribution is: Sinhalese, 74 per cent; Ceylon Tamil, 12.8 per cent; Indian Tamil, 5.5 per cent; Ceylon Moor (Muslim), 7.1 per cent; others (e.g., Parsis, Burghers, Bharathas, Malays, Memons), 0.8 per cent. The figures are taken from *Far Eastern Economic Review, Asia 2001*, Hong Kong, 2001, 15. There is some question now about the numerical strength of the Ceylon Tamil population. Diminished by nearly 20 years of fairly constant civil war, hundreds of thousands of Tamils from the Northern and Eastern provinces have emigrated as refugees, mostly to the West. The city of Toronto, Ontario alone has a Ceylon Tamil community estimated at 135,000 in 2001. The population of Sri Lanka has doubled since 1981 (*Times of India*, 18 July 2001).
2. In Sinhala, the key words are *jati* (ethnicity or race), *kulaya* (caste, from *kula*, 'colour') and *pantaya* (class). Other Sinhala nouns for caste are *variga* and, rarely, *jati*. The phenomenon of *bheda* (struggle) between these components is reflected in the phrase *'jati bheda panti bheda kula bheda'*.
3. Bruce Matthews, 'University Education in Sri Lanka in Context: Consequences of Deteriorating Standards', *Pacific Affairs*, Vol. 68, No. 1, Spring, 1995, p. 94.
4. Janice Jiggins, *Caste and Family in the Politics of the Sinhalese*, 1947–1976, Colombo: K.V.G. de Silva for Cambridge University Press, 1979; E.R. Leach, *Pul Eliya: A Village in Ceylon*, Cambridge: Cambridge University Press, 1961; Michael Roberts, *Caste Conflict and Elite Formation: The Rise of the Karava Elite in Sri Lanka, 1500–1931*, Cambridge: Cambridge University Press, 1982; Bryce Ryan, *Caste in Modern Ceylon: The Sinhala System in Transition*, New Jersey: Rutgers University Press, 1953; K.L. Sharma, *Society and Polity in Modern Sri Lanka*, South Asia Studies, Series 17, New Delhi: South Asian Publishers, 1988; S.J. Tambiah, *Sinhala Laws and Customs*, Colombo: Lake House, 1968; Jayadeva Uyangoda, *Caste in Sinhalese Society*, Colombo: Social Scientists Association, 1998.
5. The Amarapura Nikaya evolved from a visit to Burma in 1802 by *salagama* men seeking ordination. The *nikaya* was open to all castes 'in defiance of the Kandyan practice which restricted ordination to those of the Goyigama caste ... and was marked by greater flexibility and receptivity to forces of change and social reform'. See K.M. de Silva, *A History of Sri Lanka*, Delhi: Oxford University Press, 1981, p. 250. In 1865, an 'offshoot' of the Amarapura Nikaya, known as the Ramanna Nikaya was established, with emphasis on poverty, humility and scholarship (what de Silva refers to as 'Oriental learning', p. 341). It too was open to all castes. Only the Siam Nikaya was (and is) restricted to the Goigama. Once a man is ordained into *bhikkhu* status, however, he loses all caste designation. Lay folk do not recognize a monk's caste. A good example of this might be the Vajirarama Vihara in Welawatte, Colombo. Its founding clergy were Durava, but this famous temple is thronged with devotees from all castes, certainly including the Goigama.

6. Paul Younger, *Introduction to Indian Religious Thought*, Philadelphia: Westminster, 1972, p. 31.
7. Bryce Ryan, n. 4, p. 50.
8. Examples of the Kandyan 'service' castes are Batgama (palanquin carriers), Berava (drummers), Panikki (barbers), Kinnara (mat weavers) and the Gahala-Berava (funeral drummers and executioners). As late as 1950, the lowest of these castes were not permitted to cover the upper parts of their bodies. The sometime M.P. of the Ceylon Communist Party for Hakmana, Premalal Kumarasiri, has recently written of such discriminatory practices against the Beruva by the Goigama in the south. *Pravada*, Colombo, Vol. 7, No. 2, 2001, p. 15.
9. Though official statistics on Sinhalese castes do not exist, a likely breakdown is Goigama 60 per cent, Karava 10 per cent, Salagama 7 per cent, Durava 4 per cent, Batgama/Wahumpura 11 per cent, others 8 per cent. Some aver that the Goigama is only 50 per cent, and that about 35 per cent of the Sinhala population is assumed to be low caste by one definition or another.
10. Kumari Jayawardene, *Nobodies to Somebodies: The Rise of the Colonial Bourgeoisie in Sri Lanka*, Colombo: Social Scientists' Association, 2000, p. 61.
11. Michael Roberts, *Collective Identities, Nationalisms and Protest in Modern Sri Lanka*, Colombo: Marga, 1979, p. 74.
12. For example, the Karava Warusahennedige Soysa family, which began with Jeronis Soysa, who obtained the 'rents' to provide spirits to army garrisons and taverns up-country as early as the 1830s. See Jayawardene, n. 10, p. 57.
13. Jayadeva Uyangoda, *Yuktia*, Colombo, 11 May 1994 (translated from Sinhala). See also Roberts, n. 4, p. 2.
14. Tamara Gunasekera, *Hierarchy and Egalitarianism: Caste, Class and Power in Sinhalese Peasant Society*, London: Athlone, 1994, p. 1.
15. Chandrika Bandaranaike Kumaratunge became President of Sri Lanka in 1994, appointing her mother Sirimavo (Prime Minister 1960–65, 1970–77) Prime Minister until August 2000. Anura Bandaranaike became Speaker of the Parliament in 2000.
16. A.J. Wilson, *Politics in Sri Lanka, 1947–1973*, Bristol: Macmillan, 1974, p. 46.
17. Yohan Devananda (Rev. John Cooray), 'An interpretation of the Revolt of April, 1971'. Colombo, 1972 (cyclostyled).
18. Jiggins, n. 4, p. 5.
19. Bruce Matthews, 'The Janatha Vimukthi Peramuna and the Politics of the Underground in Sri Lanka, *The Round Table*, Vol. 312, October 1989, p. 427.
20. The Lankan armed forces were stretched too thin to contain both the LTTE in the north and the JVP in the south. Although the Sinhala public and polity found it humiliating, for two years (beginning in July 1987) the uninvited imposition of a division of the Indian army (the so-called Indian Peace Keeping Force) in the north probably saved Colombo from collapse. Without this intervention, the dual forces of the LTTE and the JVP would likely have overwhelmed the struggling forces of the state. The Indian army tried to defeat the LTTE at arms and hold the ground in Jaffna, but left essentially in defeat, with 1,000 *jawans* (troops) killed in action. A

churlish Colombo has never acknowledged this Indian sacrifice of life to preserve the unitary state of Sri Lanka.

21. Interview, Victor Ivan, Colombo, 2 April 2001.
22. Gananath Obeyesekere, *The Cult of the Goddess Pattini*, Chicago: University of Chicago Press, 1984, p. 500.
23. Matthews, n. 3, p. 87.
24. Sharma, n. 4, p. 21.
25. Jayawardene, n. 10, p. 166.
26. Ibid., p. 154.
27. Ibid., p. 167.
28. Christianization even spilled over into the Goigama to a limited extent. A well-known example was the family of future Prime Minister S.W.R.D. Bandaranaike. For whatever other reasons, in a politically adept move, the latter reconverted to Buddhism.
29. De Silva, n. 5, p. 422.
30. Wilson, n. 16, p. 140.
31. *Written Statement on Behalf of the UN System Represented in Sri Lanka* (FAO, ILO, UNDP, UNFPA, UNHCR, UNICEF, WFP, WHP), Colombo, January 2001.
32. *Samurdhi Authority*, Monitoring and Evaluation Division, 2001.
33. In 2000, the number of the Samurdhi Authority's Department of Poor Relief beneficiary families was 1,913,533. Samurdhi is the present People's Alliance government's replacement of the former Janasaviya programme introduced by Ranasinghe Premadasa in 1988. Janasaviya had direct access to key government ministries and departments (e.g., housing, industry, irrigation, finance). Samurdhi did not maintain this structure. It has some good points (e.g., money for food for the very poor, an insurance scheme, and a social security system of savings), but is generally considered part of the PA's political machinery. Some claim local decisions concerning recipient eligibility have been replaced by centralized political decisions.
34. Jehan Perera, 'Human Cost', *Sri Lanka Net*, 1 April 2001.
35. *Asia 2001 Yearbook*, Hong Kong: Far Eastern Economic Review, p. 198.
36. An official at Seva Lanka, a local village development NGO, estimates only 650 IT-trained specialists are currently working in Sri Lanka, virtually all concentrated in Colombo.
37. Interview, Bishop Kenneth Fernando, Colombo, 2 April 2001.
38. Interview, Victor Ivan, Colombo, 2 April 2001.
39. Interview, 30 March 2001 (identity concealed on request).
40. For example, the battle of Pooneryn, 11 November 1993; the siege of Mandaithhivu, 28 June 1995; the April 2001 'Agni Kheela' engagement, all severe losses for the armed forces.
41. Bruce Matthews, 'Counter-Insurgency In Modern Sri Lanka', in Paul Rich and Richard Stubbs (Eds), *The Counter-Insurgent State: Guerilla Warfare and State Building in the Twentieth Century*, London: Macmillan, 1997, p. 76.

5

From Differences to Ethnic Solidarity among the Tamils

DAGMAR HELLMANN-RAJANAYAGAM

'English and Vellalahood was the path to fame and fortune.'[1]

Perinbanayagam's quote sets the tone for our discussion of mechanisms of exclusion and inclusion among the Tamils in Sri Lanka, especially in Jaffna. It demonstrates that while caste played a large role in these strategies it was not the only means of differentiation.

Alongside some superficial similarities, we can see decisive differences in this regard between the Tamils and the Sinhalese. The first thing to keep in mind is that until today, the question of who is a Tamil and who is not, that is, who can claim Tamil tradition and identity and which are the determining characteristics of a Tamil, can lead to grave conflict among the Tamils themselves. We therefore have to determine two things: how do the Tamils differentiate among themselves and how do they distinguish themselves from other, non-Tamil groups?

For the Jaffna Tamils caste remains a basic feature of their social structure, and at the same time a defining feature of their identity. The caste system in Jaffna differs from that in Tamil Nadu in some small, but decisive ways and contains similarities to that of the Sinhalese. The highest caste in Tamil Nadu—Brahmin—is hardly to be found in Jaffna. They are, to put it in the words of one of my Jaffna friends, 'kept in the temples for the pucai'.[2] The dominant and most numerous caste is, as is the case with the Sinhalese, the Sudra, i.e., the Vellalar, landowners and rice farmers, who correspond exactly to the Sinhalese Goigama. Vellalar comprise 50 per cent and Karaiyar 10 per cent of the population; all other castes exist as small percentages.[3] The position which the Brahmins claimed in Tamil Nadu was occupied by the Vellalar: professions, government service, academe. Christians comprise 15 per cent of the Tamil population (of whom 80 per cent are Catholics), and they considered themselves Tamils as much as the Saivites. As long as they accepted the social structure, that is the caste system, they were themselves accepted by society. This argues against the religious foundation of caste, at least in the Jaffna context, and further observations tend to confirm this assumption.

We find in Jaffna some low castes, which do not exist in Tamil Nadu. Myths attribute their low status to migration from India to Ceylon or to transgressions which made them lose their former high, i.e., Vellalar status. These castes are the Pallar, Nalavar, and the Koviar, the latter are said to be former Sinhala Goigamas. In contrast to all other low castes, the Koviar are ritually pure. Some experts assume that these castes were excluded by the migrating Vellalar because of unusual or unorthodox ritual or social practices.[4] The east, i.e., the region around Trincomalee and Batticaloa, shows some differences concerning the caste system, because here the Mukkuvar, lagoon fishers, and the Vanniyars, former chieftains, are the most numerous and dominant and take the position the Vellalar occupy in Jaffna.

The pre-eminence of the Vellalar never remained unquestioned, either in the past or the present. The Karaiyar especially always constituted a threat. As Pfaffenberger shows, the insecurity about their pre-eminence, primarily among the Vellalar themselves, resulted from the system's own premises and mechanisms which assisted in undermining it. We can illustrate this with the well-known proverb 'Slowly, slowly, they all become Vellalar'. Anybody can become a Vellalar by acquiring Vellalar attributes. But what are these attributes? Jaffna society faces the dilemma that the nature of the caste system and its definitions make it impossible to uphold differentiations that were introduced to secure elite status for the high castes. To retain their dominance, the Vellalar tried to define and legitimize differences between castes as decisive and foundational. However, these differences were from the start superficial and marginal ones and became increasingly so as time passed. This made caste boundaries both rigid and visible, but simultaneously artificial and thus, surmountable: dress codes, hairstyles, modes of dwellings, etc. These were not differences created by birth, but by definition and coercion. The Vellalar had to invent ever-new caste differences, especially as the old ones, such as an English education, were devalued. English education was, in principle, something anybody could acquire, even though the Vellalar tried with all means at their disposal to prevent the low castes from attaining it. The reasoning for upholding these differences was that low castes were low and dirty by birth and former sins. They had no right to aspire to Vellalar attributes or to try to look and dress like Vellalar. Implicitly it was thus admitted that caste differentiations were artificial and arbitrary, Pfaffenberger even notes that this was explicitly recognized: if everybody dresses and looks like a Vellalar, it would be impossible to recognize the low castes![5]

VELLALAR, THE ESSENTIAL TAMILS

And yet, this differentiation did not really work. The ambiguity was enhanced by the fact that Vellalar were not only the highest caste, but perceived themselves, and to a large extent were perceived, as carriers and guardians of Tamil culture, as the quintessential Tamils. This perception is very ancient. It was not enough to simply be a Vellalar to be a Tamil, but on the other hand to be Tamil meant to be Vellalar. A non-Vellalar, even a Tamil-speaking one, was not considered a Tamil until the end of the nineteenth century.[6] On the other hand, the proverb shows that inclusion did occur all the time. How did this come about? The reason why Vellalar counted as the essential Tamils was not least access to and control over land. Kings of the Chola dynasty in South India are said to have sent the Vellalar as settlers to Jaffna, after other castes had settled there already. The Vellalar were supposed to create order in Jaffna and to administer the region in the name of the king. Only when Vellalar entered the region and lived and farmed there, was it considered civilized.[7] The Vellalar represented Tamil culture.

The idea appears most clearly and with a new twist in the writings of Marai Malai Adigal, a religious and social reformer from Tamil Nadu, who enjoys extreme respect in Jaffna even today. However, his understanding of who was, could or could not be, a Vellalar and thus a Tamil was fundamentally different from that of earlier writers. For him, the Vellalar were the essential Tamils, but he does not preclude that other castes can be accepted into the Vellalar. It only needs the acceptance of Vellalar ideas and values, vegetarianism and *ahimsa*. Adigal does not agree with the theory of biological caste purity. For him every Tamil can become a Vellalar, the ideal Tamil. For Marai Malai Adigal the Tamils did not increase only biologically, but also by admitting members of other groups and origins if they fulfilled the conditions of being Tamil. Vellalar is not an attribute of birth, but of choice: if you act like a Vellalar, you are a Vellalar. The extension would then be: if you behave like a Tamil, you are a Tamil.[8] He thus implicitly acknowledged the artificiality of caste boundaries, the fact that Vellalarization had always occurred and thus the truth of the quoted proverb.

Though Adigal's ideas found wide resonance, their implementation left a lot to be desired in Jaffna. The lower castes were termed *adi-Dravidas* or primitive aborigines who have nothing to do with the actual Tamils. But the idea of the Vellalar as quintessential Tamils was taken up in slightly changed form by the Catholic priest Gnanaprakasar. He declared that all Tamils, even the lower castes, were Vellalar, albeit 'Vellalar with prefix'. Originally, only true landowners were Vellalar and thus Tamils. As the same time other castes, traders, labourers and artisans were also Vellalar, but of a different and implicitly inferior kind. However, they were acknowledged to be Vellalar and in principle could claim to belong to the Tamil fold.[9]

The Karaiyar: A Case of Voluntary Exclusion?

The most ferocious opposition against the attempts by the Vellalar to exclude other castes came from Karaiyar. They are the second strongest caste in the Tamil areas. They, however, did not so much demand inclusion as equal rights on the basis of separation. The Karaiyar consider themselves as standing outside the social hierarchy of the Tamil castes, but as equal or at least not inferior to the Vellalar.[10] And they were the first among the non-Vellalar castes to avail themselves of the opportunities of English education. They were traditionally traders and fishers but were also known as the soldiers and mercenaries of the Tamil kings.

Often, they supported factions hostile to the Vellalar. They had a reputation for bravery and toughness and never accepted the low status the Vellalar tried to assign them.

When universal suffrage was introduced under the Donoughmore constitution, the Karaiyar were, apart from the Vellalar, the only caste to vote in significant numbers. And their votes counted, a fact that Jane Russell traces back to their efficient organization in the Catholic Diocesan Union. She writes:

> ... the Karaiyar or fishing caste had to a great extent engineered its emancipation from Vellalar domination by the 1930s ... the Karaiyar had used the vehicle of the Catholic Church to free themselves from the trammels of caste obligation.[11]

This self-confidence at the same time increased the tensions between Vellalar and Karaiyar. But the latter could not be antagonized, because Karaiyar votes were decisive for the election victory of A. Mahadeva in Jaffna and N. Selvadurai (himself a Christian) in Kayts, both of whom had promised to help the Karaiyar. The same applied to the victory of G.G. Ponnambalam in Point Pedro.[12] The contemporary militant movement then furnished a further chance for the Karaiyar to maintain their position against the Vellalar, this time on their very own turf: warfare and on their own conditions.

THE GEOGRAPHY OF EXCLUSION

Another kind of exclusion operates between groups of Tamils from different regions, viz., Jaffna, Colombo and the east. It is mutually enforced by all groups. On the one hand, Tamils outside Jaffna, even in the east, are sometimes seen as inferior. This again derives from caste differences—the dominant castes in the east are the Mukkuvar and Vanniyar. A traditional antagonism exists between them and the Vellalar: while the Vellalar look down upon the Tamils from the east, the Mukkuvar do not accept the claim of the Jaffna Tamils to speak for and dominate them. The antagonism has manifested itself in recent decades, especially at the level of politics.

The perceived exclusivity of the Tamil political parties in Jaffna hampered their success among Tamils in other areas of Ceylon.

Both in the east and in Jaffna itself, the Federal Party (FP) had to struggle to survive in the early years. In Jaffna the Tamil Congress (TC) was much stronger and more in line with conservative caste perceptions. For the east, C. Rajadurai, a founding member of the FP, describes in the anniversary volume with touching naiveté the difficulties and setbacks in Batticaloa where '... an unnecessary, but deep-seated hatred against Jaffna [dominates] the hearts of the people ...' and where contempt for the FP politicians who were equated with Jaffna, was so strong that he was booed and beaten up when he tried to organize a party meeting![13] This only changed in the course of the 'Sinhala Only' legislation and the colonization campaigns of 1956/58. But Rajadurai also mentions that the first success of the FP occurred in the east as well, in Trincomalee in 1952, even before it could establish a foothold in Jaffna: Chelvanayagam's defeat in Kankesanturai in that year nearly killed the party. The election campaign in Trincomalee had focused on the problem of colonization and it was this that accounted for its success.[14]

The reception and fate of the Tamil parties, particularly the FP, in the east highlights geographical exclusion combined with caste barriers. But there exists another type of geographical exclusion, which is not really related to caste. This second type has survived from the 1920s, when the Jaffna Youth Congress (JYC) derided the 'Turban brigade' Sir P. Ramanathan, a politician, and his colleagues from Colombo. Today militants and citizens of Jaffna criticize the Colombo Tamils as traitors, indifferent or just ignorant and less 'Tamil' than they should be. Only Tamils who actually live in Tamil areas are accepted and respected as Tamils. The fact that the Colombo Tamils find it difficult to negotiate between conflicting claims by the Sinhalese and the Tamils, is turned into an accusation against them by both sides.

A Different Kind of Exclusion: The Generation Gap

With the rise of the militants we encounter yet another kind of split, apart from caste and geography: the generation gap. Although this is a worldwide phenomenon known in all kinds of societies, it attained a particular virulence in Jaffna. The militant groups formed from 1972 onwards resented the cautious and slow pace of their fathers, especially because they could not foresee any results from this kind of political strategy. The teaching of the fathers had been, as always: keep quiet, study, follow tradition, then your future will be assured. Now for the first time, this tactic did not work. The efforts of the elite to lure the youth back into the fold did not work any longer. The first shock had come in 1956, with the Official Language Act (The 'Sinhala Only' Act) but the youth protest really took shape after the traumatic events of 1972. In that year a new constitution was adopted which gave Buddhism official priority. There followed protests, marches, police attacks, bombings and the assassination of the mayor of Jaffna. The old guard saw their illusions shattered and the younger generation saw that their future had been foreclosed. They considered the old strategies as leading only to a dead end. This led to real hostility not only against the Sinhalese, but also towards the older generation. The teachings of the fathers had become irrelevant. For the politicians the traditional animosity between Sinhalese and Tamils was a figure of speech, but the youth took it with deadly seriousness. The ideological conflict generated not only violence, but for the first time it also triggered a questioning of hitherto accepted social and caste norms. High castes and the old elite were equated and their values questioned. Caste abolition had been a point of the party programme of the FP as well as the TC, but until the foundation of the Tamil United Front (TUF) in 1972 it was not pursued seriously. Real change was only effected by the activities of the militants, who realized that they could not exclude nearly half of the population if they wanted to achieve their aims.

The militant groups, which established themselves from 1972 onwards, nearly all originated from youth organizations of the TUF, later renamed the Tamil United Liberation Front (TULF). At first, their members mainly comprised members of the high caste(s); however, a leavening of low-caste members dissatisfied with their traditional status joined, especially the more radical ones among them.[15] Younger members of the low castes resented the attempts of the established to speak for and co-opt them, but they had less objections to joining the militant groups. When the persecution of these groups by the Sri Lankan government began in earnest and many of the high-caste leaders of these groups went underground or were arrested, members of the low castes took over the leadership of these movements. The official history of the LTTE and the takeover of its leadership by Prabhakaran, a Karaiyar, is one such good example.

Today, the LTTE is a group not only with mixed caste membership, but, what is much more unusual and more important, with low-caste leadership. This is one reason why the LTTE seems to be the only group that endeavours to change Jaffna society, sometimes through doubtful and gruesome means. For the LTTE, social change flows like political power and redistributive justice, from the barrel of a gun. The established politicians were held responsible for the splits in society, which the LTTE undertook to bridge and close. We shall discuss these measures and their success in a moment, but first have to look at yet another kind of exclusion which, contrary to most others, was impossible to overcome.

THE UNSUCCESSFUL INCLUSION: MUSLIMS AND TAMILS

While many of the differences and splits in Tamil society could be closed after the war began, one gap between Tamils and/or Tamil-speaking groups remained—between Tamils and Muslims. Chelvanayagam had quite deliberately spoken of Tamil-speaking groups, not Tamils, in order to include the Muslims in his appeal. The LTTE has as well in several pamphlets and programmes highlighted some special rights and privileges for Muslims in their envisaged state. Neither of the efforts impresses the Muslims, who had been alienated from the Tamils since the end of the nineteenth century, when Ramanathan had tried to subsume the Muslims under the Tamils in order to claim a higher number of representatives in the Legislative Council. This claim had come at a time when Muslims from Arabia and Egypt had tried to enhance Muslim consciousness in Sri Lanka and to make them consider themselves a separate ethnic group. It had never been possible to overcome this split, especially as it was cleverly exploited by the government. The LTTE did not help when it expelled 50,000 Muslims from Jaffna in 1990 (the reasoning that it happened for their own protection and to prevent espionage was not widely accepted) and when mutual massacres occurred among Muslims and Tamils in the east which were routinely blamed, without real evidence, on the LTTE and the Special Task Force of the government. The argument of a common culture and language does not work here; on the contrary, the Muslims deny the existence of this common culture and the significance of language for a feeling of commonality.

CASTE AND THE MILITANTS: BRIDGING SEPARATION?

How did the militants now try to overcome the caste system? The Karaiyar stepped in where out of ignorance or indolence the Vellalar (and the TULF) feared to tread. The changes introduced by the militants and the Karaiyar are however, not always as radical as they seem, they continue a development that started at the beginning of the twentieth century: the horizontal and vertical extension of the concept of the 'Tamil' and the awakening of ethnic consciousness.

Surmounting of caste barriers means for the LTTE a reform of society at large. Among these is education for all, which is still, even after the demise of Vellalarhood, considered the entry ticket to a better life (though it is no longer exclusively in English; Jaffna has one of the best mother-tongue education systems in South Asia). It also includes the emancipation of women and the interdiction of taking or giving dowry. The LTTE has pursued both policies with great vigour. It encourages women to join its cadres and to actively fight in the war. Female suicide bombers have attained sad fame. But in many cases, women themselves seem to perceive membership in the militant group as a form of liberation, primarily because it is said to be a protection from rape by the ubiquitous rampaging Sinhalese soldiers.[16] Simultaneously, heavy penalties are proclaimed and enforced against the forbidden custom of dowry. People acting against this decree, mostly from the high castes, are severely punished. Houses of Vellalar, who have fled abroad, are confiscated for the LTTE.

Have these measures really changed society? Doubts might be justified. In spite of the mildly Marxist rhetoric, the LTTE appeals to the population on the basis of a national and traditional programme. Indeed, it has declared itself the guardian of this tradition. The LTTE initiated societal changes by demanding social justice with traditional categories of argumentation. That means their terms and models of identification were those of the Vellalar. The Karaiyar usurped the ideals and traditions of the Vellalar and thus they became the 'true' Tamils instead of the former, while the framework of the constituents of Tamil society remained the same. Like the rhetoric of hostility to the Sinhalese, the Karaiyar youth took the rhetoric of the safeguarding of tradition seriously, revived this tradition and preserved and interpreted it in their own fashion. Because the Tigers are perceived as guardians of the tradition, they were able to retain popular support in the teeth of many drawbacks and in spite of their harsh methods. The new social ideals are the old ideals and the new society is the old society in a new disguise, or at least that is the idea the LTTE has managed to put across.

This did not signify the destruction of caste. On the contrary, the shifting and redefinition of caste boundaries indicated a strengthening of the concept. Caste hierarchy, however, had taken a blow—it was devalued or at least made irrelevant.[17] Castes are equal as castes, not individuals as individuals. Individuals can only be equal as members of a group. Low castes no longer 'slowly, slowly' become Vellalar, they do not want to be Vellalar any more. They demand equal rights and dignity as castes—Karaiyar, Akampatiyar, Nalavar. In this regard, they have taken on board the traditional attitude of the Karaiyar. Given that the Karaiyar want to uphold tradition, it seems that they would also include the traditional restriction on women as the carriers of culture. Decrees to this effect have been published. Reports from Jaffna stated that posters with 10 commandments for Jaffna Tamils had been posted on walls and trees (ostensibly by the LTTE), of which most were directed at women. Among others, it was demanded that women should not ride bicycles and not ride pillion on a bicycle with men who were not their husbands (the bicycle is the ubiquitous means of transport in Jaffna and it would severely inconvenience women if they could not use it). Also, women should give up western dress and only appear in public in sarees and wear their hair long.[18] The LTTE has categorically rejected the suspicion that it was responsible for this decree and blamed the rival Eelam National Democratic Party (ENDP), a former militant group now ruling Jaffna with the help of the Sri Lanka government, for using its name to detract from its reputation. It may be doubted whether the LTTE really would publish posters to this effect, but it has some strange bedfellows and its emphasis on Tamil tradition may bring all sorts of ideas out of the woodwork.

Though the social system and the situation of the low castes have changed considerably over the last hundred years, we cannot talk about an 'equal' or egalitarian society even today, and have to ask whether the changes effected now will survive an eventual end of the conflict. Or will the LTTE share the fate of the Jaffna Youth Congress (JYC) and be forgotten? But the Vellalar are not giving up without a fight. They had considered Karaiyar dominance as conditioned by and dependent on the war and so of limited duration. In times of peace these conditions did not apply. Until the mid-1980s the Karaiyar conformed to their role as fighters and bodyguards. Only after 1983, when they also began to seriously engage in attempts to change social conditions, did the armed bodyguards become more than that. They began to challenge the Vellalar on their own turf instead of just doing their dirty work, and the backlash from the latter was swift and ferocious. It could not be allowed that a low-caste youth of doubtful origin took over not only the military, but also the social initiative. The counter-attack was vicious—defamation of the militants and their methods and a rapprochement with the Goigama on the Sinhalese side for 'talks'. Vellalar expatriates often seemed to find more reprehensible the LTTE's violation of caste boundaries and abolition of social customs than the LTTE's alleged cruelty on the battlefield and in revenge against the Sinhalese. Rejection of the LTTE was rejection of the rise of the Karaiyar. Even an alliance with the Sinhalese seemed a lesser evil. The current generation of expatriates, worried as they are by the conflict, are far more concerned with maintaining an 'orderly' society, giving their children a proper education and preventing them from transgressing caste boundaries in friendship and marriage than with the war and its effects. Two or even three post-independence generations have grown up in Jaffna and the worldwide movements for equality, human rights, social justice have completely passed them by. Marriages between different castes were (and still are) the exception in the late 1970s, when many forms of discrimination, especially in education and profession, had disappeared. Such marriages could lead to the ostracism of whole families in Jaffna, if they occurred. A few years ago a poignant description was presented about the fate of 'brides for export', Tamil girls of high caste who in order to leave Jaffna were prepared (or their family were prepared) to undergo incredible hardship and insecurity just to marry any expatriate (and mostly unknown) Vellalar. The graphic illustration of the misery and unhappiness often resulting due to betrayal, cheating and ill-treatment was heart-rending.[19]

Until now the Vellalar elite has not managed to dislodge the 'bodyguard' from the position of power it has obtained and to return to the status quo ante. The counter-attacks of the Vellalar are so fierce for precisely this reason, they know they fight on lost ground. Many of them have drawn the corresponding conclusion and left for greener pastures abroad, where they can live with their social system undisturbed.

But the pressure on them is increasing even in the diaspora. The diaspora is increasingly varied, and splits have already emerged overseas among different caste and political groups. It is now impossible in Jaffna or outside, to openly defend the caste system. The system might not be shattered, but its reputation is. There are twofold reactions to claims that the caste system endures. The youth mostly deny categorically and often indignantly that it still exists; they claim that the LTTE has managed to destroy it. But these claims are implicitly contradicted by the marriage advertisements in the diaspora Tamil papers, even those sympathetic to the militants, which bear eloquent testimony to an enduring caste consciousness. But publicly, Tamil solidarity regardless of caste has to be demonstrated. Even the Vellalar have to fall into line, though they support the LTTE through clenched teeth. While reports of the demise of the caste system in Jaffna are vastly exaggerated, the war has thrown up a new elite and a new dominant caste.

THE PRESSURE TO UNITE

The exclusionary policies of the Tamils have led the Sinhalese to believe that they could widen the gaps and split the Tamils. They very correctly perceived the social and cultural differences among castes in Jaffna and among Tamils from Jaffna and the east. They began with small measures, trying to create gaps among the Tamils by directing their conversion efforts specifically at the low castes. As expected, this provoked fierce protests from the Vellalar, but it did not have the desired effect on the lower castes, because the Sinhalese overestimated the depth of the splits among Tamils. They thought they would be able to exploit caste and other differences religiously and politically and tried to widen the gaps. Politically, they tried to insert the mainly Sinhalese parties into the Tamil areas in order to wean the people away from the Tamil parties.

They highlighted the attempts of the Vellalar to retain dominance. The high castes, to some extent, played into their hands. The fierce resistance against temple entry and other rights for lower castes raised doubts about the legitimacy of the struggle in Jaffna for equal rights for the Tamils, because this struggle could just as well be seen as an attempt by the Vellalar to uphold an unjust and oppressive social system in the name of culture.[20] It seemed to justify the accusation of the Sinhalese against the Tamil parties that their demands for fair treatment and greater autonomy were nothing but the attempt of the high castes to safeguard their privileges. This argumentation was supported by the shortsightedness of Tamil politicians when dealing with caste problems. Vellalar intransigence also appeared to confirm for the Sinhalese that the call for Eelam was nothing but the call to exclude non-Vellalar from democratic rights and opportunities after independence. This argument was only effectively refuted by the militants many years later.

The strategy worked well with the Muslims: many let themselves be persuaded to support the Sinhalese government against the Tamils. But the strategy could not work with the Tamils, because the concessions granted the Muslims were not given to the Tamils. Simultaneously, the Sinhalese neglected to use or exploit an important characteristic of the Tamils from the east which could have worked in their favour. Batticaloa was for centuries a fief of the king of Kandy and before that, of Ruhuna, though its population was overwhelmingly Tamil. These ties were close and loyal. But they were completely ignored. For example, de Silva never mentions this fact in his study on the 'homelands'.[21] Instead the government alienated even potentially friendly Tamils through its colonization schemes. In the end, the differences between Tamils from Jaffna and those from Batticaloa were not grave enough to prevent closer ties in the face of Sinhala oppression. The Tamils from the east even began to accept the idea of Eelam, which for the longest time they had rejected. The development resembled that among the Sinhalese in the 1920s when the British tried to separate lowland Sinhalese from Kandyan Sinhalese with remarkably little success and instead brought all of them closer together.

Internal and external pressure replaced the centuries-old caste solidarity with an ethnic solidarity which is, however, still perceived in caste categories. But it did something else too—it prevented the lower castes from acquiring an independent self-perception, identity and goals versus the upper castes. The aims of the lower castes were still defined within the terms of reference of the Vellalar ideals. It also prevented coalitions of low castes across the ethnic divide, e.g., with low castes among the Sinhalese. Both LTTE and EPRLF at one stage tried to form an alliance with the JVP because they perceived ideological and social similarities, but these were brought to naught by the developing ethnic antagonism and the war. The low castes in Jaffna were forced into an alliance with the upper castes against the Sinhalese, in pursuance of high-caste aims. The Karaiyar leadership, however, has preempted this hegemonic development by putting itself at the top of the heap and claiming Vellalar goals as its own. The Vellalar were left behind.

Conclusion

Among Tamils the internal exclusions have become less severe as the 'ethnic' differences from the Sinhalese were emphasized. The bond that Tamil equals language, though not sufficient, was strong enough to separate Tamil from non-Tamil. Conflicts and exclusion among Tamils can nowadays be defused and marginalized with the argument of a common language and culture. Conflicts that may arise among Tamils are therefore not as there enduring as those between Tamils and Sinhalese.

Language became the lowest common denominator, the core of Tamil identity, and this is never threatened by conflicts among Tamils, thus these can in principle be solved. When the meaning and content of the term 'Tamil' change, language becomes an integrating bond for all Tamils.[22] Other border markers like religion, domicile, origin and caste do not vanish; indeed, they can be activated for exclusionary purposes again if the need arises, but they become secondary. Language can both enhance and weaken, so to speak 'dilute' other potential boundary markers, sometimes it does both things at the same time. Within Tamil society it nearly always dilutes internal boundary markers. The original linguistic marker 'Tamil' is then additionally tied to other markers which enhance the exclusion: religion, culture, territory. A group feature only becomes an ethnic boundary marker if it contains Tamil in its description, to which it adds an additional defining, limiting characteristic perceived as immutable. This immutable feature is language.[23] Language is brought from the core to the boundary of the ethnicity. 'Fuzzy borders' thus become definite lines of separation, boundaries and barriers.

Nowadays, the militants and, increasingly, the marginalized moderate parties propagate a type of cultural nationalism that openly excludes and separates the Sinhalese. The Tamil 'cultural nation' arose in the confrontation with the Sinhalese. Behind the nationalism of the militants we see an understanding of national characteristics as 'essential', 'congenital' and immutable. The LTTE stands for a concept of nationalism that emphasizes nearly exclusively the ethnic and essential component of a nation, its inescapability and its 'manifest destiny'. One cannot escape one's national affiliation, which shows most intensely in the fact that Tamils who do not conform to this position or cooperate with the Sinhalese are considered traitors who have to be punished.

While Tamil nationalism can be considered *sui generis*, the particular type of nationalism the militants represent can be seen as a reaction to a similar concept on the Sinhalese side. The use of history to justify violent national struggle and their interpretation of the nation as nearly biologically determined finds its mirror image in certain Sinhalese parties and movements, who much earlier planned and justified the oppression and expulsion of the Tamils by pointing to historical precedence.[24] We could talk about a negative convergence on both sides.[25] A decisive difference remains. Despite their brutality, the nationalism of the militants—unlike that of the JVP—is not directed against the annihilation of the Sinhalese as a people or as individuals by reason of their perceived ethnicity. The right of the Sinhalese to live in Sri Lanka is never questioned, but the same is claimed for the Tamils, and that means, in a state of their own. Their violence, they claim, is merely employed to repel Sinhalese aggression. The claims may be propagandistic rhetoric, but they do indicate an important ideological difference between extreme types of Tamil and Sinhala nationalism which is only too easily overlooked.

Eelam comprised two things for the militants: an independent state and a just, because equal, society. Their aim is national as well as social liberation. As I have argued elsewhere the militant struggle was thus a struggle in two directions: against the suppression by the Sinhalese, but at the same time also against the suppression led by the high castes in Jaffna. Caste consciousness therefore is tied to ethnic consciousness. This means that within the caste-oriented and caste-dominated social system of Jaffna the development of a more comprehensive group identity and consciousness is already prefigured, which in time ends in nationalism which subsumes caste and instead highlights race or ethnicity. The hegemonic groups in a Gramscian sense changed, when the Karaiyar appropriated the symbols and ideas of Tamilness and Tamil tradition from the Vellalar. This extended the notion of who and what is a Tamil. But this change is still in progress and accounts to some extent for the problems of legitimization of the militants. The enduring social structure long resistant to change worked against the efforts of the militants. We can still observe these fissures today. But they are increasingly becoming irrelevant in the light of the death and destruction wrought by the Sinhalese army and affecting all Tamils regardless of caste and status. These are the surest way to secure Tamil unity under the banner of the LTTE.

NOTES

1. R.S. Perinbanayagam, *The Karmic Theater: Self, Society and Astrology in Jaffna*, Amherst: UMP, 1982, p. 87.
2. Washbrook describes similar conditions in contemporary Tamil Nadu. See 'Caste, Class and Dominance in Modern Tamil Nadu: Non-Brahmanism, Dravidianism, and Tamil Nationalism', in F. Frankel and M. Rao (Eds), *Dominance and State Power in Modern India*, New Delhi: Oxford University Press, 1989, pp. 204–64, Especially, pp. 211–15.
3. Bryan Pfaffenberger, *Caste in Tamil Culture: The Foundations of Sudra Domination in Tamil Sri Lanka*, Bombay: Vikas, 1982, p. 47.
4. Phillippus Baldaeus, *Beschryveninge van het Machtige Eÿland Ceylon*, Den Haag, 1672, pp. 817–18 (Private Collection).
5. J. Pandian, *Caste, Nationalism and Ethnicity*, Bombay: Sangam Books, 1987, p. 23. He puts it more sharply, 'In practice it was sheer brute force which kept the Untouchable jati groups outside the system of Hindu hierarchy. *As there was little or no physically distinguishable difference ... various methods were adopted to denote or identify Untouchable ... groups*' (Emphasis added by author).
6. S. Gnanaprakasar, *Ancient History and Religion of the Tamils*, Jaffna, 1912, pp. 19–22 (in Tamil).
7. S. Pathmanathan, *The Kingdom of Jaffna*, Part I. (circa AD 1250–1450), Colombo: Anul M. Rajendran, 1978, p. 185.
8. Pandian, n. 5, p. 31.

9. S. Gnanprakasar, *The Tamils, Their Early History and Religion*, Jaffna, n.p., 1910.
10. Simon Casie Chitty, *The Ceylon Gazetteer*, Kotte, 1834, p. 247.
11. Jane Russell, 'Communal Politics under the Donoughmore Constitution 1931–1947', *The Ceylon Historical Journal*, Vol. 26, Peradeniya, 1982, p. 13.
12. Ibid., pp. 83–84.
13. C. Rajadurai, 'History of the development of the party in the East', in the *Commemoration Volume for the Silver Anniversary of the Ceylon Tamil Government Party*, Jaffna, 1974 (Tamil and English), part II, pp. 5–8.
14. Hansard 1956, DO 109/46. Amirthalingam was MP for Vattukkoddai, Chelvanayagam for KKS, Vanniyasingam for Kopay, and Ponnambalam (TC) for Jaffna.
15. Dagmar Hellmann-Rajanayagam, 'The Tamil Tigers—Armed Struggle for Identity', *Beiträge zur Südasienforschung* 157, Heidelberg, 1994, pp. 37–38.
16. Ann Adele Balasingham, *Women Fighters of Liberation Tigers*, Jaffna: LTTE International Secretariat, 1993, pp. 8–9.
17. Neither here nor in Tamil Nadu do we find demands to totally erase the system and institution of caste.
18. Tamilnet 2000; Neloufer de Mel, 'Agent or Victim? The Sri Lankan Woman Militant in the Interregnum', in Michael Roberts (Ed.), *Sri Lanka: Collective Identities Revisited*, Vol. II, Colombo: Marga Institute: 1998, pp. 199–220.
19. Sivaloganathan, Conference Sri Lanka Studies, Peradeniya, July 1997 (Unpublished).
20. Bryan Pfaffenberger, 'The Cultural Dimension of Tamil Separatism in Sri Lanka', *Asian Survey*, 21, 1981, pp. 1145–55.
21. K.M. de Silva, *The 'Traditional Homelands' of the Tamils of Sri Lanka: A Historical Appraisal*, ICES Occasional Paper 1, Colombo, 1987.
22. Dagmar Hellmann-Rajanayagam, *Tamil—Sprache als politisches Symbol*, Heidelberg: F-Steiner Verlag Stuttgart, 1984, p. 208f.
23. Immutable here means that anybody who renounces the Tamil language or denies the primacy of Tamil, is no longer considered 'Tamil'.
24. See Bruce Matthews in this volume, Chapter 2.
25. Dietmar Rothermund, *Geschichte als Prozeß und Aussage*, Heidelberg: Oldenbourg, 1994, pp. 214–15.

An idealized image of a hero's resting place.

Reprinted from an LTTE pamphlet published on the occasion of Prabhakaran's birthday celebration (November 2001).

Selection of Tamil Poetry

They Go on to Live as History

They go, the great heroes, they go—Having
Won the war with the enemy they go to their death

The big army of the ruler arranged to march in rows
In the sounds of music they dissolve—In a vehicle
Decorated with flowers, wrapped in the red flag
Go the ones who command respect.
Having paid the big debt to the soil of the good Tamil Mother
Crowned with the golden band they go—Their
Mothers to wail and our country's people
In sobbing rows they go.

Consciously having given their own body for the land,
The life for Tamil, they go—Courageous with the
Pride of youth in their body
Flower bedecked they go—in the house's
Garland a lamp, the filled jar of perfection, the black flag,
A string of coconut leaves to hang over the
threshold, so they go—having
Created an epic like to the deep sea
Go the heroic guardians.

Before the heroic war tigers sink into the ground
Thousand tigers sprout
Having beaten their chest having lived in honour these
Unbowed they go—great heroes
Unsullied, having given their lives for the life of our village
To seek the final resting place they go—their
Names mentioned they go on to live as history
In the hearts of the Tamils tomorrow.

Ko. Tirunamam

***

A Few Tears for the Darling Resting in the Sepulchre

Brother when you became a soldier
I was just a little girl—but
Now the feelings
You had, all the courage
Are for me now—Did you
Really forget that—that time
While I as a soldier
Walked into the camp
Why did you come
With eyes swimming in tears
Close to my ear
You came and asked!
Oh ... Brother the meaning
Of the words asked that time
Now you understand, do you not?
Brother even though you perished in the war
For the liberation of the country, your goal
And your weapon already your own sister
Took for herself
Having thought about that tears of joy
You shed, did you not?

Brother! Then indeed
You knew—You
Forever to kiss the ground
You go, having said that,
Because of that indeed from the string of poison
Shaking at your throat
Having put one round my neck
After embracing me tightly and kissing me
Even if you were no longer your
Goal to fulfil was necessary
Because you said that your name
I had to adorn
With a handshake you received
From me the leave to depart
Now where are you

Unending rest you take, do you not
Brother ...! Not even once your
Glorious face you show?
Near your tomb
Having given you leave to depart
As the little sister have I come to linger here, have I not?
Brother, once open your eyes
With your name—and
With the poison garland you gave and
With your weapon—and with
Whatever ideal you carried—with the
Pursuit of that same ideal near to you
Have I come to linger.
My desire oh Brother ...!
Do you rest in loneliness ...?
Do not worry—near you
Your comrades also sleep—from now
In a few days near to you I also
Shall come to my rest—for me, too,
Near to you a place has been marked.
In your footsteps I, too ....

Cevvanam

***

SUPPORTERS OF THE SOIL

... one day came
They entered inside decked with flowers.
From the opening a voice asking,
Eyes seeing,
Life pulsating.
Whose saying, to term these dead and gone?
Whose saying, to term them rotten bones and dung?
They will not come, instead
In the dark hole the rule over the realm of shadows.
Kartikkai twenty-seven
Is the day to give life to the country.

The ground will have gone cold.
With flowers we shall go, pure shadows.
Slowly approaching
We shall wash the sepulchre with tears.
It is the time to light the oil lamp
Precious eyes will open.
Laughing will be heard.
Will obtained
In the language of silence
To cool they will speak
Therein thousand meanings are unbound.
'Word has become our sigh'
In the song dissolving the saying
Shivering we shall turn into statues.
'Having done the task, we sleep,
You go the rest of the way'
Say the disembodied voices of the godlings
'For us there are no flowers ...
For us there are no lamps ...
For us there is not even this song ...
For us there is only freedom,
For us there is only the liberation of the country'
With this great sound rising on the wind
The sepulchres close.
In the direction of the light the path is clear.
The door is open to come out
The ground opens.
Our journey will continue
Until the dream of the supporters of the soil becomes reality.

Putuvai Irattinaturai

***

Speak the Truth

Mother!
For your eldest son
Who learns to skip and walk

When you sing him to sleep,
How for the liberation of our race
The own body has become dynamite—our
Black tigers' story tell.

Standing still in the sand of the yard
Enjoying the rays of the full moon
Children's stories to hear—for your
Youngest daughter,
Blown up in the air—of that
Courage of our darlings tell.

Having built a house of sand, having cooked sand rice
To your daughter happily playing
Of the sons loving the land—of the fierce
Tamil heroes guarding the Tamils' honour,
On land and sea the story that becomes an epic
Unhesitatingly and with certainty tell.

Mother!
These who carry flowered dreams
For the love to the people
To let the soft wind of freedom blow in Ilam
They have become a national storm, these—speaking
Our life's bright dawn of day
Our soil's jewels of never fading lustre
Apart from this news still
Many unspoken truths
Not hiding their light speak.

Ka. Karttika: Warrior

***

How You Alone …

Not all who fell became seed
How you alone …

As admirable humans
Glorious form attaining
How you alone …

To give the crown to liberty
This is our wish, too
But how you alone ...
As freedom's people!
On the way we travelled
Our journey unfinished
For the coming of the dawn we
Merely empty pledges*.
With questions that find no answers
In vain we are here now.
We are the answer ...
How you alone!

By entering the camp of the leader indeed—the Tamil race
To make prosper you risked your head!

On the battlefield the seed of the race to guard
Heroes grown in the womb of the Tamil mother!
Rather than leading an obscure life abroad—we
praise and honour in our hearts you
Who are living in the motherland.

Arts and Culture Association, Germany

***

All poems are from the Heroes' Day celebration
pamphlet of 27 November 2001.

The translations are by
Dagmar Hellmann-Rajanayagam.

* Literally: anticipatory fasting.

6

The Rise of Militant Tamil Nationalism, Its Assumptions and the Cultural Production of Tamil Women

SIVAMOHAN SUMATHY

This chapter raises some specific questions about militant Tamil nationalism and its intersection with a growing consciousness about gender among Tamil women in Sri Lanka. I look at the social and discursive structures of the liberation struggle waged by sections of the Tamil minority against the Sri Lankan state, the militarism of the Liberation Tigers of Tamil Eelam (LTTE/Tigers), the military/martial feminism of the women cadres of the Tigers and the overall emergence and limitations of women's movements. My analysis inevitably revolves around the idea of violence: the epistemic violence: of the post-colonial, which in the narrative of post-colonialism becomes a collective violence of the body, of the nation, class and gender. By mapping a terrain of post-colonial feminism through the national struggle of a particular group of Sri Lankan Tamils (largely northern Sri Lankan Tamils), I seek to map my own political stances with regard to feminism and its multiplicities ideologically and historically.

Nationalism has been both hailed and condemned as either liberating or destructive. In the nation under scrutiny we need to locate nationalism within history and within those discursive structures that help shape interlocking trajectories of nationalism and women's cultural production. Without going too far back into colonial history and the independence struggle against the British, in general Sri Lankan women's movements were tied to the Sri

Lankan independence movement. Ideologically and socially such movements were manifold, ranging from reformism to trade unionism and communist party activities. They all sought to bring about development. More recently, we find the militant nationalism of the Sinhala and Tamil youth. It is this militancy within nationalism that was an enabling force initially, mobilizing diverse groups of women. Now it is almost a destructive one.

In the initial phase of militant Tamil nationalism, the 1970s and 1980s, 'armed militancy' emerged as the mobilizing force. During this period, women's consciousness vis-à-vis the Tamil nation and nationalism found its nascent expression. Although low-key, it was full of possibilities for alliances with other radical subversions related to caste and class. Around this time, several active young women's groups emerged alongside the growth of militant nationalism.

The national liberation struggle was and is a destabilizer of hierarchical structures of class, caste and gender. In some ways gender has been the most dynamically active of these three social forces. Despite the fact that militancy was heavily informed by the middle-class thinking of the emancipation of a bourgeois nation and of national social mobility backed by the capitalists, a high-caste intelligentsia, and a socially mobile expatriate community, the mobilization of people at different levels led to a challenging and exploration of hierarchies including that of gender. In the first flush of revolt, nationalism created a space for a militant women's consciousness to emerge. This I oppose to the militarism of the mid 1980s onwards when the LTTE, with its centralized militarist strategy, came to predominate.

The cultural production of Tamil women grew, with the women's movements attached to the growth of the national movements. The Women's Study Circle, comprising women in and around Jaffna University, was one with an academic setting. There was also the more popular Mothers' Front of the mid-1980s, which served as a model for the Mothers' Front of southern Sri Lanka in 1989–90 during the suppression of the youth upheaval in the south led by the Sinhala-dominant People's Liberation Front (JVP). The Front consisted of all classes of women as reported in the now classic document on the growth and crisis of Tamil nationalism, *The Broken Palmyrah*, where accounts of women's responses and varied forms of resistance to militarism are recorded.[1] The Mothers'

Front resembled a popular front similar to the nationalist movements. The subcultures of women's wings in the militant movements were also part of this activity generated by nationalism. Poorani Women's Home, established in 1989 as a home and resource centre for women rendered destitute by war and loss as well as others in need, is another instance of how women's initiatives both within militant and military nationalism arise to the occasion to build structures supporting women's issues, their sense of agency, and analysis.

Any analysis of the women's movement, women's consciousness, and negotiations with dominant historical trends has to deal with the social composition and development of structures. In this respect, I look at the discourse as fixed by hegemonic operations on the one hand and a competing activist dimension on the other. I look at the discursive structures framing nationalism, its engagement with the construct of the woman, and the interaction of women's production with such a structure to see how the social dynamism of women may clash with the discursive constructions of 'woman'. This approach is important to me and to my construction of a feminist praxis as I seek a social and discursive space for resistant struggles.

Both Sri Lankan nationalism and Tamil nationalism are laden with the metaphor of woman as land and land as woman, which has a powerful hold on the nationalist consciousness as nationalism rapidly moves towards armed militancy. How are women positioned and understood in relation to the nation? I look at a particular construct of women's military action, which Peter Schalk, the Swedish scholar on Sri Lanka and Tamil and Sinhala nationalism, has termed 'martial feminism'.[2] Why 'martial feminism'? For Schalk martial feminism denotes the militarized politics of armed struggle waged against the Sri Lankan state by the LTTE, where women have, in recent times, participated in forming military units within its ranks. Also, they have attracted international attention by taking part in suicide bombings. Martial/military feminism is a 'localized' struggle for Schalk, which he sees as authentic and non-western as opposed to the efforts of women who stand outside of the nationalist paradigm which he terms 'western'.

It is interesting that Schalk validates the ideological persuasions of the least politicized and most militarized nationalist group, the LTTE. Much of the LTTE's energies go into developing its military arsenal while it has not simultaneously developed a sophisticated critical political consciousness regarding class, gender and even nation. For instance, the movement did not have a political wing until 1989, which even then did not have any autonomous operation. The martial feminism of Schalk's construction evolves out of this predominant militarization of militant nationalism by the LTTE. The LTTE's women fighters were called 'Birds of Freedom', and have now developed into a highly trained and dedicated women's section of the army and its suicide squad.

Adele Balasingham, who records the story of women fighters from within the movement, hails women's militarism as the articulation of Tamil women who, oppressed by patriarchal conditions, are coming into their own within nationalism.[3] In her opinion, it is the most liberating act for contemporary Tamil women.[4] Schalk, as a spokesperson for the LTTE and with access to internal publications of the LTTE, has this to say about Tamil women's martyrdom:

> The major battlefields on which women met their deaths are regarded as historic by the LTTE. Annually they observe a National Heroes' Day and a numerical account of their martyrs is published for internal circulation.[5]

This factual/statistical account of martyrdom as the inevitable, and therefore desirable, end for women is what has become the most liberating potential of Tamil women's militancy within nationalism—a political future of quantified glory. Here, women, express a certain glorification of and preoccupation with militarism instead of militancy.

Known for its rigid control over the sexuality of its cadres, the LTTE has given a particular twist to the gendering of the military discourse. The LTTE and following it, the media, have repeatedly projected the image of the woman as fighter and martyr. The LTTE focuses on the woman fighter as an imago-signifier and, in doing so, has kept up a public emphasis on the control of the sexuality of its cadres, both men and women. From the time of its 'official' inception in the mid-1970s it has publicly celebrated the celibacy of its cadres (men) as a virtue. Since then it has been boastful of its rigid control over the sexuality of its cadres, both men and women. The deployment of celibacy as a hegemonic signifier serves to allay the fears of a moralistic Jaffna public (initially the high seat of Tamil nationalism) and to re-inscribe the aspirations of society onto what is considered its progeny and, by extension, onto the LTTE as well. According to Nirmala Rajasingham (previously called Nithiyanandan), a much-acclaimed activist associated with the LTTE in the early 1980s, the LTTE felt that its strictures on sexuality conformed to the moral sensibilities of the Jaffna public.[6] In some respects this control endeared it to the moralistic middle classes of Jaffna in the 1980s. That the organization was able to maintain this public image of celibacy by prohibiting love relationships and marriages testifies to the rigidity of its centralized command and its politics of renunciation and self-control.

The difficult issue of sexuality became more acute when women began to be trained as fighters in large numbers from the mid-1980s onwards. In a culture which restricts the movement of unmarried women and burdens them with family concerns of dowry and property, women have to be aggressively chaste in preparation for marriage. In this context, the formation of units comprising young unmarried women who have left their homes or their traditional dwellings, poses new questions for militant/militarist/nationalist operations. While this must have been a problem faced by all the different armed groups, the LTTE found a solution to it through its characteristic strictures on sexuality—regulating women's desires by segregating their camps from the men. This set-up could have created a great deal of agency and control for the women. In fact, women leaders did emerge from within the ranks of women cadres. But women's agency is not controlled and/or activated merely by the dictates of a central command.

In order to understand the effective control over women's sexuality and their agency, we need to look at these paradigms and their operations in Tamil society. Schalk sees *katpu* (chastity)—a concept of virtue highly valued in the Tamil community—as a discourse of power for women fighters. For him, containing the woman fighter's sexuality allows her to take on the role of an avenging female empowered by her chastity/chaste womanhood. For the archetypal signifiers of this virtue Schalk says that the LTTE women look to the anti-colonial martial heroines like India's Rani of Jhansi and Illakumi Visvanathan, the South Indian Tamil leader of the Rani of Jhansi regiment in the army of the militant

Indian nationalist leader, Subhas Chandra Bose. Both the Rani of Jhansi and Illakumi Visvanathan are signifiers of martial chastity.[7] Following this, Schalk chooses to draw upon a constructed and yet authentic mythological resonance for equating *katpu* with martial justice. In the nationalist imagination, according to him, the women fighters are engaged in a 'just' war where the sexual energies of the woman have been transmuted into military power through their containment.

Following this mode, Schalk translates the practices of national liberation by Tamil women as martial feminism, particularized within the context of war, and therefore, tangential and opposed to what is commonly considered feminism, which he rather arbitrarily calls western feminism. In the propaganda of the LTTE, and in an overarching sense, in the discourse of the nation itself, nationalism is the only valid site of social struggle. Hegemonic militarist-nationalism, upheld as authentically non-western by Schalk and by Balasingham, sees nationalism as the only site of struggle through which women are able to express themselves and proposes the armed struggle of the LTTE as the liberating movement of the Tamil people. For Schalk, who uncritically supports the LTTE's practices and control, the culture of sexuality exemplified in the idea of chastity and chaste womanhood gives power and agency to women fighters from within a space opposed to western feminism. In his view, the authenticity of chaste womanhood channels sexual energy into military valour, it works against a putative western feminist conception of subject formation which is realized through individual sexual liberation. For Schalk, and the LTTE probably, martial chastity becomes a resistant power by opposing the imperialism of western feminism and by embracing a revolutionary nationalism. In contesting Schalk, I do not want to dismiss the sense of agency women fighters have and may claim as women's consciousness. But what I explore is that agency in relation to the political and sexual economy of the Tamil nation and its class- and caste-inflected gendering.

I turn to the analysis of popular culture, since *katpu* as a sexual virtue is disseminated through popular films, stories, and gossip. This understanding of culture is important if we are to figure out how it plays an important role, changing in meaning with time. Dominant Tamil culture is a mish-mash of popular understandings of the idea of Tamil and Tamil heritage serviced by a pedantic curriculum of a perceived high culture. This is clearly brought out in Sumathi Ramaswamy's treatment of the rise of Tamil nationalism in Tamil Nadu, South India, in an interesting study of the invention of 'Tamil Tai' or 'Tamil Annai' (Tamil Mother), paralleling the independence movement, which develops into the anti-north, anti-Brahmanic nationalism of the Dravida Munnetra Kazhagam.[8]

The understanding of *katpu* among Sri Lankan Tamils is an inheritance of colonial and post-colonial signification of Tamil culture and heritage, a construct passed on by word of mouth and popularized by South Indian Tamil cinema and the Bollywood industry in general. This very fluidity of culture informs the term with multiple political meanings.[9] The cultural investment in chastity is an indication of an ideological operation that connects it to colonial and post-colonial developments of Sri Lankan Tamil societies. This is where I would like to look at the antecedents of *katpu* in the Tamil imagination within its political and sexual economies. Here I want to draw upon the figure of Kannaki, a mythical female figure of Tamil culture. In the *Silapathikaram* (The Lay of the Anklet), a classical Tamil epic, Kannaki—one of the heroines—burns down the city of Madurai with the power of her chastity when her husband Kovalan is wrongfully accused of stealing the anklet of the queen. For me, the figure of Kannaki is a more lasting figure of martial feminism's contradictions than Illakkumi Visvanathan or the Rani of Jhansi. Sitralega Maunaguru writes of how Kannaki, along with others, has been evoked in the mobilization of women in Tamil nationalism. She comments on the caption of a photograph of women marching and picketing in the 1960s underlining the rhetoric of the Federal Party (moderate Tamil nationalist party which demanded a federal state for the north and east and later became part of the Tamil United Liberation Front). The caption reads as follows:

> Kannaki of the past rebelled against the injustice of the Pandya king. Thousands of young women have rebelled against the injustice of the Sinhala state.[10]

This rhetoric has not changed substantially. In many ways, the image of Kannaki is a highly popularized image of womanhood itself and of its power. She resonates with the connotations, not so much of the quest but of how chaste womanhood is perceived and internalized in popular national imagination. In the imagination of the middle class, whipped up by the rhetoric of the nationalists, the act of Kannaki's revenge blurs into insignificance, while the power of her chastity carries strong mythical allusions.

However, Kannaki's chastity is of a strange order. She occupies a liminal place in Jaffna Tamil culture. She is virtuous, but still her husband steals away with her wealth and leaves her for Mathavi, a learned courtesan whom he abandons when he has spent all the money and then returns to Kannaki. Kannaki occupies the status of a saint and a goddess, not an actual woman. For instance, in a culture where names carry a lot of meaningful and auspicious significance, few people in Jaffna (I don't know of any) name their daughters Kannaki. In the economy of Jaffna Tamil culture tied to marriage, very few would like to wish upon their daughter a life of marital chastity such as Kannaki's. As I was growing up in the 1970s and 1980s in middle-class Jaffna, high-school class debates and inter-school debates over which heroine is more virtuous, Kannaki or Mathavi, were not uncommon. Such a preoccupation sounds strangely quaint today. But this quaintness does not mean that we have moved very far from its ideological implications. For me it only marks a crisis in the Tamil consciousness.

If chastity is a loaded signifier, then its contemporary manifestations too would carry those contradictions along with it. This is widely apparent in stories about why women take up arms. The gossip about Dhanu, the LTTE suicide bomber who detonated herself to kill Rajiv Gandhi, a former Prime Minister of India who was on an election tour in South India, is the most spectacular of all. As Nirmala Rajasingham says, 'they (LTTE) let it be known that Dhanu avenged herself by killing Gandhi because she had been raped by members of the Indian Peace Keeping Force (IPKF) in Tamil Eelam. A suicide killing is sanctioned as an act of avengement for a raped woman. Here the raped woman is contrasted with the chaste woman'.[11] The LTTE here restates Tamil society's anxieties about its national purity and cohesiveness by foisting the traditional stigma of pollution on the suicide killers. About this incident Maunaguru says:

> A raped woman is considered one who has lost her chastity: the 'super virtue' of a Tamil woman. She is not only violated

> but polluted. She cannot regain her purity by any means except by negating her polluted body .... In other words, by killing Rajiv Gandhi, she not only tackles revenge against the enemy, but also performs an ancient purification ritual—the agnipravasam (immolation by fire).[12]

In Maunaguru's view, the suicide killings of Rajiv Gandhi as well as of other enemy presences by metaphorically raped women is an act of purification of both the body of the woman and the body of the land-nation. To get back to the Kannaki–Mathavi story, if women's militarism is metaphorically caught between these two classical Tamil heroines, Kannaki and Mathavi—the undesired virtuous wife or the educated 'whore' (and in our case the unchaste raped woman), where does the community see a fulfilment of its aspirations and quests through chastity? At this time of crisis for the Tamil community and its national longings, chastity and its marital manifestations are also in crisis and in collapse; they lead only to acts of purification of the women's bodies and their deaths.

Marital chastity and martial feminism are not, as Schalk implies, constructions of authenticity by progressive nationalists. Authenticity itself is in crisis here. In my view, martial feminism reasserts the nation's biases of class, ethnicity and gender, where actual militarism, chaste womanhood and suicide-killing are part of a contradictory and difficult terrain and are reserved for those who are poor, destitute, abandoned like Kannaki or Mathavi, or, allegedly and conveniently, 'raped' by the army.

In yoking the discursive to the social, I maintain their indivisibility at given moments of time. For me, any question of chastity where women are concerned cannot be dissociated from the predominant feature of Jaffna middle class's means of capital accruement, dowry. Dowry is the single most important factor governing exchange in the semi-agricultural and predominantly professional economy. Selvi Thiruchandiran traces the history of dowry in Jaffna from its matrilineal roots to the frittering away of the rights of the landowning women of Jaffna in colonial and later post-colonial times.[13] I believe that the crisis of the agricultural and professional economy which fuels Tamil nationalism unleashes the crisis of dowry for the woman as well, which has served to imprison Tamil women in a rigid patriarchal ideology.

Thus, dowry is an important economic and semiotic signifier within the general terrain of post-colonialism.

The connections between Tamil society and the structures of Tamil nationalism are obvious here. Traditionally, and to an extent even now, dowry is conceived of as primarily land. But in recent times the conditions of war and migration have changed the terms of dowry, which has in most instances gone 'international'. As the Tamils are increasingly scattered all over the world, the terms and transactions of dowry also take place internationally. Transactions between the respective families of the bride and groom are not confined to the giving and procuring of land in the Tamil areas; (Tamil) land as dowry has lost its significance. This is ironic given the fact that land—an authentic homeland—is seen as the end point of the nationalist struggle. Only a gnawing emptiness reigns at this disjuncture between discourse and the momentum of social mobility.

The crisis of the nation for the Tamil public involves the crisis of land, dowry, its economy and women. The discourse of feminism, authentic, martial, resistant and chaste, has to be examined in relation to these shaping crises of the social. What does the concept of chastity mean in terms of dowry in relation to women cadres who are seen as virgin women going towards their deaths in heroism and purity? What exactly does chastity mean when the virgin woman is married off to death, carrying around her neck the cyanide capsule like the *Tali* (sacred thread worn around the neck—a symbol of marital status for the woman) and is seen as married to the cause and its leader, Prabakharan.[14]

In such a conjuncture of forces acting upon the nation, chaste womanhood leading to a valorization of the spectacle of women's martyrdom can only mean a crisis in the meaning of 'woman' itself. Its resolution in a hegemonic concept of authenticity yokes woman to land violently and destructively (leading to the mass death of women and others) and erases any sense of women's emergent subjectivity and consequent rupture with the nation. The tension between the radical emergence of women's movements and the nation's quick capitulation to a monolithic sexual norm bespeaks a problem far more overarching and globally longreaching, than does the simple binary opposition of western and western-resistant. The way chaste womanhood has been articulated by the practices of the LTTE and by Adele Balasingham and

Schalk, points at something crucial concerning the viability of the nation and its 'authenticities'. The containment of the sexuality of LTTE women, the discourses of chastity and rape, of land and woman and the spectacle of the suicide bomber's death rehearses over and over the Tamil middle class's sexualized desires of land as dowry, brought along by the wife-woman, and recruited into the narrative of the nation-land-woman continuum.

Women and the Nation

While Schalk extols the liberating potential of the contained sexuality of women, the nation fritters away the potential of women in its militaristic denial of the validity of women's resistant action within the nation. This denial excludes the possibilities of multiple sexualities as well. While the LTTE's strategies are geared toward containing heterosexual desire, segregation can be argued as favouring homosexual desire. But the multiple possibilities of women's desire created by segregation are thwarted by the LTTE's celebration of sexual containment and the channelling of sexual energy toward the cause and, more importantly, also toward the male leader. Desire is merged into the strategies of a gendered discourse of nation, family and struggle. In this respect, any fracturing of the nation displayed by women through a resistant consciousness and practice is translated as breaking faith with the chaste mother/woman construct. Against an independent alternative structure within and outside of nationalism, the rigidity of Tamil nationalism holds out martyrdom as the liberating potential for Tamil women.

This containing idiom is pervasive. Even where independent women's organizations have emerged they have been hamstrung by having to toe the LTTE line. The Mothers' Front is a case in point. In the mid-1980s it heroically battled against the government of Sri Lanka to secure the release of youth held under the Prevention of Terrorism Act (PTA), but capitulated to the demands of the LTTE and fasted at its bidding to kick-off negotiations between the LTTE, the government and the IPKF.[15] Thus, women's movements have a chequered trajectory within nationalism. The heroism of the Mothers' Front and other women's collectivities, some of which were spontaneous gatherings, is commemorated by Rajani Thiranagama:

> Even in the community, women have come out strong during the war. In many instances of confrontation with the Indian army, they have stood out as individuals or as small groups, exposing their atrocities and violations of dignity. On the other hand it was mainly women who, in the midst of war, pleaded and argued with the militants for their families and the whole nation. Again it is women who have braved the guns and sat in a fast to save others. Thus, when one appraises the political bleakness that confronts this community and this land, women's history has a triumph. There is powerlessness, disappointment and disillusionment, but also hope. We have done it ... a little bit ....[16]

But even as she salutes women's efforts, a sense of disillusionment persists in and dominates her writings until her death in 1989 at the hands of the LTTE. Her poem 'Letter from Jaffna' written at the height of the LTTE–IPKF war concludes with these lines:

> *Fear? Now we know of Rape.*
> *I'd like to get together with the other women.*
> *But I know of nobody to get in touch with.*
> *All of us are scattered.*
> * * *
> *15 years of war—*
> *And now a hopeless halt.*
> *Our society has no will to organize.*
> *...The era demises with so much loss*
> *and bitterness all round.*[17]
>
> (p. 8)

Working within a Tamil national framework, even if not a nationalist one, the poem sees a connection between the breakdown in women's networking and the breakdown of the cohesion of Tamil society. In relation to these fragments of the nation, her position can be viewed as being traumatized. Thiranagama does not see any easy solution to the problem of women, particularly that of *katpu*, nor does she accept nationalism as a valid site of struggle even as she operates from that location. I see this as the post-colonial predicament, which operates within a site of competing and conflicting ideologies and social movements. This presentiment persists in her writings until the very end.

One of Thiranagama's personal contributions to *The Broken Palmyrah*, the postscript, underwrites this selfsame sense of struggle between the self and the nation. She asserts, 'objectivity, the pursuit of truth and propagation of critical and honest positions, was not only crucial for the community but was a view that could cost many of us our lives. It was only undertaken as a survival task.'[18] This is a cry of subjectivity seeking a position outside of nationalism: the position of 'objectivity'; the subjectivity of the woman here articulates itself only in participation in the struggle and by positioning itself/herself in relation to the nation and, as a result, outside of it.

From the many writings on women by women, and from the formation of women's organizations within and outside the militant movements, it can be seen that women's discourse gains greater currency within a 'resistance culture' than in the discourses of independence–nationalism. The co-optation of women, initially and predominantly middle-class women of the intelligentsia, paves the way for women to articulate and grasp the concept of struggle from a position mediated by gender specifics. In Gramscian terms, I would say that the articulation of women's subjectivity is a negotiated position that falls both inside and outside of the nation. Yet women's cultures, even in those instances when they teeter on the edge of personal freedom, remain subsumed under the dominant ideology of Tamil nationalism.

The discourse of the nation hints at the crucial cleavages and impasses within its constructions for trajectories of gender. In the gendering of the nation the woman's independence and dynamism is thwarted and contained, much like her sexuality. The history of the short-lived Mothers' Front serves as a reminder of the shortcomings of how the nation is gendered. For the Tamil people, discursively, the mother conceived as the mother of the nation's sons and possibly as the chaste Kannaki, avenging the death of her husband Kovalan by burning the city of Madurai, offers a choice between just two possible directions of development for women. One is to carve out an independent ground where the mother's role would be more dynamic than that of handmaiden to the militants; in a sense the language of land as mother and the woman as chaste expressed quite different desires from those formulated by the binary of man/woman within the nationalist discourse. Conversely, the other is be subsumed under the rhetoric of nationalism with its dominant discourse of motherhood as only that of a passive and inert being waiting to be protected by her sons or to heroically defend her womanhood in the name of patriarchy.

My ambiguously binary model of options for Tamil women underscores the tragedy of hundreds of Tamil women dying as martyrs today. The inability to opt for the former and to construct motherhood/womanhood as something other than a construct of the male/female, the inability to conceive of mothers as mothers of daughters and mothers of children (before gender), and as women moving in an internationalized trajectory of feminism, speaks to the crippling limitation of Tamil nationalism today. Any conception of motherhood that would have displaced the rigid masculine/feminine binary in nationalism would have rendered co-optation by militant movements difficult. The Mothers' Front's easy acquiescence to LTTE's dictates is clearly a case in point here.[19] The formulation of 'woman' within the nation remains intact and monolithic in the binary structure outlined above. Opposed to the monolithic homogenizing of gender and its relation to the nation as undertaken by the apologists for the nation, Sara Abraham examines the double-edged role of women's movements within the nationalist context and the tightrope they walk in negotiating for a space for women within the post-colonial trajectory and through the maze of nationalist ideologies and their operations.[20]

This struggle within draws upon a certain consciousness of gender as a separate category. I call this common strand of feminism the internationalized trajectory of feminism; the cultural production of Sri Lankan Tamil women and their expression negotiates with these confusingly competing ideologies of the post-colonial dynamic of the local and the global, the national and the international. In this sense the international dynamic of feminism, which produces from within the nation a consciousness of gender as an active social force, situates women in a critical relation to nationalism but within the local, and yet, connected to the international.

I make this argument as a response to Schalk's treatment of the national and western as simple dichotomies. Replacing 'western' with 'international' I would like to say that women contesting narrow patriarchal and imperial chauvinism are conscious of an international movement in which the west may predominate, but also in which politically dangerous binaries are replaced by a nuanced understanding of how the world operates today. Through an understanding of women's struggles in black America, in the Chicano movement, in Kenya, India and China, to name of few, women of the Tamil nation can see a way of deconstructing the confining framework of the imagination of the Tamil present. Internationalization also links women to struggles of class and sexuality in several ways. To oppose these interlocking moments by positing a narrow authenticity of experience that serves to exclude not the west but the marginalized sections of the Sri Lankan population is myopic and is suggestive of collective suicide. In many ways we see this politics of suicide as a predominant theme of Tamil nationalism today. The politics of suicide is an offshoot of the LTTE's military programme, which revels in its vortex of cyanide suicides and suicide bombings. It is pervasive in the entire consciousness of Tamil nationalism. The inevitability of death becomes the resolution of the nation's dilemmas. Rajasingham comments on this extensively in her understanding of suicidal martyrdom and its persuasiveness in the writings of the women fighters.[21] The predominant theme of death and nihilism locked in battle with the viability of the nation is a recurring one in women's writings. The culture of women's production is informed by this pessimism, nihilism, and a preoccupation with death.[22]

WOMEN'S WRITINGS

Women's literature in general is subsumed under the Tamil nationalist paradigms—the conditions of war, resistance, militancy, and deprivation. 'Struggle' takes on a resistant tone in its articulation of deprivation; the deprivation of land leading on to the loss of civil liberties. At the reformist end, short stories and plays are written/produced specifically on women's concerns, such as dowry, education for women, the plight of abused women, widowhood, etc. This illustrates the concern of some sections of society for the deprived lot of women.

In expressive nationalist discourse poetry takes on a powerful form. Several women writers have attempted to express their aspirations and experiences through poetry. Poetry, as R. Cheran's article demonstrates, has been the most powerful cultural form of resistant nationalism.[23] Although Cheran looks upon this in an ambivalently sympathetic sense, I adopt a more estranged position on this. Poetry becomes capable of expressing resistance when the cultural milieu of nationalism employs an objective and yet emotive discourse of the struggle. At the same time, I must say that in many ways, poetry has allowed women to forge resistance too, even if in a marginal sense. In the context of our analysis I look at a few selected poems of this period of high militant/militarist nationalism. I begin with two poems by Bhanu Bharathi and Anichcha, both titled 'Lullaby', published together in the weekly *Saringar.*[24] Both are about the war-torn situation of the northern peninsula. These two poems definitely draw upon the oral tradition of lullabies, which has been made popular through South Indian cinema.[25] In Bhanu Bharathi's poem, the mother gently coaxes the child to sleep although, as she says, the tranquillity and security necessary for sleep are no longer there. The poem is uninteresting if we are looking for a counter-hegemonic stance. The woman's position is undoubtedly seen as that of deprivation and insecurity without men. The second lullaby, by Anichcha, is a slight variation on the former in structure and content. The rhythms of the lullaby genre are broken by a more discordant structure. The child, a daughter here, is the hope of the future.

Rolling in the heavy rain clouds,
you my little girl,
are a child of war time.
You have come to give me
a new lease of life.
Sleep my baby sleep.

On the whole, the 'lullaby' here stays within the discourse of the images of war. The use of a lullaby as the poetic mode is very pertinent to the construction of a subject-position for the woman. The discursive formation revolves around that of family, community, and extended to its ultimate, the nation. But there is a reversal of the mother–son relationship. It focuses on the girl, daughter of the nation.

Another, later poem by Anichcha is less sanguine. It is the third poem of a four-poem series called 'Four Poems About Our Nation: Ten Years to the 21st Century', centred on the woman's political role as an activist who stands up against the brutality and impersonality of the gun.

You did not stay crippled
claiming womanhood
Did not laze away life's energy, eating, sleeping,
You clasped our hands tight
to show the way to the light.
...
They shot you dead
threw the bones
across the way
to close it off
Took the ashes
Threw them against the wind
To silence it.

There's life beyond silence;
Struggle beyond the
Bounds of death.

The poem is about the death of a woman activist and leader–nurturer; it speaks of resistance to the culture of violence. But it cannot name that violence. Specifics about the context of the death of the activist seem somehow unimportant although I read it as an oppositional, counter-hegemonic poem. But, given the celebration of suicidal martyrdom on the one hand and an overpowering sense of disillusionment with political process/progress, even oppositional women's strategies end up being swallowed up by a celebration of death. Thus, even in this tragically hopeful poem, the poet feels compelled to celebrate death as resistance to the violence that precedes it. The resolution seeks answers beyond the pale of life, in death.

Thiyagaraja Selvanithi (known as Selvi to many) wrote a poem in 1988 which reproduces this very sense of disillusionment but through a more thoroughgoing discordance with the dominant sentiments of militarist hegemony. The dominant tone is ambivalent and traumatized about the jubilant cries of a doomed nationalism. Here I reproduce lines from the poem 'In Search of Sun'.

My soul, full of despair
yearns for life
...
primitive humans
yellow toothed, ugly mouthed

thirsting blood, slit flesh
saliva adribble
cruel nails and horrifying eyes.

Bragging and jubilating
over victories are not new
legs lost from long walks for
miles and miles
in search of a throne
days wasted waiting for full moons
only boredom lingers ....[26]

Selvi was a political activist until her detention by the LTTE in the early 1990s. After distancing herself from nationalist politics in which she had been active as a member of a militant nationalist movement, the People's Liberation Organization of Tamil Eelam (PLOTE), she allied herself with factions that critiqued nationalism. Given her continued disappearance in LTTE custody (presumed dead), her poem here sounds strangely prescient. In contrast to nationalist jubilation, the writer yearns for life, its unities and harmonies, seeking the sun amidst the scatter of 'slit flesh, saliva adribble/cruel nails and horrifying eyes'.

In 1986, the Jaffna Women's Study Circle released a slim volume of 24 poems by 10 women, called *Sollatha Sethigal* (Untold Messages) edited by Sitralega Maunaguru. Since then, women's literary activity, as a separate phenomenon, has attracted considerable notice. This volume represents a concerted effort to express a 'feminist' ideology as it stands in relation to the dominant culture. One of Sitralega Maunaguru's poems, 'Viduthalai Vendinum' (Towards Liberation), written under the pseudonym Sangari, articulates a desire for a female existentialism, appropriating metaphors normally associated with male ideologies, such as 'the space air craft Odyssey' in her poem. Her poems translate the signifiers of the nation, here national heritage, into a feminist consciousness by transcending nationalist ideologies and invoking the construct of a universal woman. In another poem, 'Avargal Parvaiyil' (In Their Eyes), which she writes as Sangari, she looks down at what goes on an earth, in the city, in the village, within the nation. As she says:

I have no
face

heart
soul.
I have in their eyes,
two breasts
long hair
slight waist
broad hips.

Cooking,
spreading beds,
bearing children
are my tasks

They'll talk
of chastity
of Kannaki
And while they
talk so
They'll keep on gazing
at my body
This is habitual
from shopman
to husband.

Sangari's poem here cuts through patriarchal ideology, focusing on the male dominant practices of the nation–family. This powerful poem bemoans the lack of space for a woman to function outside of the family–nation nexus, which is exhausted by the continuum from husband to shopkeeper, from home to the streets. There is a difficult and unnamed strive for a beyond, beyond nationalism to talk of women's issues as women's issues.

In this light, Rajani Thiranagama's writings are much more unequivocal. In 'A Letter from Jaffna', she names the problem and the contestants directly. That she was one of the first of the academics and feminist civil activists to be murdered by the LTTE is noteworthy. The forthrightness with which she accosts the suicidal politics of Tamil nationalism of the different groups challenges the core of the LTTE's operational practices. The death of Rajani in 1989 coincides with the takeover of the north by the LTTE for six long years followed by the fleeing of many activists to the south and the deaths of others who stayed behind. Yet others, both activists and other inhabitants, continued to function by adjusting their lives around the soaring prices controlled by the state and the LTTE, curfews, acute shortages of staple food items, military operations, illegal migrations, and the LTTE's military dictates. The expulsion of Muslims in 1990 and the way their belongings and property were promptly confiscated and sold by agencies of the LTTE, reasserts the group's bid for homogeneity. In 1995, when the Sri Lankan army regained control of the northern city of Jaffna and the surrounding regions, the Tamils this time were forcibly evacuated by the LTTE. Some of those who remained were harassed and even killed afterwards.

With this experience of war in mind I quote from Rajani's poem. Being closely associated with her writings, having co-edited this poem along with Nirmala Nithiyanandan-Rajasingham for publication in *Outrite* (a feminist magazine in Britain), in 1987, I make no claims to being non-partisan here. Written during the war between the LTTE and the IPKF (called 'Innocent People Killing Force', by the people), her poem captures a sense of the internal conflict of the construct of the 'nation' itself. Here, the contest locks the people and Tigers in battle. I, who know her voice well, can hear her passionate plea for reflection and her anger at the rhetorical gestures and military intimidation of the LTTE in these lines:

Our great brave defenders and freedom fighters
lure the enemy, right to our door-step,
to the inside of the hospital,
start a fight,
ignite a land mine,
fire from near each and every refugee camp,
escape to safety.
And then come the shells, whizzing whizzing.
Bloody hell,
Tigers have withdrawn, while
We the sacrificial lambs
drop dead in lots.

The young poet Sivaramani writes of the slow draining of all initiative as the war progresses with great ferocity. She writes:

Finally,
Our last thinking human is dying, slowly.

The door is closed to all
dissent.
You leave your children
the legacy of darkness;
the crumbs of culture
preserved in the traditions
of a six-yard cloth.[27]

This poem of 1990, written just after the LTTE regained control of the north and parts of the east were once more witness to heavy military operations, captures the sense of dearth of all critical activity and initiative. In these lines she sees the culture of nationalism emptied of dissent and intellect and instead, preserved by the conservative idea of tradition. The analogy she uses is related to women—the *sari* (6-yard cloth)—a sartorial signifier of womanhood. Sivaramani makes these slight attempts to displace the discourse of nationalism from struggle to dissent, nation to gender, and thereby from martial feminism to a critical consciousness because that is the only terrain of opposition possible within the binary of western/martial feminism proposed by Peter Schalk. Sivaramani undercuts that binary, weaving her way in and out of a woman's consciousness of nationalism that is nevertheless steeped in pessimism. Her disenchantment with the national struggle just before her suicide in 1991 demonstrates the contradictions that the intensity of war brings to her humanist ideology, rendering it indeterminate and intimately dangerous. In her poetry the echoes of the gun can be heard shattering the complacence of the unity of the nation.

I do not have words
for a solution
like a leaflet in bold print

Dreams
their meaning is lost to me
who is uncertain
whether the sun will rise tomorrow

While a gun
aims at society's
umbilical cord,
the dreams

of a butterfly
resting delicately
on the tip
of a fragile flower
are merely
an occurrence.

In my attempts
to be humane
I would rather leave
the flowers
on the trees.
Now,
the beautiful night
shaped by the day
is only a dream.[28]

The reconstruction of struggle and praxis does not end here; it goes on in my own work and other people's works, many of whose lives and work are unsung by Peter Schalk or Adele Balasingham. Yet they serve to fashion a critical space for a post-colonial feminism to emerge and grow within and outside of a Tamil nationalist trajectory.

NOTES

1. Rajan Hoole, Daya Somasundaram, Sritharan and Rajani Thiranagama, *The Broken Palmyrah: The Tamil Crisis in Sri Lanka—An Inside Account*, 2nd ed., Claremont: Sri Lankan Studies Institute, 1991.
2. Peter Schalk, 'Women Fighters of the Liberation Tigers in Tamil Ilam. The Martial Feminism of Atel Palacinkam', *South Asia Research*, 14, 1994, pp. 163–83.
3. Adele Balasingham, *Women Fighters of Liberation Tigers*, Jaffna: LTTE International Secretariat, 1993.
4. This speaks of the general contempt in which the LTTE holds the public. This attitude of the LTTE towards the Tamil public is symptomatic of its entire politics regarding civil society. It is merely one side of the coin of the LTTE's relations with the Tamil people. Any analysis that closely examines the LTTE's politics regarding opposition to it from within the Tamil people would show that it is determined to snuff out, by threat and by force, all women's initiatives coming from independent and alternative quarters.

5. Schalk, n. 2, p. 166.
6. Nirmala Rajasingham, 'Construction of Gender and Political Agency in Nationalism: The Experiences of Tamil women', MA Thesis, London, SOAS, 1998, p. 13.
7. Schalk, n. 2, pp. 176–78.
8. Sumathi Ramaswamy, *Passions of the Tongue: Language Devotion in Tamil India, 1801–1970*, Berkeley: University of California Press, 1997.
9. Chastity as a hegemonic signifier popularized by film has been examined by a number of Indian film critics including Vijay Mishra and Rosie Thomas. Mishra and Thomas take the text and the inter-textuality of the classic film *Mother India,* to explore the operations of hegemony through popular culture. In Rosi Thomas's analysis the signification of 'chastity' in the film plays a big role. But unlike Schalk, Thomas does not take the concept of 'chastity' at face value. The diverse meanings of the 'chastity' of Radha, the heroic-subaltern mother in the film, rests on the lack of 'chastity' in the political underpinnings and receptions of the film. In my reading of chastity in the context of Sri Lankan Tamil culture I connect it to a signification of political and sexual economy.
10. Sitralega Maunaguru, 'Gendering Tamil Nationalism: The Construction of "Woman" in Projects of Protests and Control', in Pradeep Jeganathan and Qadri Ismail (Eds), *Unmaking the Nation: The Politics of Identity and History in Modern Sri Lanka*, Colombo: SSA, 1995, pp. 158–75.
11. Rajasingham, n. 6, p. 27.
12. See n. 10.
13. Selvi Thiruchandiran, 'The Construction of Gender in the Social Formation of Jaffna', *Nivedini,* Vol. 4, Issue 2, 1996, pp. 50–83. See p. 66.
14. See Rajasingham, n. 6, pp. 17–18 for an analysis of the relations between the LTTE supremo Prabakharan and the women fighters.
15. See *Broken Palmyrah* (n. 1) and Schalk's article (n. 2) for conflicting approaches to this event. Also Maunaguru, n. 10, pp. 160–63 and 167–68.
16. *Broken Palmyrah*, n. 1, p. 330.
17. Published in the Rajani Thiranagama Commemoration Volume, London: South Asia Salidarity Forum, 1989, pp. 8–10.
18. *Broken Palmyrah*, n. 1, p. 408.
19. Kumudini Samuel, 'Giving peace a chance: women's activism and marginalisation in the peace process', *Options,* Vol. 21, No. 1, 2000, pp. 3–8. In her *Options* article on the Womens' Movement, Kumudini Samuel salutes the efforts of the Mothers' Movement. Perhaps an activist journal like *Options* catering hopefully to mass circulation needs to underscore the courage that goes into the moves of women's activism. But at the same time, I would also like fellow feminist activists to put under analytical scrutiny, women's agendas and the likes.
20. Sara Abraham, 'Under the shadow of the land', *The Thatched Patio,* Vol. 6, No. 1, 1993, pp. 15–33.
21. Rajasingham, n. 6, pp. 30–31.
22. Rajasingham embarks on a socio-cultural study of the Tiger women, focusing on the significance of suicidal martyrdom and how it pervades the writings of the women fighters. I draw upon her insights widely in my

reading of women's militarism in Tamil nationalism and its socio-political content.

23. R. Cheran, 'Cultural Politics of Tamil Nationalism', *South Asia Bulletin*, Vol. XII, No. 1, 1992, pp. 42–56. See pp. 50–55 for the point I am making here.
24. The poems by Bhanu Bharathi, Anichcha, M. Sitralega (pseudonym Sangari), Nirupa, and Pamini are translated from Tamil by me for this study.
25. Popular Indian film is a major agent shaping cultural discourse in India. In turn, popular Sri Lankan Tamil culture is permeated by the song and dance culture of South Indian films. Music, song and dance are parallel texts of the average Indian film. Mainstream Indian film is relentlessly intent on producing the roles of the family within community. Lullabies sung by the mother and sometimes the father or some other closely connected member of the family are part of a discourse based on filial relationships.
26. T. Selvi, 'In Search of Sun', Neloufer de Mel (Ed.), *Options*, Vo. 1, No. 1, 1994, p. 10.
27. Sivaramani, *Sivaramani Kavithaigal*, Toronto: Vizhippu, 1994, p. 58. Translated by me for this study.
28. Ibid., p. 59. Translated by a group of poets from Tamil.

III

The Struggle to Build a Better Life, a Better Society

The transformations of the last 50 years have shifted the distribution of power in society, in part by creating new resources and devaluing the old and in part by paving the way for new organizations claiming the right to speak for the formerly powerless. Such shifts in power involve contestation and conflict.

In Ratnapura district, the combination of government initiative in creating the State Gem Corporation, which provided training in gem assessment and processing, and the expansion of the international market for new types of gemstones, broke the previous monopoly control of marketing. Labourers in the gem pits, and others who had previously lacked opportunities, were able to enter the gem trade, prosper and improve their social status. The fortuitous convergence of a government programme with developments in the international gem market has been a boon for Ratnapura.

The Tamil estate workers, who had been exploited for generations and victimized in ethnic attacks, are finally gaining in power. The growth of the urban market for vegetables, which grow best on the high estates in small plots, has created an alternative to estate work. With the government administration of the estate schools, improved education has opened the door, a little, to new opportunities. And the government's concern that the Tamil estate workers might join with the Tamil militants in the north has supported the restoration of citizenship and the improvement of wages, working conditions, housing and social services for the estate workers. But the persistent discrimination by both government and private agencies fuels a potentially explosive situation among the young.

Government housing policies, NGO relief measures and attempts at organization in the urban slum of Mahaiyawa have failed to build a community capable of collective self-help. Power continues to be concentrated in the hands of municipal politicians eager to move the slum dwellers out of a potentially prime piece of urban real estate. Rapid urban growth trumps the housing claims of the minority Tamils, who are clinging to housing leases and packing in even more fellow Tamils in the quest for physical security. National policies, which led to the deterioration of ethnic relations, have helped create a slum and aggravated the low status and weak bargaining power of the residents.

The organizational innovation of the development NGO has helped shift power from the government to civil society. Satyodaya is one such development NGO. The founder of Satyodaya traces the changes in the operating environment, both domestically and internationally, since its inception in 1972. The new realities of local development problems, the new relations with the 'People', the new relations with donors have led to constant adjustments. From the down-to-earth experience of Satyodaya, there has grown a vision of how the NGOs, as part of an expanding civil society and with the help of their international partners, can share in rebuilding a fairer society within Sri Lanka.

All across the country, changes in the distribution of resources and capacity are altering the ways in which people relate to each other and to the previously dominant institutions. Our authors write of a 'fractured society' or a more 'fluid society' and many are concerned that it might lead to a 'disintegrating society'.

7

Struggling to Create Self-Help Organizations in an Urban Slum: Mahaiyawa

SRI RANJITH

Mahaiyawa is the largest slum community in the inner city area of the municipality of Kandy. It is one of 52 slum communities scattered around the municipal area but is distinct from other communities. The distinction is important for understanding community dynamics, power relations and other social and political factors of the community. These help to explain why the community is so poor. And it also helps explain the relationships that undermine the improvement of the people's quality of life and how they are oppressed by the existing social, administrative and political structures. This chapter discusses individual and household capacity to organize and build up contacts beyond the household through various links, in order to overcome the difficulties that hinder the betterment of the community.

The core of the city of Kandy is divided into four municipal wards. Mahaiyawa is one of them, located in the north-west of the city. Mahaiyawa is the slum community closest to the core of the city. Trinity College, an elite fee-paying school, is to the east and the newly constructed road from the city centre to Katugastota is to the south. The Kandy cemetery is to the north and a home for elders is located to the west. The land area of this community settlement is about 10 acres in extent and consists of some steep slopes and flat land. The eastern edge is a steep hilly area where the population density is relatively low, and the flat land area is closer to the Kandy–Katugastota road where the population density is higher.

Mahaiyawa, like other slum communities, developed through various processes and stages of conflict. These evolutionary stages of slums in Kandy are closely associated with their social, economic, political, cultural, ethnic and religious affinities. A few historical documents are available regarding the Mahaiyawa community. Information given by the Community Development Officer (CDO),[1] and some residents of the community, whom we interviewed, helped us to understand the evolutionary changes and various stages of expansion of the community. Originally, the location was known as Mahayaya, which means a large plot of land. In fact, this is the largest single plot of undivided land located in the inner city area. The origin of the slum goes as far back as the 1860s, the period in which British colonization flourished, thanks to commercial crops, mainly tea. The shortage of labour during this period led them to hire cheap labourers, who were ethnically Tamils from South India. The estate owners employed most of these labourers as estate labour but others were employed as city sanitary workers. Free housing was provided for the municipal workers by the government, and those houses were popularly known as 'line rooms'—low-cost houses with shared walls and amenities, built along the roads or footpaths in lines. Mahaiyawa settlement is one such community.

Mahaiyawa King Quarters, which is also a part of this community, has a different historical background. This was originally a settlement of only a few families, who had been settled there by the kings of the Kandyan kingdom even before the South Indian Tamils came to Mahaiyawa. They were given quarters as servants to the king and were also expected to perform certain duties for the Buddhist temples around the city. These people were Sinhalese. However, Tamils in Kandy have a long history, dating back even before the British first hired labourers from South India. Tamil and Sinhalese have had a close relationship with each other socially and culturally.[2]

SOCIO-ECONOMIC CONDITIONS

The total number of families in Mahaiyawa is approximately 900, and the total population numbers about 4,200. Almost 90 per cent of the residents are Tamil, a national ethnic minority. The remaining are Sinhalese (3 per cent) and Muslims (6 per cent). Religiously, most of the Tamils are Hindu, while about 7 per cent are Christian, 3 per cent are Buddhist and 2 per cent follow Islam.[3] There are three Hindu temples, nearly 100 year old, located within the community premises. There is also a Buddhist temple and a mosque. The caste system within the community is not a significant factor for segregating people since many other commonalties such as poor economic conditions, ethnicity, culture, and religion overlap. However, caste becomes a significant factor in certain cases for particular groups of people, usually the community leaders, for building up network relationships with actors outside the community.

The most intimate social level in the community is the household. In some cases, economic life could encompass more than one family living under the same roof. The second level is that of inter-household relations at the lane, neighborhood and community levels. These relationships are important for inter-personal and inter-household reciprocal assistance. All these elements of community social life are the sources of the indigenous social cohesion of the Mahaiyawa community.

Community Based Organizations (CBOs)

At present, there are several CBOs in the community. One of the active organizations is the Mahila Sangamaya (women's society), which undertakes women's empowerment programmes such as training programmes and related services for small-scale home-based self-employment activity, childcare and nutrition programmes conducted by the Kandy Municipal Council (KMC) Health Department. However, the effectiveness of this society has been undermined by internal conflicts and incompetent leadership. This was reflected by the fact that some members were trying to separate and form another women's society. This division seemed to be spatial—based on proximity to neighbourhood rather than ethnicity or caste.

There are religious societies, are based on people's religious affinities, which support the temples and mosque and organize religious and cultural events. However, religious societies do very little for people's empowerment and solving their problems of basic services. There is also a youth sports society known as the Green Park Sports Club. They are reluctant to use the name Mahaiyawa because it has been stigmatized by outsiders. The club is mostly involved in promoting recreational and sports activities, primarily among males. They have access to the community centre in Mahaiyawa, which is maintained by the KMC for holding meetings and keeping societal sports properties. This centre is also available for other CBOs to hold meetings and other communal activities. In addition, some recreational facilities are available for children at this centre. They arrange sports events with outside societies in the municipal area, which in turn helps to build social network relations among the younger generation.

The major weakness of the community lies in the lack of competent leadership. Community leaders are more concerned about their individual interests, cultivating personal contacts with politicians and officials to fulfil their own desires rather than addressing community needs and group expectations. They are not trustworthy, as community members have learnt from past experiences of broken promises, corruption and misuse of societies' money. The participation of individuals and households in collective efforts to benefit the community has been discouraged due to the loss of trust in their leaders.

Apart from these formally constituted CBOs, there are a number of other small groups that are concerned with their particular issues only. For example, there are labour unions and pension unions. Some people are members of other groups outside the community. These groups are mostly based on their employment and trading activities in the informal sector of the city. Head-load carriers, cobblers and street vendors know each other very well from working together for a long time. They have their own social networks and unions for day-to-day informal sector activity. This in turn has weakened the process of social networking within the community as ties have been built to outsiders which meets the needs of some individuals only.

Although there are frequent quarrels and bickering related to the common use of public utilities, tight kinship, neighbourhood relationships and ethnic bonds make all disputes only temporary, with social relations soon returning to normal. Furthermore, there is a broad pattern of mutual assistance and exchange among neighbourhood families and community groups, such as the use of sleeping space in neighbouring households to accommodate visitors and borrowing money or household items for short-term use. They respect each others' cultural and religious affinities, organize in an emergency or in times of distress such as a funeral or an illness and can mobilize resources within a short period of time in terms of finances, labour and material or equipment, regardless of the caste, kinship or ethnicity of the families who are affected. These are the most valuable social and cultural ties that exist in the community in the absence of functioning formal institutions.

EDUCATION

Although there are several well-regarded and well-equipped government schools in the city, the children in the Mahaiyawa community have limited access to these schools due to the high fees and other related expenditures. These schools are usually attended by children of powerful rich and middle-class families, senior government officials and the elite of both rural and urban areas. The poor community children are educated at small and poorly-equipped government schools. According to survey sample data, only 15 per cent of the population has an education above the grade 10 level, and 65 per cent are below the grade 5 level. Therefore, in general, the level of education in this community is poor. Very few have been educated through the high school level. Although people do have minimum literacy, this is inadequate to gain access to formal sector employment in the government or private sector. The dropout rate among Mahaiyawa children seems to be relatively high in the early stages of education, as they leave school to work.

Access to information and communication facilities is relatively poor in this community, though the use of radios and TVs is common. However, people generally use these for recreational purposes such as listening to music and watching films, rather than as tools for access to information and education.

HEALTH AND MEDICAL FACILITIES

The health conditions of the people in Mahaiyawa are relatively poor. According to the Medical Officer at the KMC Health Department, controlling diseases such as diarrhoea and malaria in the Mahaiyawa community is a serious concern. The main causes seem to be the lack of health education such as awareness of diseases and preventive measures, and lack of basic amenities to maintain standards of sanitary hygiene in the settlement and its environment. The necessity of adequate basic services, especially water and sanitation (toilets, effective sewage system and solid waste management system) is obvious, given the high density of population in this community. Roads and footpaths within the community are used to dispose of solid waste. Children play on the roads and footpaths, and elders gather by the roadside and within the small spaces left between lines of houses. Individual houses do not have their own backyards or compound areas. Some houses have as many as 15–17 individuals per house, which may include two to four households, although the housing space is not adequate even for a single small family consisting of four persons. Usually, this density has an adverse impact on health and the environment.

According to the information given by the KMC Health Department and the Mahaiyawa families, health education programmes on childcare, nutrition and midwife and maternity clinic services are currently carried out in this community by the KMC Health Department through the women's society. In addition to this, all families in this community have access to Kandy General Hospital, which is maintained by the Ministry of Health. Although the facilities are public, the actual access to expensive medicine, equipment and consulting specialist doctors is possible only through personal contacts with hospital workers or high-ranking officials. Poor people are poorly served—this is not unique to Mahaiyawa, but holds true for all who are poor. According to my own experience and observations, Kandy has well-established private sector health centres and hospitals. Most specialist professional doctors who are officially appointed doctors to the government hospitals are hired by these private sector hospitals. Thus, poor people's chance of consulting such a specialist depends on his or her income.

ECONOMIC BACKGROUND

Mahaiyawa families' survival strategies benefit from the location of the slum community in the city. Most of the Tamil people in Mahaiyawa are working as labourers at the KMC, as sanitary workers, in cemetery maintenance and other related activities.

Some families have supplied workers to the KMC for generations. A new labourer is supposed to work for at least five years on a temporary basis in order to be qualified as a permanent worker. The permanent workers are entitled to receive pension payments after retirement. The current salary scale for a labourer at KMC is around Rs 3,000–3,500 per month, which is a relatively low salary scale in the public sector and merely covers the cost of living. These labourers are much concerned about their pension payments upon retirement and about holding on to their housing in the Mahaiyawa settlement. In addition, they need to be involved in some other self-employment activity to meet living expenses. Many of them work in informal employment, such as head-load carriers, who perform menial tasks such as carrying loads for people, or work as street vendors, cobblers and casual workers such as cleaners in hotels and other private sector businesses.

Other families are involved in making food such as hoppers, string-hoppers, short-eats and sweets for commercial purposes, and they supply these to the hotels and other small canteens and groceries in the city. Some are engaged in various small-scale home-based production and service-oriented business activities such as typing/computer shops, rubber seal shops, grocery shops and movie rental shops. Other are cobblers, barbers or tailors. Women mostly participate in home-based income-earning activity while caring for their children.

In addition to all these economic activities, some small segments of the community seem to be involved in informal and illegal income-earning activities, such as the production and selling of illicit liquor, gambling, hawking and prostitution. Except in the case of municipal labourers, the levels of income of these families are difficult to estimate. Their level of income often fluctuates, is mostly irregular and difficult to predict. No records or documents are maintained regarding these income earnings. Although poverty alleviation programmes were launched by both the present and previous governments, the Mahaiyawa community did not really benefit from either of those programmes.

POLITICAL DYNAMICS

Mahaiyawa seems to be an active community as residents make great efforts to solve their problems regarding land tenure, housing and basic amenities. At the same time, these people have been manipulated by politicians for several decades in the past through unrealistic political promises. For instance, the Mahaiyawa Rural Development Society, which was initiated at the beginning of the 1980s with the intention of helping families to get their deeds for lands, upgrade houses and develop basic services and other community infrastructure, collapsed due to the lack of government support and political will at its initial stages of development.

Each political party has supporters from the Mahaiyawa community. The United National Party (UNP) is the dominant political party within Mahaiyawa. It was the central government ruling party during a previous regime, then formed the opposition and is now back again as the governing party. This party continues to be dominant in the Central Provincial Council, which includes Kandy district, as well as in the KMC. The other powerful political party is the Sri Lanka People's Alliance (SLPA), which is a multi-party coalition that is now the main opposition in the national legislature. Other than the two dominant political parties there are some minor political parties whose supporters are not very active in the community. The Ceylon Workers Congress (CWC) is one of them for which a majority of the supporters are plantation workers.

Politicians know that Mahaiyawa is a pool of votes and that if they can convince the voters, it will work to their advantage during elections. They know the strategy to convince people is to promise improvements in basic services such as housing, water, sanitary and other infrastructure services. As long as these problems remain unsolved, people need to beg for the politicians' support. Politicians use this situation to recruit socially powerful individuals to lead and organize the community by promising to improve these services. These agents of politicians ultimately benefit from the support given by politicians in solving their individual problems rather than communal issues. After that the politicians are not seen again by the people until the next elections are scheduled. At present, people are disappointed with politicians due to past experience. Nevertheless, this process continues as the people have no other alternative.

SOCIAL COHESION IN MAHAIYAWA

Although Tamil people have lived in Mahaiyawa throughout the ethnic conflicts, no move has been made against them by the

Sinhalese who live within the same community. The main reason is equal socio-economic background: all are low caste and poor, so the community tends to ignore ethnic differences and share whatever basic services are available for the community. Moreover, the similar social backgrounds improve social cohesion among families, which collectively resist any confrontation with outsiders. Therefore, Mahaiyawa has been a safe area for most of the poor Tamils. For this reason, migration to this slum settlement has increased over the last two decades. Although the population increased during this period, the living space available for them as well as the basic services facilities have not expanded. Extended families from the original settlers and the coming of new migrants have overcrowded the settlement.

The Mahaiyawa slum community is different from other slum communities in Kandy. These differences are mostly shaped by the location of the community, its ethnicity, and the historical relationship with the KMC. As Mahaiyawa is the slum closest to the city centre, the land it occupies has a higher commercial value. Ethnically, the majority of inhabitants are Tamil whereas in most of the other slum communities the majority are Sinhalese. Therefore, the relationships between the inhabitants and outsiders are relatively weaker than is the case with other slum communities. Many families in the Mahaiyawa community have lived here for over three generations. Other newer slum communities have grown on vacant land available in the peripheral areas of the city. Furthermore, the Mahaiyawa dwellers traditionally worked for the KMC as labourers, whereas no other slum community in the city has such a long-term relationship with government institutions. This long-term relationship between the community and the KMC shapes the land tenure and the economic survival of the inhabitants.

LAND AND HOUSING

The land occupied by Mahaiyawa is legally owned by the KMC. However, the community has resided there for many generations and possesses a history as old as that of the KMC, which was established by ordinance in 1865. The people who lived there in the past as well as those living there now have worked for the KMC as labourers and minor workers. Yet, they have not been given land ownership. The land security of present residents has been limited to a 30 years' land lease from the KMC, renewable for another 30 years. Upon the leaseholder's death, the lease is transferable to a family member previously nominated by the leaseholder. According to the KMC, this system of land tenure has been effective for over a century now. It includes various conditions upon which people have to build and maintain their houses. Some strict conditions of this land tenure can be summarized as follows:

- Shall and will pay the rental of Rs 120 (US $1.50) per annum each and every year.
- Shall not sublet, sub-lease the premises or in any manner to a third party.
- Shall not effect any structural alterations, improvements or renovations without the prior approval in writing of the Municipal Commissioner.
- Shall keep the said premises in a tenantable condition.
- If the said premises are required for any purpose of the Lessor Council (KMC) and the lessee upon receiving three months' notice from the Lessor Council must surrender, yield and give up possession of the premises without claiming any damages or compensation.

[Source: Official leasing deed issued by the KMC.]

Out of a total of about 900 families, 834 families are descendants of the original settlers, according to the KMC statistics. But of these only about 275 families have a lease. The balance of the descendant families without leases are categorized as 'unauthorized settlers' by the KMC. Because of the rules and regulations of the KMC, these families have no rights to land or to upgrade their houses. According to a proposed community development programme initiated in a collaboration among the KMC, Urban Development Authority (UDA) and the National Housing Development Authority (NHDA), the families that do not have the leasing tenure have been asked to agree to relocate to another location about 12 miles from the city.

Housing in Mahaiyawa is an unsolved issue. About 625 houses are occupied by nearly 925 families. In an extreme case, one house is occupied by five families even though the house does not have enough space for a single family. There are only a few houses with a separate kitchen, bedroom or living room. About 90 per cent of the houses are in poor condition, lacking adequate space, ventilation and natural or electric light. These houses have no clear demarcation of kitchen, dining room, living room and bedroom, and all are confined to one or two rooms. Except for one or two chairs, a table and basic appliances, the houses lack furnishings. Families cook with expensive as well as polluting fuel sources such as firewood and kerosene as they are not able to pay the initial costs for gas cookers. Electricity connections are not possible due to the low quality conditions of the houses, otherwise costs would have been lower in the long run. In certain cases, people make illegal connections from street lines despite the possible risks of electrocution.

A few houses do have tiled roofs, two storeys, bricks and cement-plaster and painted walls. These houses are owned by community leaders who enjoy close relationships with politicians and other influential groups outside the community. In addition to the better quality of houses, the residents have a little space for flowerbeds, vegetable plants and animal husbandry as well. The second standard of housing is occupied by the employees of KMC. These are 'line rooms' which are not as good as the community leaders' houses but are still in relatively good condition. The space and structure of this type of a house is around 150 sq. ft. with no extra land space available. These houses are made of low-cost building materials, but are relatively permanent. For a normal family of five to seven members, the space in this type of house is inadequate. There are about 250 houses like this in the community. The latecomers and the extended families without leases—presently the majority of the community—have the lowest standard of housing. These are temporary and have no particular plan, or no foundation, erected wherever space is available. The situation has led to overcrowding and a lack of space for laying down infrastructure such as footpaths and steps. Building materials for these houses are the cheapest—cardboard, polythene, asbestos, used wood and paper. There are more than 400 houses belonging to this category which are the most unhygienic and in the most poorly serviced area of the community. These houses are located on steep slopes, next to garbage collection spots, the walls of communal toilets or bathing spots, and on sewage canals covered by wood or plates. Naturally, this leads to a very poor quality of life.

Availability of Safe and Clean Water

One of the essential services for any community is water. The only possible source of water for this community is pipe-borne water supplied by the KMC. At present, only about 80 families have private water connections to their houses. They only have access to the communal standpipe water supply. Problems relating to water vary in this slum community. These problems are usually the inadequate and interrupted water supply, rules and regulations of the KMC, public washing in proximity to the water pipes and inadequate maintenance. There are only 26 standpipes available for water and they are scattered around the whole community. In extreme cases there are 15–20 families using one water pipe, otherwise one pipe is used by 10–15 families on average. There are six bathing spots available for communal use. At each spot, six persons can bathe at a time. But often at least one or two showers are broken at each spot. Some families have easy access whereas other families have difficulties fetching water due to the lack of footpaths or flights of steps to their houses. People must wait for water and the use of water pipes over time makes the location unhygienic since people wash their dishes, pots and pans, and clothes at the water point. Usually the used water flows to open sewage canals which are often blocked by solid waste. Issues regarding water use, cleaning and maintenance are critical.

In addition to the inadequate number of water pipes, the constantly interrupted water supply is another problem. Each household must store some water in containers in case the water supply is interrupted. This causes waste of water through evaporation, leaking and spilling over from containers. People complain to the KMC that the water is supplied only in the morning hours and after that taps are dry for the rest of the day. According to the KMC, the problem is due to the lack of capacity or the pressure of the water pumps. However, this is not a problem for the well-off families who live in higher elevation areas elsewhere in the city. This problem is specific to Mahaiyawa due to the absence of adequate pumps. But since there is no politically powerful intervention, nothing is done to upgrade the service.

The problem of inadequate provision of basic services in Mahaiyawa is common to most of the low-income communities. However, the extra disadvantage of the Mahaiyawa slum community is the lack of acceptable alternative means to provide those services. For instance, some low-income communities in peripheral areas of the city have access to well water, stream water, and more space between houses than in the Mahaiyawa community. Furthermore, in other slums the relationship between the community and outsiders is relatively better. Also, similar ethnicity helps in finding part-time employment, contract work or entering into mutual assistance programmes with neighbouring communities.

SANITATION, SEWAGE AND SOLID WASTE

There are about 82 latrines available for communal use, while only about 40 families have their own toilets. Each toilet is connected to a septic tank which is rarely emptied. These toilets have been used since as far back as 1948 and have not been renovated or expanded despite the increasing population. Therefore, the toilets are overused and they overflow. Some toilets cannot be used and are malfunctioning due to contamination. The CDO and the KMC health officers agree that the toilets are in inadequate for the existing population in Mahaiyawa. Alternatively, some people use open sewage canals for defecation, so that the maintenance and cleaning of the sewage system has also become difficult. Usually toilets do not have electric lights, so that safety concerns make it difficult for women, children and aged people to use these toilets during the night.

Municipal labourers, who are also members of the community, are reluctant to clean the sewage system and the toilets due to health risks. The labourers are often treated with antibiotics by the KMC Health Department as a protective measure. Furthermore, the KMC allocates only 10 labourers each day to clean the whole area within a four-hour work session, which is not adequate to serve the area properly. Labourers complain that the KMC does not issue the necessary cleaning equipment whereas the KMC suspects the labourers of selling the new equipment to outsiders at low prices whenever new equipment is issued. Garbage collection procedures are irregular and inappropriately performed. Except for a few houses along the roads, most other houses do not have access to the solid waste collection system. Therefore, people have been asked to bring the garbage to the roads where tractors can pick up the garbage. But due to the lack of containers in each house, people often throw garbage into the sewage drains.

The Power Relations between the Community and Outsiders

There are several CBOs in the Mahaiyawa slum community, such as women's societies, religious societies and youth sports societies, but none of them have worked successfully for the improvement of their living conditions. Even though many attempts have been made since the 1980s by the CBOs in Mahaiyawa to upgrade and provide basic services to this community, all attempts have been ineffective. Perhaps they were not powerful enough to draw the attention of the officials in the institutions and other responsible parties such as politicians and NGOs. For instance, even with some assistance provided under the Urban Housing Sub-Programme of the Ministry of Housing, which assists in housing and infrastructure facilities for low-income communities, Mahaiyawa enjoyed no great improvement in facilities except the creation of a pre-school, library and community centre. This can be compared with other low-income communities such as Menikkumbura and Dodamwala, which were able to benefit more from this programme and build up their own houses and other infrastructure facilities successfully. The inability of the Mahaiyawa community to mobilize resources and other benefits for the betterment of the community is a continuing problem.

Power relations and contacts with outsiders to the community are mostly on an individual basis, rather than through the CBOs. Although it seems that the community is lagging behind in terms of influential relations with outside actors, some particular groups of people in the community, especially higher status Tamil families, are relatively active and have more social and political relationships with outside actors. These families have gradually become better off due to their connections, which helped them gain land leases, housing loans, employment and admission of children to better schools. They are usually the leaders of the CBOs and are relatively better educated than the other families in the community. Some are supporters of party politicians. The local community leaders serve the interests and expectations of these outsiders and in return they make personal gains rather than working for the well-being of the community. The majority of the CBO members whom I interviewed are critical of these selfish community leaders who are no longer trusted. Nevertheless, members are scared to criticize them openly. The people know that they are being cheated by the promises of politicians but they feel powerless.

The long, historical relationship between the Mahaiyawa community and the KMC has three different forms: first, people in Mahaiyawa traditionally work as employees doing the lowest level work for the lowest pay; second, they are tenants of the KMC; and third, some are voters helping to elect members to the KMC. However, none of these links, separately or in combination, have been strong enough to draw the attention of the KMC officials to the problems of Mahaiyawa and encourage solutions. Instead, these institutional relationships have limited the options that the community might follow to improve conditions. Only a few officials I interviewed at the KMC understand the situation and the importance of addressing the problems of low-income communities through community-based development projects. However, they cannot extend their support due to the various constraints imposed by politicians which impede such efforts.

At present the CDOs, who are young and only educated up to high-school level, are the agents who maintain the link between the community and the KMC. They mostly bring messages and orders from the officials rather than forwarding the problems of the community to the officials. Although they may or may not be members of slum communities it does not necessarily mean that they are actual representatives of the community. They have been appointed by the KMC as employees on a temporary basis. In addition to reporting maintenance issues of the community, they organize meetings and workshops whenever the KMC wants to inform the people regarding health issues, childcare and family planning.

Within the larger society of Kandy, the people in Mahaiyawa have been stigmatized by the richer and middle-class people. Outsiders see this area as socially hazardous and the residents as ill-behaved. The people of this community are known as 'Mahaiyawa people'. They are excluded from the benefits of labour legislation, and are politically manipulated to maintain the status quo. Due to incompetent leadership, they cannot develop influential contacts with outsiders who could truly mobilize resources and political action. They are safe as they are a large community and are ensured of the status quo by their long-term relationship with the KMC. Because of the ongoing conflict between Tamil separatists and the Sri Lankan government, the ethnicity of the residents further impedes the relations between the community and the larger society, including bureaucrats, influential politicians, religious leaders and other elites.

Obviously, most of the people of Mahaiyawa feel trapped. They have the physical and emotional security of living in the midst of other Tamils, the low cost of housing, the employment possibilities with the KMC or, within easy walking distance, in the centre of the city. All these factors converge to keep them in Mahaiyawa. Making a move away from the community even more difficult is their lower standard of education and income-earning skills. Within the community, they stand together against outsiders and the police. Short-term neighbourly help is provided when needed. But joining together to work for a community benefit has failed so far.

Undercutting community self-help efforts are the politicians of the KMC with their connections to the national ministries. The reasons are well known. The expansion of the business core of Kandy has been forced to bypass the land occupied by Mahaiyawa. In recent years this land has become some of the more valuable in the city. The municipal councillors would like the tax revenue from a commercial development and want the residents of Mahaiyawa to move out. The KMC is not seriously interested in encouraging the development of strong community organizations or undertaking programmes to improve living conditions for the residents.

Effective community organization needs both the confidence that all the participants will share fairly in the costs and benefits and that the goals set for the organization can be reached. The buying off of the community's few leaders and the stalling of improvement projects keeps Mahaiyawa a slum. It is only a matter of time before it is replaced by high-rise commercial buildings, as has happened elsewhere in Kandy city.

Notes

1. The name of the CDO is not mentioned for reasons of anonymity. However, his personal characteristics and performance will be used to explain the relationship between the local authorities and the community.
2. Unfortunately, regional conflicts within Sri Lanka have been misinterpreted as ethnic conflicts in history by the foreigners who invaded Sri

Lanka due to their lack of understanding about the social and cultural ties among ethnic groups. This misinterpretation was continued by the Sri Lankans themselves in later periods and what were once political issues have turned into ethnic issues. The ongoing ethnic conflict, which evolved into a war during the early 1980s, is one of the consequences of these ideological changes.

3. No recent survey or research data are available for socio-economic conditions in Mahaiyawa community. The figures given in this chapter are estimates based on information supplied by the CDO and my own field research carried out in 2001–2.

8

Expanding World Demand for Gems: The Old Poor and the New Rich in Ratnapura

KARUNATISSA ATUKORALA

Sri Lanka was internationally known for its valuable gemstones from the pre-Christian era. References to the gemstones of Sri Lanka have been made in the Mahabharata, the Mahawamsa and other historical chronicles. Throughout its long history, the gem industry has played a significant role in the social, economic, political and cultural life of people of gem-mining areas.[1] It is not an exaggeration to say that in the history of Sri Lanka no other single product has attracted so much outside attention as gems. Accounts of various early foreign visitors to Sri Lanka refer to gems as a valuable product of the land.[2]

Gem-mining is carried out mainly in the area known as Ratnapura (gem city). Of the total active labour force of the district of Ratnapura, 60 per cent is directly or indirectly engaged in the gem industry.[3] During the post-independence period export earnings from the gem industry made a significant contribution to the gross national product of the country.[4] However, recent statistics show that earnings from the gem industry have declined gradually over the last two decades even though the world gem market has expanded. This does not mean that gem ores have been exhausted but that the marketing of gems is done through informal channels so that figures of actual sales do not get reported. This decline in gem earnings reported by the government is observed to be a direct result of the entry of buyers from Thailand into the gem market in Sri Lanka. They purchase gems and smuggle them out of the country though informal channels. The Thai invasion of the industry has had both a positive and negative impact on the gem industry, society and the economy of the Ratnapura district.

The gem industry in Sri Lanka has a number of features that make it a typical system of production. One characteristic is the organization of property relations. In the gem industry the workers and the owners are not clearly separated on the basis of the ownership of means of production. This unique situation makes the class relationships in the gem economy very complex. Another important characteristic that makes the gem economy different from other industries is its hidden and illicit character. Despite government attempts to regularize gem mining, such activities are still carried out without legal sanction in some areas. In gem trading there is a very large element of secrecy involved and the pricing and valuing are done with utmost secrecy.

Though gem mining has been an important vehicle for upward social mobility, sociological research on the industry is limited. This may be due mainly to the difficulties experienced in gathering reliable information about the industry. However, the technical and operational aspects of the industry, such as the geographical distribution of gem deposits, valuation of gemstones, technology associated with gem mining, cutting and identification of gemstones and so on, have received more attention. Much of the available literature on the socio-economic aspects is in the form of historical discussions. A study of the marketing and cutting of gems appears in the report of the Sub-Committee of the Executive Committee on Labour, Industry and Commerce in the 1930s. This policy study systematically analyses the marketing aspect of the gem industry in the pre-independence era from a sociological point of view.[5]

In 1984, a sociological analysis was carried out by Weeramunda.[6] In this study he explains the historical development of gem mining in a selected village in Monaragala district. He describes the historical process from era to era and explains how the village agricultural economy was replaced by the growth of gem mining in the 1970s. He sees the emergence of social classes based on gemming in the village. This in turn weakened the administration, disorganized the water management system, led to the decay of formal organizations for self-help and finally to signs of social anomie. By the 1980s he detects the emergence of a 'mass culture and Westernization'. These limited studies on the social aspect clearly indicate that the industry has changed. And as the industry increasingly supplies the external markets, it has had a growing direct impact on the producers. Such changes are seen especially in the gem market, which links village producer to international market via several types of networks.

This chapter focuses on the changes in the market forces and the formation of a new class in the gem-mining area of Ratnapura and how the formal gem market converted into an informal market as a result of the globalization process. Further, attention is also paid to recent developments in the industry, such as the migration of gem miners from Ratnapura to Madagascar for gem mining.

Colonization to Globalization: Their Effects on the Gem Industry

The industry has been changing its shape from era to era. In the pre-colonial period gems were often sent as a tribute or as gifts to foreign rulers. Reference is made in the epic Mahabharata to Vibushana, king of Ceylon, whose tribute to king Yudhisthira consisted of gems and pearls of great value. Further, the Mahawamsa records that king Devanampiya Tissa sent precious stones as part of a gift to Emperor Asoka, who was overjoyed to receive these unique gifts.[7] The Sri Lankan kings were able to develop good international relations and get the support of neighbouring rulers by gifting valuable gems to them during this period. In the colonial period there was no longer a king to patronize the gem industry but traders had by then fully realized the value of Sri Lankan gems. The Moors had begun to take over the gem trade and this was the beginning of the present day gem trade. By the time Haeckel visited the island in 1882, the Moor men were cutting and polishing gems.[8] In the meantime the British administration declared that a license was necessary for locals to engage in gem mining. In addition foreign companies were undertaking gem mining. The companies commenced large scale gem mining using coolies and villagers as labourers. These ventures and the continued Moor monopoly in gem sales did not lead to satisfactory economic returns to the local economy. As the foreign ventures were unsuccessful, by the early 1900s locals increased their share in mining. The gems found by the villagers were sold to the gem-pit financier who then sold them to the village headman. The village headman sold them to Moor dealers in the small towns or the capital city of Colombo. A dependency was formed through the market monopoly enjoyed by Moor traders. This system of profit distribution continued because the financier for the gem-pit usually was a member of a village elite on whom the majority of villagers were dependent.

Significant changes in the gem industry were observed after independence, especially after the establishment of the State Gem Corporation (SGC) in 1971.[9] The establishment of SGC has expanded the industry in many ways. Before the setting up of the SGC, the domestic market for gems, the cutting, polishing and valuing and contacts with foreign markets were mainly handled by a few traders and families largely from the Muslim community. The non-Muslim producers had very little opportunity of bargaining for good prices. As a result of the SGC stepping in as a purchaser, the bargaining position of the village seller of uncut and unpolished gems was considerably strengthened. The SGC's operations benefited the small-scale rural gem miners. Functions such as issuing of gem licenses, leasing of government land for gem mining, purchasing of gems and exporting through state monopoly led to drastic changes within the industry. As the rural producers profited more than ever before, a degree of material development became visible in the villages.

The initiatives taken by the SGC and the training it offered in the cutting, polishing and processing of gems and manufacturing of jewellery were eagerly welcomed. The lapidary courses held by the SGC in the gem producing areas have contributed to the break up of the technological and business monopoly enjoyed by the Moors. The equipment used for cutting and polishing gems was not expensive, so those seeking employment opportunities could either buy a set of equipment or be employed at an established workshop until they could afford to set up an independent workshop. Thus, the gem industry was now open to the hitherto unemployed poor Sinhalese youths. This provided new job opportunities for the young educated job seekers. At the beginning only the urban youth entered this activity but gradually even the rural youth took an interest in training.

As a result of being trained in the valuation of gems, many small-scale businessmen, especially in the urban sector, became involved in the gem market as middlemen (termed as *erottu karaya*). They approached gem sellers coming to the market and brought them to their patrons. If a transaction took place they received a commission from the patron. Gem-buying involves high risk and ready capital. The middlemen were unable to afford such a risk or to invest money in the transaction. However, in these transactions, a dealer in the *erottu* group did not lose money because he did not invest his own money in the risky transaction. With the earnings from this transaction, they started buying less valuable gems and started making some profit. Some visited gem pits, villages, and small towns to buy less valuable gems.

Both the *erottu* traders and the rich Sinhalese gem merchants made visits to gem-mining sites in order to buy gems. The Muslim merchants, who commonly had other lines of business, usually conducted transactions at their shops and did not visit the gem pits. They did not show any interest in participating in gem auctions held at the village level. The other characteristic observed among the Muslim gem merchants was that they were buying gems on which they could turn a big profit and they were not interested in competing with the new Sinhala buyers for a small marginal profit. Engaged with their other business, they gradually moved away from the gem industry. With the entry of Sinhalese buyers into the trade, the Moor monopoly of the market declined. This resulted in a more competitive gem market that provided opportunities for producers to obtain a relatively higher price for their products. Most of the Sinhalese traders who are today millionaires became rich in this manner. The spread of knowledge about valuing gems strengthened the bargaining power of the rural producers as well. As the industry grew, some of the elite in the village who earned money from the trade migrated to the city where more facilities were available. Those large-scale merchants who moved preferred the capital city, Colombo, where they invested their money in more diverse enterprises. Due to the geographical mobility of the richer traders, a large fraction of the income from gems did not remain in the district of Ratnapua.

The SGC was unable to control the industry's activities for a reasonable period of time as expected at the time of establishment of the corporation. Its control over the purchasing and export was surpassed by the private sector within 2–3 years of commencement of the corporation's activities. The gem buyers were able to influence the officers of the corporation to stay away from the gem-marketing activities. At the beginning, the gem-pit labourers made more money since the valuation officers of the Corporation participated in the gem auctions if they were invited by any share holder of the gem-pit. However, they later cooperated with the gem merchants and stayed away in the expectation of a financial pay-off. Though the production of gems increased rapidly, the profit distribution still benefited the gem-pit owners. The share received by the gem miners was still marginal (about 3 per cent).[10]

After the liberalization of trade in 1977 when the SGC became less important, private merchants began to engage actively in the export of gems. The increased involvement of the private sector opened the door to increased gem smuggling and the free entrance of international dealers. According to the Customs Reports, a higher number of smuggling attempts have been detected after 1977. Although there is a reported decrease in export-earning after 1977, there is no evidence of a parallel drop in gem mining or other related activities. The value of gems smuggled out of the country could be very high but these transactions were not recorded officially.

The control of gem marketing, seems to have been taken over fully by the private sector as a result of the decline of the activities of the SGC. The Corporation that purchased gems worth Rs 152 million in 1973 purchased only Rs 1 million worth of gems in 1983. The SGC exported less than 5 per cent of the total recorded gem exports after 1977. By the 1980s it declined to about 1–2 per cent. The corporation's control is evident only from 1972–75 and since then the corporation has been displaced by the private sector.

Competition among the buyers provided gem producers in the rural sector a relatively better price. This resulted in the formation of a class of the newly rich in the rural sector as well. The traditional social organization, based on the caste system, was on the decline, now individuals of all castes were able to increase their power and position in the village by entering the business and earning money from the expanding gem industry. The poor mine-workers became further dependent on the rich as the share received by them remained marginal.

The entry of Thai nationals into the gem market after 1977 is an important event in the recent history of Sri Lanka's gem industry.

Thai nationals came in large numbers to purchase a semi-precious stone by the name of 'geuda'. They used a technical process and converted the 'geuda' into blue sapphires. The Thai intervention has affected the gem industry of the country both positively and negatively. On the positive side 'geuda', which was considered a stone of no value, started fetching a fairly good price and created a new enthusiasm in the industry. The Thai buyers entered the market with the help of the *erottu* group without obtaining permission from the relevant authorities. As far as the distribution of the profit within the entire network—from village to international level—is concerned, based on my case study, the international traders receive half the share of the profit while the local trader/manufacturer receives one quarter of the profit. Of the rest, 20 per cent is distributed in the city for wages and other costs, 4 per cent goes to the dealers in the small towns and the other 1 per cent, goes to the village.

Entry of the Thais into the gem market negatively affected the rich Sinhala gem traders. The network of relationships between the small traders (*erottu* class) and the big gem-buyers at the city level was disrupted by the competition of the Thai dealers. There were incidents where a group of local merchants physically beat up some Thai buyers.

RECENT DEVELOPMENTS

As the world gem market expanded, Sri Lanka had to compete with several other gem-producing countries. Although export earnings from gems continue to fall, production is observed to have increased. During the last decade, Thai buyers continued buying 'geuda' and exporting it through formal and informal channels. With the arrival of the technology of heat-treating 'geuda', Sri Lanka was able to earn foreign exchange from stones which previously had no market value.

The other recent development is the migration of gem merchants to Madagascar. As the Madagascar gem market opened up, groups of Thais and Sri Lankans started visiting Madagascar to buy gems. A group consists of gem merchant, valuer, cutter and polisher. This venture is completely different from the earlier practice in Sri Lanka. Gems from Madagascar are either brought to Sri Lanka to be cut and sold here or they are taken to Bangkok

TABLE 8.1
'Geuda' Exports

Year	*Carat*	*Value (in millions of rupees)*
1988	8,919,337	528.6
1989	10,432,868	534.4
1990	4,343,053	597.1
1991	11,227,880	634.1
1992	7,138,280	456.0

Source: M.S. Rupasinghe and P.G. Cooray (Eds.), *The Sri Lankan Geuda*, Kandy: Institute for Fundamental Studies, 1993.

and sold there. With the expansion of the world gem market the process of mining, cutting, polishing and selling of gems has gone beyond country boundaries and the identification of gem by country is lost. In this process, buyers may return to their country with capital and invest in various businesses. Others remain overseas and may operate their businesses far away from their place of birth, participating in the international gem market. The impact of this process is yet to be studied.

CASE STUDY 1

Loku Bandara was the *Gammuladeni* (village headman) of the village of Maragala since the 1930s and belonged to a high caste and lived in a big house constructed in the early 1900s. Of his two daughters and two sons, the daughters were married off outside the village. One son received higher education and became an engineer. The other son, who was addressed as 'Appo' (respectable high caste persons are addressed by this term in this area) remained in the village after his father's death. He had only passed grade 10 and was able to get a teaching post in a nearby school prior to the death of his father. However, he was later sacked from the job on disciplinary grounds.

Appo then entered the gem industry as a gem-pit manager. In the early 1970s he was able to earn some money by gem mining. Around 1975 he bought all the shares of the mine and became a gem-pit owner. With his earnings he continued the business. It is said that a low-caste villager found a gem while engaging in illicit gem mining. This stone had been sold to Appo for Rs 500, who had resold it for Rs 75,000. The money received from this sale was spent on buying valuable gemstones. All his workers were either low-caste or poor, high-caste persons. They would accept any amount of money given by Appo. He built a big house after demolishing the old ancestral house. Villagers believe that he has interests in illicit gem mining. Although people are taken into police custody if caught engaging in illegal gem mining, if one has police support, it is very easy to carry on such activities. The usual practice is to give a share of the profit to the policemen who help. Towards the end of the 1970s, Appo is said to have bought land in several areas, in and outside Ratnapura district. He married a woman from a high-caste family in the same district.

With the introduction of the liberal economy after 1977, Appo bought some buses and started a private transport company. In the 1980s, when his children reached school-going age, he moved to Colombo. He bought a big house in a neighbourhood where well-to-do families lived. While living in Colombo, he paid frequent visits to his village as all his gem-mining activities were still based in Ratnapura district. By this time he received income from several sources: gem mining, trading in gems, commercial agriculture and the private bus service.

Appo had by then become a very influential gem merchant not only in the Ratnapura district but also in Colombo. He visited gem auctions in the area to buy valuable gems. In some auctions he would simply say 'I want to buy it.' Usually no other trader cared to compete with him. He did this especially at auctions at his own gem-pits or at auctions in his village. The gem miners did not complain even if they felt that the price offered was very low. Many gem miners told me that despite the low prices they had no alternative but to accept his offers. He was able to exercise this power because of social prestige, his strong financial position and the support of the police. Appo is now planning to join politics.

When special events such as a funeral or a wedding are held in the village, Appo is usually invited as the chief guest. At funerals, he himself pays a visit and offers money or some other support. He is always the chief guest at the annual ceremony of the village temple. He is the chief guest and the main financier of the village New Year festival and many other functions. Every year many of the villagers visit him during the New Year and he gives money and clothes to everybody who visits him during this period.

It may appear that he uses his powers to exploit the villagers. This is correct to some extent but it is also true that he does this with the support of the existing social structure and social organization. There is a dependency relationship between him and the miners and poor villagers. The villagers can always invite other traders to the gem auctions, or sell gemstones to other traders in the town, but they do not do so because they depend on his help in many other ways.

CASE STUDY 2

Somadasa was born into a low-caste family in another village. As a youth, he worked at a tea estate as a wage labourer and also as a labourer in the village paddy fields from time to time. During this period a man from a nearby village collected shares and opened a gem-pit on lands belonging to poor low-caste people in his village. In 1970, Somadasa entered the gem industry as a gem-pit worker even though wages of gem miners were very low in comparison to wage labourers in the tea estate. He then gave up his estate job and invested some money he had earned on gem-pit shares.

In 1977 Somadasa applied for a gem-pit licence and organized the shareholders. He kept a few shares for himself and took on the task of manager. The yield of the gem-pit was very satisfactory, so he received the licensee's share and the manager's share in addition to money received for his few shares. Then he invested his money in his own gem-pits, where he owned all the shares. In this way he was able to receive a large sum of money from gem mining.

Somadasa built a big new house in the village. He became the strongest supporter of the ruling political party. Through his gem transactions, he developed close connections with the large buyers in the city. Thus, he gradually became the most powerful man in his village. However, since he belonged to a low caste he did not receive social recognition from the village folk. He was in a position to buy a brand new car for himself but he first bought a car which had belonged to a high-caste person in the area, for a relatively higher price than its market price. He hired a high-caste driver. He offered jobs in his gem-pits to poor high-caste people. Somadasa donated Rs 25,000 for the improvement of the school building in the village. He also built a temple with his own money and invited as incumbent a Buddhist monk belonging to

Ramanna Nikaya, which serves the lower-caste communities. He collected a lorry load of food items and cloths to be given to flood victims in another area and received publicity for his generous act. Through these actions he was able to get some recognition from high-caste persons.

Somadasa later bought a big old house (a *walawwa*) that belonged to a high-caste family in Ratnapura city for a very high price. He settled down in this house after it was renovated. Even though he moved in, the house was still called a *walawwa* (prestige place) by the people and so he used to tell people that he was living in the *walawwa*. This was a very wise step that he took to hide his caste position. Thus, he could gain the desired recognition from the city folk. Prior to changing his place of residence, he changed his name including the 'ge' name that implied his caste. He bought a number of brand new lorries and buses and wrote his new name and address on those vehicles. He later married a poor woman of high caste from an area far away from his place of birth.

Summary

Gems have been mined in Ratnapura district for centuries but it was after independence that the greatest changes occurred in the industry, followed by the social consequences. The creation of the State Gem Corporation in 1971 led to the entry of a new class of poorer Sinhalese into the gem business, which led to the displacement of the Moor traders who had held a near-monopoly over the trade. The liberalization of the economy after 1977 opened the way for more local investors and for Thai buyers to enter the gem market. Two case studies of Appo and Somadasa illustrate this process. The entry of the Thais further strengthened the position of the middlemen and encouraged Sri Lankans to enter the rapidly growing international gem trade. Now Sri Lankans are joining hands with Thais to exploit the gem fields in Madagascar.

Notes

1. As there is no suitable sociological definition of the gem industry, I provide the following definition: 'The gem industry is the process whereby a person

or persons extract(s) gems from the earth, in legal or illegal operations, with or without the aid of the standard gemming technology. It also includes the process whereby the stones are marketed, cut, polished and set into jewellery. In short, it is the chain of actions through which gems are extracted and processed for the market.'

2. *Economic Review*, Colombo: People's Bank, September 1977, p. 3.
3. Tissa Atukorala and others, *Socio-economic Survey of Ratnapura District*, a report prepared for a training programme conducted by the Research Institute of Management Studies, The Netherlands and the National Institute of Business Management, Sri Lanka, 1984, p. 49.
4. The export share of the gem industry increased significantly with the establishment of the State Gem Corporation (SGC) in 1971. By 1973, gem exports became the third highest foreign income earner.
5. *Report of the Sub-Committee of the Executive Committee of Labour, Industry, and Commerce on the Marketing and Cutting of Ceylon Gems*, Colombo: Ceylon Government Press, 1939.
6. A.J. Weeramunda, *From Chena Plot to Gemming Pit: Case Study of Okkampitiya, Monaragala District*, Sociological Aspects of Rural and Regional Development, Research Paper Series, No. 3, Colombo: University of Colombo, 1984.
7. W. Geiger (Trans.), *The Mahawamsa*, Colombo: Ceylon Government Information Department, 1950, p. 59.
8. Ernest Haeckel, *A Visit to Ceylon*, Colombo: Tissa Prakasakayo, 1975, p. 218.
9. The State Gem Corporation was established by Parliamentary Act No. 13 of 1971. According to the Finance Minister's budget speech, the SGC was designed to provide opportunities for the poor man to mine, to provide training facilities in modern methods of cutting and polishing gems and to provide facilities for any one to have gems tested and valued. Combating smuggling and earning foreign exchange were other objectives. In order to achieve these objectives the SGC was granted a complete monopoly in the export of gems.
10. The miners of a gem-pit receive a share (*karuhaula*) which is 34 per cent of the profit of the total receipt. If it is assumed that an average of 10 miners are working in a pit, the share per miner is about 3 per cent. The pit owner gets the highest share (34 per cent), the licence-holder gets 7 per cent, and the landowner gets 25 per cent. The ratio of profit between the pit owner and the individual miner is roughly 1:10.

9

Bonded Tea Estate Workers: Still Waiting at the Gates

M. SINNATHAMBY

Sri Lanka has long been recognized for its high levels of achievement in the development of its human resources. The country, well known as a leader among developing countries for its human development record was one of the first developing countries to understand the importance of investing in human resources and promoting gender equality.[1] On the strength of its human development achievements the country has been ranked high among South Asian countries in the United Nations' Human Development Index (HDI) and in the middle in socio-economic indicators for many years.[2] The HDI rating of the country is 0.735 and it ranks 91st out of 175 countries. This is nine places above its ranking in terms of real per capita income. The country, despite its low per capita income, has been able to achieve such a high level of human development mainly because of the widespread state welfare system that has been in place since the early 1940s. The welfare system consisted of subsidized rice and flour distribution and rationing, free education, relief for the poor, subsidized or free medical care and several other welfare measures. These welfare measures contributed to a fall in mortality rate from 22 in 1945 to 6 per 1,000 live births in 2000. During the same period, maternal mortality rate dropped from 165.2 to 2.4 per 10,000 live births and infant mortality rate declined from 140 in 1945 to 16.9 per 1,000 live births in 1996.[3] Life expectancy at birth climbed from 43.9 to 76 years for women and 41.6 to 71 years for men while birth rates declined from 4.1 to a near replacement rate of

2.1 births per woman between 1980 and 1996. The literacy rate increased from 17.4 in 1947 to 94.3 in 1997.[4] These laudable achievements, however, are not evenly distributed, neither across the country nor among the ethnic communities and social groups. In other words, pockets of backward regions and social groups exist within the country.

This chapter is concerned with one such social group, namely, the Tamil estate workers who form the majority of the Indian Tamil community, also known as the Tamils of Recent Indian origin in Sri Lanka. They are also known by various other names such as the 'Plantation', 'up-country' and 'hill-country' Tamils. The different names by which this group of Tamils are known is indicative of the identity crisis they face. Daniel, for instance, argues that the

> ... identity of the Estate Tamil, more than that of any of the others is caught in the throes of both history and heritage and that heritage provokes an identification with the Tamils of Southern India. They are still in search of an identity but are moved by the contingencies of situations to assimilate, integrate or separate vis-à-vis the others.[5]

'Estate' Tamil and 'up-country' Tamil are two terms that have come to have the widest currency in recent years. The term 'Estate' Tamil emphasises their origins as workers on tea estates. Since their social, economic, political and cultural life has taken place primarily on the plantations it is not surprising that their identity is constrained by it. However, it should be noted that not all 'Estate' Tamils live on the estates. 'Malaiyaha' Tamils, which literally means 'hill-country' Tamils, is yet another term that has come to be accepted as standard self-appellation but this ethnic identity occurs only in the Tamil language.[6]

Estate Tamils make a substantial contribution to the wealth of the country. In the past, it was the surplus generated from their labour that contributed to the development of the country's infrastructure and enhancement of the physical quality of life of the rest of the population. Their sweat and labour continues to make significant contributions to the country's Gross Domestic Product (GDP) and the scarce foreign exchange earnings of the country. Until recently, it also contributed to the bulk of government tax revenue. But despite these contributions they have been denied the opportunity to enjoy a fair share of the country's social achievements, referred to earlier.

Within the multi-ethnic fabric of Sri Lankan society, Estate Tamils form the majority of the Indian-origin Tamils in Sri Lanka. (In the last reported Census of 1981, they numbered 818,656, or 5.5 per cent of the total population—Eds) They are the descendants of the immigrant workers brought from South Indian villages by the British to work in the plantations opened and managed by them in Sri Lanka. These people, who suffered from a combination of high population pressure, loss of employment due to the extinction of rural handicraft industries (caused by discriminatory British trade policies), landlessness, indebtedness to landlords, caste oppression etc. in their villages in India volunteered to migrate to Sri Lanka. Although the estate Tamils have a linguistic and religious affinity to the other Tamils who had settled on the island centuries ago, they have developed their own distinct identity by working and living within the plantation or estate system. The estates, with their residential system of labour are described as a total institution that encompasses the entire existence of the workforce.[7] The estate provides jobs, living quarters, education, health facilities, vegetable gardens, shops and even the burial grounds—all located within the boundaries of the estate.[8] In short, they offer a 'package deal' in return for which the workers have to live and work within the plantation enclave, virtually in conditions of semi-slavery. The tying of residence to employment served as a constraint on their mobility. In this respect, it is said that the estates are comparable to organizations such as army camps, hospitals and prisons. There is a strict hierarchy marked by housing, style of dress, and levels of pay and benefits. They have a corporate culture with strong notions of inferiority and superiority.

The Condition of the Estate Tamils

Estates are located in 9 out of 24 districts and 6 out of the 9 provinces in Sri Lanka. Central Province has the largest concentration of the Estate Tamil population, for it holds 46.5 per cent of this population while Uva and Sabaragamuwa, two other Provinces hold 16.9 per cent and 15.9 per cent respectively. Within the Central

Province the concentration is in the Nuwara Eliya district, the heartland of the plantations, where they form 42.7 per cent of the district's population. After the Anti-Tamil Riots of 1977 more than 40,000 Estate Tamils fled to the Tamil-dominated northern districts of Vavuniya and Mullaitivu in search of a secure environment away from the violence directed against them. They form around 19.5 per cent and 23 per cent respectively of the population of these districts. In most cases, they live as squatters and landless agricultural workers in these areas and many of them live in refugee camps. A few months prior to the countrywide Anti-Tamil Riots of July 1983, the refugee camps of these estate Tamils were attacked by the security forces and the refugees were subjected to harassment, torture and rape. Many of them were driven out of these districts and were forced to return to the tea estates where their relatives and friends continue to live.

The migrant Tamil estate workers in Sri Lanka possess some characteristics of indentured labour. Once they arrived in Sri Lanka after a difficult journey from India they were settled in various estates in what have come to be known as estate line-rooms built for them by the companies that employed them. In these rooms, approximately 10 feet by 12 feet in dimension, entire families cooked, slept and carried on with their daily lives. The majority of the descendants of these workers continue to live in these old and dilapidated line rooms even today. There are around 163,000 houses of the line room type constructed over 70 years ago, of which 49 per cent are back-to-back lines and the rest are single lines. The line rooms—dark, damp, ill-ventilated and devoid of kitchen facilities—create much hardships for the residents and especially for the women. Other types of accommodation (that is, twin or single cottages) constructed more recently total up to 30,200 units. About 85 per cent of the lines are now totally dilapidated and beyond repair. They are not worth upgrading and instead should be demolished. About 98 per cent of these rooms did not have electricity until very recently. The floor is made of mud and when the roof leaks during the rainy season it becomes wet and damp. While the interior of these rooms is swept and kept tidy, the surrounding common areas are dirty with stagnant water, open sewers and fly-infested garbage pits. Due to overcrowding in the lines, newly married couples, elderly parents, babies, infants, grown up girls and sick persons live together, deprived of any privacy (Ministry of Housing, Construction and Public Utilities, 1996).

Estate workers, who produce a significant proportion of the country's wealth, are the least fortunately placed in economic terms as well as in terms of education, social acceptability and cultural opportunities among all groups in the country. In the field of education they lag far behind. The spectacular expansion of education in Sri Lanka during the 1930s and 1940s bypassed them as the responsibility for their education was left in the hands of the estate management, which assigned a very low priority to schooling. In the thinking of the day, an educated labour force was not required for estate work. The important role that literate people and an educated labour force could play in the social, economic, demographic, political and cultural development of a country was not understood. The educational situation remained unchanged until the state took over the estate schools in the 1970s. In 1973, for instance, only 7.7 per cent of the residents in the estate sector had achieved more than primary education whereas in the rest of the country it was 37 per cent. While significant developments have taken place in the education of plantation children over the past two decades in terms of number of schools, pupil–teacher ratio and other education indicators, much remains to be done to bring their education up to the national level. The level of education on the estates lags behind that in urban and rural sectors due to inferior infrastructural facilities in Tamil-medium schools in the estate areas and the socio-economic backwardness of this community. Lower access to education persists at all levels—primary, secondary and tertiary—with relatively low participation rates in secondary and tertiary education and school avoidance among children in the age group 5–14 years. Unfortunately, in the past few years the trend of improvement in education has slowed down and even reversed.

A number of state agencies are involved in providing housing, electricity and water supply, health services and other benefits to the estate community under their respective sectoral programmes. However, these services do not reach them the way they do with other communities in the country. Furthermore, many of the services provided by the Ministry of Social Services, such as care for the aged or services to disabled persons are scarcely available to the estate workers. It was suspected that the lack of a proper mechanism to coordinate the programmes and activities of these agencies in the estate sector may have been responsible for this. In consideration of the hiatus, in the coordinating mechanism the first People's Alliance Government (1994–2000) established a separate Ministry of Estate Infrastructure specifically to function as the coordinating body to ensure that the benefits of various government programmes reach the plantation workers. This Ministry is also expected to fill in existing gaps in these facilities with its own resources so as to ensure that the quality of life of these workers is brought into line with the rest of the community.

ETHNIC RELATIONS IN THE ESTATE AREAS

The opening of plantations in the central hills of Sri Lanka during the nineteenth century ushered in a major change in the land-use pattern of the area. The land was divided into two main types of agricultural activities—plantation agriculture and peasant agriculture. The former consisted of large-scale production units using imported labour and capital and exporting a major part of output to foreign markets, while the peasant sector consisted of small-scale farms and cottage industries, using mostly unpaid labour and producing primarily for subsistence. Consequently, hardly any economic transactions involve purchases or sales or exchange of labour developed between the two sectors. Furthermore, as most workers on the plantations were Hindu Tamil immigrants while the peasants were Buddhist Sinhalese, the two communities remained isolated from each other. Such isolation was due partly to physical factors and partly to differences in language, religion and culture. This isolation was further reinforced by the policies of the British planters, which effectively prevented the entry of outsiders into the estates. Outsiders had to obtain the permission of the planters before entering any estate. Trespass laws were enacted for this purpose. Facilities in health, education, etc., were provided separately for the two communities. Thus, having very little economic or social relations, communication or cultural exchanges with each other, the two communities existed side by side—physically isolated and socially segregated. Nevertheless, they coexisted peacefully during the pre-independence period with no major open conflicts. A number of developments since the country gained independence in 1948 disturbed this peaceful coexistence between the rural Sinhalese and the estate Tamils and created various strains and stresses in their relations. Some of the noteworthy developments are discussed here.

DENIAL OF CITIZENSHIP RIGHTS TO THE ESTATE TAMILS

Disagreement on the definition of citizenship prior to independence resulted in the country gaining independence with a constitution that omitted a definition of citizenship. The Citizenship Act No. 18 of 1948 enacted by the first independent government assigned citizenship by descent to all persons born in Sri Lanka. But unlike the other communities, the community of Indian-origin Tamils, including the estate workers, was asked to produce the birth certificates of their fathers for the award of citizenship rights. Since systematic registration of births and deaths started only after 1895, most of these people were unable to produce such certificates and this was used to deny them citizenship rights. Subsequently, their right to vote in General and Local Government Elections was withdrawn and they were disenfranchised. The citizenship problem of the Estate Tamils thus stems since the time of independence. In the meantime, they were also rendered 'stateless', as India refused to take back those who were denied Sri Lankan citizenship. As a group of stateless persons they were subjected to various disabilities in their everyday life, especially in their dealings with the government. A good example is selection for government jobs. Gazette notifications inviting applications for vacant positions in the public service stipulated that the applicant must provide proof of citizenship of Sri Lanka by descent or registration. This effectively kept them out of jobs in the public service. Deprived of citizenship and all other accompanying rights, estate workers became a community under siege with little access to justice or redress for their grievances. Thus freedom from colonialism instead of leading to greater fulfilment of the aspirations of the estate workers, only made their position infinitely worse. Despite all the odds, a tiny percentage of them succeeded in obtaining citizenship of the country under the provisions of an act passed in 1949. However, this legislation was so restrictive that as of 1964 only 164,000 were able to gain citizenship under it and they too were categorized as citizens by registration. Thus, Sri Lanka became one of the few countries in the world that upheld two different types of citizenship, citizenship by descent and citizenship by registration.

Deprivation of citizenship rights and the denial of the right to vote at National and Local Government Elections precluded Tamils from participation in the country's mainstream politics for almost four decades until these rights were restored to them in 1988. The denial of citizenship rights had serious consequences on them as individuals and as a community. It marginalized them economically and politically. At the time of independence the estate workers were already one of the most underprivileged groups on the island and the continued denial of political rights led to the deprivation of economic and social rights as well. It denied them access to government welfare programmes. It also had negative consequences for their employment and training, as non-citizens were not allowed in the public sector and semi-governmental organizations. Even private sector employment was hard to find, as private employers also conformed to government policy. Civil and political rights, particularly the right to political representation, flow from the enjoyment of citizenship rights. By the loss of citizenship rights they also lost the right to parliamentary representation. This is well brought out in the following example. In the first parliamentary elections after independence when they enjoyed voting rights they were able to return seven members to the Parliament and also influence decisions in 20 other electorates. As against this, the denial of voting rights in 1949 left them with no elected representatives in the Parliament. Their non-representation in Parliament and at the local government institutions prevented them from participating as equal citizens in the main development process going on in the country. Without political representation they had to be content with being mere onlookers while the rest of Sri Lankan society was making rapid strides in social development. This invariably made it difficult for them to escape from their underprivileged position. Between 1960 and 1977, they had just one solitary Member of Parliament and it was only after the grant of citizenship in 1988 that they were able to elect nine members to represent their interests. However, in the 1994 parliamentary elections this number was reduced to five primarily due to leadership rivalries among the political (or rather, trade union) organisations that claimed to represent their interests. In the most recent elections, because of the unity forged among some of these organizations, they were able to secure eight seats.

In the absence of political power through the electoral system they came to rely heavily on trade unions as their sole representatives for ensuring their rights and needs. Membership in these unions was based more on their ethnic status as Estate Tamils rather than their status as exploited workers.[9] This, in turn, reinforced the already existing perception among some sections of the majority community that these people were aliens to the country, and this perception was shared even by some radical elements in the country like the Janatha Vimukthi Peramuna (JVP) or the People's Liberation Front, which claimed to liberate people from the capitalist exploiters. In spite of the fact that the overwhelming majority of the estate workers were proletariats in the true sense of the term, the JVP identified estate labour as part of an Indian expansionist drive and viewed them as a reactionary group rather than as a revolutionary force. They further argued that national economic emancipation could be achieved only by expropriating and closing the foreign owned plantations and turning over the land to Sinhalese villagers for growing food crops. In the light of this, it is not surprising that the land reform measures that paved the way for the takeover of much of the plantation lands were introduced soon after the JVP Insurgency of 1971.

Nationalization of Estates and Communal Violence against Tamils

The second development to seriously affect these workers were the land reform measures of the early 1970s. These resulted not only in the takeover of large foreign-owned plantations but also those owned by nationals exceeding an area of 20 hectares (or 50 acres). The latter category of lands were mostly located in the mid-grown tea areas where estates and traditional Sinhala villages are situated in close proximity to each other. The post-reform institutional arrangements introduced for managing these lands aimed at promoting cooperative or collective forms of agricultural production there. The Tamil workers resident on these estates, because of their status as non-citizens, found themselves ineligible to become members of these cooperatives as the laws governing membership of cooperatives in the country required one to be a citizen of the country. This led to the expulsion of a large number of these workers who failed to gain membership of the cooperatives that were set up to manage these lands. Many of them simply got evicted from the lands on which they had lived and worked for three to four generations. Such eviction was also accompanied on some estates by threats and actual physical violence against them. Sinhalese villagers, encouraged by local political leaders, often looted them of their meagre possessions. The eviction of Tamil workers was justified on the grounds that the British rulers had stolen these lands that belonged to the Sinhala villagers more than a century ago to open the plantations. Such evictions and attacks, in fact, marked the beginning of the ethnic violence against these people which became a common feature in the post-nationalization period. Hitherto, they had remained insulated from the tensions and physical attacks on Tamils that began in 1956 with the enactment of the Official Language Act (the Sinhala Only Act of 1956). But with the nationalization of the estates they became exposed to ethnic violence and physical danger. During the communal violence of 1977, Estate Tamils became victims of pogroms in many areas. Since then, there have been several rounds of organised and unorganised attacks on them, often as a reaction to the conflict in the north. The 1977 attacks were followed by larger scale attacks on some estates in the southern parts of the country in 1981. This seems to have been the backlash to racial clashes in the Eastern Province. The July 1983 riots were more widespread, covering many estate areas as well. Sporadic attacks have also taken place on individual estates, as happened on an estate in the Ratnapura district in September 1998. The line rooms of 300 Tamil families were burned and destroyed as revenge for the stabbing to death of two Sinhalese youths allegedly by Estate Tamil youths over some private dispute. Similarly, large scale riots and destruction took place in Talawakelle and Hatton areas soon after the massacre of 26 Tamil inmates in a detention camp (Bindunuwewa Camp) which included two detainees from estates in the Talawakelle area.[10] In all these hostile activities, the worst affected was the small group of Estate Tamils who had ventured out of estate employment and were living in villages and towns.

ETHNIC CONFLICT AND ESTATE TAMILS

The third development that has had serious repercussions is the ethnic conflict between the majority Sinhalese and the Sri Lankan Tamils. The ethnic conflict in its present form (a militant secessionist movement) marked the culmination of a process of estrangement of relations between the Sinhalese and the Sri Lankan Tamils over power-sharing since independence. The intensification of grievances of the Sri Lankan Tamils eventually led to the demand for a separate state and an armed struggle to achieve it. Some of the grievances of the Sri Lankan Tamils, such as discrimination against official use of the Tamil language and in the distribution of economic opportunities, are shared by the Indian Tamil community. In 1977, the killing of 13 Sinhala soldiers in Jaffna by Tamil militants led to the outbreak of countrywide violence against Tamils. The ethnic conflict escalated after 1977 and took the form of an armed struggle to set up a separate state in the north and east of the country. The prolonged ethnic conflict and the ongoing civil war have had their spillover effects on the Estate Tamils, who support neither of the parties involved in the conflict. The Estate Tamils have been made unwilling participants in the conflict and have become the target of Sinhala chauvinists simply because of their Tamil identity. Furthermore, in the name of national security Estate Tamil youths are often taken into custody by security forces on mere suspicion of having links with the northern Tamil militants. These people also bear the brunt of official discrimination, harassment at checkpoints on the roads leading up to the hill country and to searches and suspicion if they happen to live outside the plantations, and particularly in big towns such as Colombo and Kandy. The estate youth become particularly liable to arrest and detention as they lack appropriate documentation such as an official identity card (ID). On the other hand, they experience difficulties in obtaining IDs since this requires the submission of their birth certificates. In many estates, documents relating to births maintained by estate management have been destroyed during periodic bouts of ethnic violence. Many youths without IDs have been taken into custody and kept for long periods without trial and are also subjected to torture. Having remained in prisons and detention camps for several years some of them have staged hunger strikes in recent months, demanding that they be either charged and produced before the courts or released if there are no specific charges against them.

CONTINUING PROBLEMS FOR TAMIL ESTATE WORKERS

Despite the violence, the community has been able to improve its status over the past 10 years. The key development was the restoration of citizenship rights to the majority in the late 1980s. It has helped them to strengthen their position as a minority group, though the community's citizenship problem is yet to be resolved fully. At the same time, there are many areas where they are lagging behind other communities, particularly in tertiary and technical education and job recruitment (specially in the public sector), and land distribution. And of course, security is a crucial area of concern to them.

There has been a considerable improvement in the primary and junior secondary level of education of the estate children in recent years. However, the acute shortage of qualified teachers to teach subjects such as science and mathematics in the Tamil medium in the area schools is a serious drawback. Most secondary school students fail the General Certificate of Education, Ordinary Level (GCE O/L) examination because of their inability to secure passing marks in science and mathematics. Since a passing marks in the GCE O/L examination is the minimum requirement for any post-secondary education—General, Technical or Professional, very few of these children pursue their education beyond GCE O/L. The number pursuing post-secondary education is below 1 per cent of the cohort of children who enter the primary cycle.

Technical and vocational education is another area in which they seriously lag behind. An increasing number of students who study up to the O/L, but fail to complete that examination, drop out of schools. Unlike their parents, they do not wish to become estate workers and aspire to a job with higher status and dignity. Unfortunately, they find that they are not adequately qualified academically, technically or professionally. Even if they possess all the necessary qualifications and training they often face ethnic discrimination in the selection process. This has resulted in the under-representation of Estate Tamils in the public services and the semi-government sector. Many of the government service jobs in the estate areas, such as the police, post office, the cooperative society and the bus service are staffed with Sinhala officers while the estate youth remain unemployed. In the past, youth unemployment in the estate sector was the lowest compared to those in the urban and rural sectors. While this situation is improving now, unemployment remains a serious problem among estate youth.

Land distribution is another area in which they face serious discrimination. In the colonization schemes, through which new settlements are set up on tea Estates, the Estate Tamils are deliberately overlooked. In some cases, estate workers have had to move out of their homes in order to make room for such settlements. Land being an important source of economic activity in Sri Lanka, their exclusion from land settlement schemes acts as a serious drawback to their development.

Security is also an area of vital concern. They have suffered a great deal due to ethnic riots on numerous occasions. Killing, looting and arson have destroyed the future of many estate worker families. Even when they want to settle outside the estates, they are compelled to choose the place for such settlement with extreme caution as some areas are considered unsafe for them. Still worse is the insecurity they face even inside the estates, where they are subject to occasional attacks. (See description of Tamil migrants in Mahaiyawa slum in Sri Ranjith's chapter—Eds)

Youth unemployment, lack of socio-economic mobility, low recruitment to the public service, harassment by the security forces and frequent communal riots, both inside and outside estates, are creating an explosive situation among the estate youth. If meaningful steps are not taken to improve the youths' life prospects, the emergence of youth militancy on the plantations in the near future will be inevitable.

NOTES

1. World Bank, *Sri Lanka Country Brief*, 2000.
2. The Human Development Index is made up of three indicators: long life, educational level and low-levels of infant mortality. See UNDP, National Development Report, Sri Lanka, 1998.
3. Ministry of Health and Women's Affairs, Population Information Centre, *Population Statistics of Sri Lanka*, 1990. And Ministry of Health, *Annual Health Bulletin*, 1997, Colombo.
4. Central Bank of Sri Lanka, *Consumer Finance and Socio-Economic Survey Report*, 1996/97.
5. Valentine Daniel, *Three Dispositions Toward the Past: One Sinhala and Two Tamils*, Colombo: The National Library of Sri Lanka, 1992.
6. D. Bass, *A History of Ethnic Conflict in Sri Lanka: Recollection, Re-interpretation and Reconciliation: The Estate Tamils*, 2000 (Mimeograph).

7. G. Beckford, *Persistent Poverty: Underdevelopment in Plantation Economies of the Third World*, New York: Oxford University Press, 1972.
8. S. Bastian, 'Plantation Labour in a Changing Context', in C. Abeysekara and N. Gunasinghe (Eds), *Facets of Ethnicity in Sri Lanka*, Colombo: Social Scientists Association, 1987, pp. 171–91.
9. Charles Kemp, 'Unions in Plantations: Do Basic Needs matter?' IDS Bulletin, Vol. 18, No. 2, 1987.
10. Programme Support Group, 'Economic and Social Impact of Privatisation of Plantations', Colombo: *Satyodaya Bulletin*, No. 187, May 2000.

10

Satyodaya, NGOs and Civil Society: Mobilizing across Class and Community in a Globalizing Economy

PAUL CASPERSZ

Sri Lanka has sometimes been called the Paradise Island. From the early 1970s, however, there has been so much unrest, conflict, violence and war that Paradise has nearly gone up in flames. Within its area of 65,610 square kilometres, in a total population of around 20 million, the Sinhalese comprise 74 per cent, the Tamils 18 per cent, Moors and Malays 7 per cent, while there are also a small number of Burghers (descendants over several generations of the Portuguese and Dutch with a generous admixture of Sinhalese and Tamil genetic influences) and others. Religionwise, the Buddhists are 69.5 per cent, Hindus 15.5 per cent, while the Muslims and the Christians account, nearly equally, for the remaining 15 per cent. Languagewise, Sinhala is the mother tongue of the majority, Tamil of the Tamils and most of the Moors, while about 5 per cent of the Sinhala and Tamil-speaking people also use English at home, and a few hundreds would be trilingual. No wonder therefore that Sri Lankan society has been described as a microcosm, a mosaic, a palimpsest—ethnic, religious and linguistic.

The Case of Satyodaya

Living in such a diverse society, and fully aware of the problems of inter-group cooperation, on 11 February 1972 we formed a group which came to be called Satyodaya (from *satya*, truth and *udaya*, dawn). Our primary purpose was to share ideas and to attempt to understand the reality following the trauma of the 1971 JVP insurrection, which made clear that violence also existed on our island. Only secondarily and indirectly did we seek to change the reality, which we tried to analyze. The thought of an organization of any kind was still over the hills and far away. On that day in 1972, we met for the traditional boiling of milk in a clay pot. The milk has to boil over so as to augur a prosperous future. But on that morning as one of us kept stoking the fire, there were beads of perspiration on some of our faces. Was there too little fire or too little milk? Was the pot too deep? Would it ever overflow? If not, the omens would be bad, our friends whispered to one another. Finally, however, with much encouragement from the stoker, the milk finally boiled over.

This was much like a prophecy of the next 30 years: hope in the midst of struggle, doubt, anxiety, pain of mind and heart—at first, concerning the Tamil plantation people, the inter-ethnic, countrywide conflict; today, concerning the future of donor-partner funding—but also great joy and a spirit of camaraderie in the Satyodaya community. Yet we have no illusions. The struggle will go on until the Dawn of Truth rises again, never more to fade.

On 11 February 1972 there was no thought of social action, but only, as the name Satyodaya indicates, of social research. In July that year came the first Law of Land Reform, which began the process of nationalizing the tea and rubber plantations, the best known of which were British-owned. The process was welcomed as an anti-imperialist and socialist measure. As the then Trotskyite Minister of Finance said, it was incongruous that the 'commanding heights of the economy' of an independent country should continue to be managed by those who had exercised unwelcome colonial power over it. In its implementation, however, the law came to be racialist and directed against the Tamil plantation workers. These workers had been brought into the country from the impoverished villages of South India in the nineteenth century to work on the plantations of coffee and later of tea and rubber. 'We have sent the white men away', the mobs, instigated by scheming politicians, shrieked at the hapless Tamil workers, 'now out you go too'. It was then that Satyodaya felt compelled to take notice of what was happening on the plantations and to the plantation workers.

I distinctly recall the day—a turning point in my life—when I went one evening at dusk with a Tamil university undergraduate student to interview the Tamil plantation workers who, often driven out of the estates with hardly a day's notice, were roaming the streets of the big towns, seeking shelter and what food they could find, even in refuse bins. At the end of about three hours of interviews, we met a Tamil worker, about 35 years old, who was very vocal. We decided that we would take him to a small teashop to talk with him and seek relief from our own weariness and hunger. It was also a period of extraordinary food shortage in the country and good food was hard to find in the small shops. As soon as the Muslim shop-owner saw us, he said, 'We don't have food for you two but we can satisfy the Tamil man.' 'How's that?' we asked. The man said, 'We have only *rotti* (a cheap local flour cake) and some of the morning's potato curry.' 'That's just what we want,' we replied, and the three of us took our seats at a table in the teashop. My undergraduate friend and I were ravenously hungry and thirsty, but we both noticed that the *rotti* was stale and the potato curry rancid. Our Tamil guest ate his portion very fast and noticed that we were pushing our food away, sipping only the boiling hot black tea. 'Why aren't you eating?' he asked us. 'We are not really hungry,' we lied to him, 'we only wanted a cup of tea.' 'Then may I take your portions to my wife and my three children who are in the *kovil* (Hindu temple) premises for the night? They haven't had a morsel for the past two days.' We of course readily consented. I can still remember the almost religious fervour with which he silently folded the four ends of the banana leaf over the *rotti* and the potato curry to take it away to his family. To this day I am haunted by the picture of that man folding the leaf over what was to be for his wife and children a festive meal. There is no turning away from the struggle for justice as long as the incident remains in my memory.

So Satyodaya was forced into action to mitigate the sufferings of the plantation workers and to work with them to secure their human rights. With the beginnings of social action came the need for organization. But even then it was keenly felt that the organizational aspects of Satyodaya should be as little organizational as possible and should always be flexible, built more on trust than on rules. Rather than being listed as an NGO, Satyodaya strove and still strives to be a people's organization, or indeed not an organization, but a movement participating in the achievement of national and international justice and equality.

In 1974 Satyodaya gave birth to the Coordinating Secretariat for Plantation Areas (CSPA), a federation of organizations and groups that after the horrors of 1972 began to show concern for the Tamil plantation people. Then came 1977, with its fearful all-island communal riots. Satyodaya led the way in providing support and relief to the Tamil victims. A good friend cabled Oxfam: 'Send Satyodaya funds. It is working for the victims without funds.' Oxfam immediately sent £5,000 (which today would be worth £50,000 at least). With our idealistic volunteers and idealistic outside support, Satyodaya helped about 10,000 estate families who had lost everything, or nearly everything, they possessed. Satyodaya and CSPA pondered over what had to be done. Finally, they in turn gave birth to the Movement for Inter-Racial Justice and Equality (MIRJE). Satyodaya changed from being only a socialist research centre to being a centre for social action as well.

At its birth, on 11 February 1972, Satyodaya hadn't once considered the possibility of obtaining aid from foreign donor agencies. But the money from Oxfam was the beginning of the Satyodaya–Donor relationship. There was idealism in both places, inspired by the post-war emergence of the Third World, the Second Vatican Council and the radicalism of the World Council of Churches. The idealism remains at Satyodaya. What remains of it in the donor agencies is a question we shall address later.

Over the past 30 years Satyodaya has confronted three main problems in its work: (*a*) the inter-ethnic, which grew ever more intractable with each passing day (until December 2001, when signs of a possible peace process began to appear); (*b*) poverty, which is the lot of the majority and is aggravated by the current Structural Adjustment policies imposed on the country (a small class of the rich, has, however, never had it so good, so that the problem of the poor cannot be taken on in isolation from the problem of the rich); (*c*) the resultant social disintegration of values, family life and ordinary social intercourse.

The Constitution of Satyodaya sets out its chief objectives as follows:

- to strive to create peace-founded-on-justice among the people;

- to strive to promote the cultural, economic, civic and social activities of the people living on the plantations, in the villages and in disadvantaged urban areas;
- believing that Sri Lanka is, and should continue to be, a plural society, to strive for concord and mutual understanding;
- to strive to eradicate unjust and unfair divisions and cleavages that exist among the people.

The history of Satyodaya's fieldwork divides into three phases: (*i*) until 1975, when Satyodaya's objective was to work for the people; (*ii*) from 1975 to 1995 when it sought to work with the people; (*iii*) from 1995 onwards, the people take the lead and work with Satyodaya.

The transition from the first phase to the second phase took place because of a situation that is worth recording. We began the first of our social work programmes with a health clinic run by a committed doctor in a poor urban area (an area also written about in Chapter 7), Mahaiyawa. Many children were affected by scabies. Our doctor prescribed the standard scabies lotion. Within three days the scabies disappeared, only to appear again in about two weeks. We discovered that this was because, as the cure proceeded, the children wore the same infected clothes. So, in discussions with the people, we gradually discontinued the scabies lotion and instead gave each family a large piece of washing soap, instructing them to wash the clothes often as the cure proceeded and to dry them in bright sunlight. Satyodaya thought that it had to do its work for the people with the people, and scabies has since ceased to be a problem in the community.

As the self-confidence of the plantation workers, the villagers and the urban poor grew, we had to review our self-understanding and our relations with them. This led to the third phase, which is the one now in progress. The people take first place and seek our assistance only when they think it is necessary. The programmes are theirs. There is no name board to indicate that Satyodaya is around. As the present leader of Satyodaya says, 'We have to be the doormat on which the People tread in order to achieve their own liberation.' He goes on to say: 'Even the doormat is too good for us. Let us be the dust below the doormat.' Our success comes whenever the People rise up and say, as Lao-tse said in 700 BC, 'We have done it ourselves!'

But all action is located within a framework of understanding, which carries us back to the original, primary aim of Satyodaya—'seeking to understand reality'. Our understanding has changed from 1972 and we now see the society and, necessarily, the world within which we have to act as being different. The world has changed since 1972 and so we must change our tactics and strategy.

A FRACTURED WORLD

We live in a fractured world. There seemed to be grounds for hope of a new and better world as nations began to be formed five or six centuries ago out of the coming together of local communities and as our ancestors began to understand and direct the forces of nature and harness them to the tasks of what we now call development. There is abundant evidence that, so far as the great majority of our race is concerned, we have largely not succeeded.

Economically, despite the accelerating pace of production and the sober statistics that that there are now in the world more than sufficient resources to feed, clothe and house every woman, man and child of the 6 billion who now live on our planet, we all know that there are millions of people, hungry, homeless and improperly clad. In our Third World countries, where more than one billion people live far below the lowest poverty line that can be drawn, we do not have far to go to see with our own eyes the evidence that burns into our hearts and minds as we walk along our streets.

Educationally, we have reached high levels of literacy: the newspapers, radio, TV, telephone and computer are everywhere. Yet, though we have made giant strides forward in knowledge, we have stagnated in wisdom and also nearly lost all the wisdom of our ancient forebears. Religion remains a force all over the world, and especially in the Third World, but its formal institutions and its hierarchies are distanced from the rank and file and are in many places compromised and discredited and seem to have lost forever the prophetic voice of truth and justice. The nuclearization of the family is demanded by industrialization and modernization but the process of nuclearization has been left completely to laissez-faire and, where it has taken place, it seems impossible to salvage the positive communitarian values of the extended family system.

The events that took place in the United States of America on 11 September 2001—though in themselves flea bites in comparison with Hiroshima, Nagasaki, Rwanda, Iraq—and also their aftermath show up our world as politically and morally not just immature but nearly bankrupt. Our markets are flooded with medicines that cure and other things that prevent disease and even postpone death. But there are millions even in the rich countries who cannot afford to buy these medicines and other things and even those who do buy them do not seem to be happier, healthier, or less anxious. Over continents and oceans there is a vast network of travel facilities, transport and quick communication and yet our human family is more sharply divided than ever, and we understand one another less and less. The bureaucracy seems more and more geared to serve the interests of the minority rich, not those of the overwhelming majority who are poor; in many places of the world the bureaucracy is dilatory, inefficient and corrupt.

CIVIL SOCIETY AND NON-GOVERNMENTAL ORGANIZATIONS IN A FRACTURED WORLD

When the formal structures of society—the economic, political, religious, educational, familial, and bureaucratic—have not delivered, or delivered only in a broken, haphazard and very unequal fashion, it seems to be time to give the fluid institutions of civil society an opportunity to enter vitally into the arena. In point of time they antedate the formal social structures by several millennia. They need to be brought back, this time consciously and deliberately.

Sri Lanka—one of the smaller countries among the nearly 200 listed in UN publications, yet one that held much promise when it received constitutional independence in 1948 (our benchmark for this study)—is also prey to this fracture. In it too, civil society may yet play a role, not indeed to replace or weaken formal social structures, but to support them and render them more compliant with the legitimate demands and aspirations of the citizens.

Prominent in civil society today are the NGOs. The trouble is that both terms, 'civil society' and 'NGOs', are hazy. They are not completely defined and are, it would seem, inescapably and inherently fluid. While they cover some of the same things for all who use the terms and think about them, they also cover some different things for different persons. For Michael Edwards, civil society refers to 'all organizations and associations between the family and the State with the exception of business'.[1] In the same journal Jude Howell of the Institute of Development Studies in Sussex does not quite agree. She says civil society can be defined as the 'arena of association located between the State and the household' (thus far agreeing with Edwards) but then goes on to include in civil society formal organizations such as religious bodies, chambers of commerce, trade unions, NGOs and trade associations as well as informal types of associations such as mutual support groups and burial societies.[2] Other writers locate civil society between the State and the market and are not sure where the family fits in. The difficulties of definition are perhaps inherent in the concepts. However, though civil society, at least in the present state of the social sciences, cannot be precisely defined, it may be described.

Civil Society then appears to be that part of society which lies outside, beyond, or in the interstices of, the following societies which are also part of society:

- political society or the State with its structures of parliaments, parties, the courts of law, electoral processes and all that concerns the shaping and sharing of political power;
- economic society or the market institutions whether big or small, public or private, businesses and firms, stock exchanges, banks, production and product distribution, both within each nation and between nations;
- religious society consisting of churches (in Sri Lanka, Buddhist, Hindu, Christian and Muslim and minor others), with their multifarious chains of command and rituals;
- educational society with its networks of primary, secondary and tertiary schools, formal and informal, government-controlled, government-assisted or private;
- family-based society with its networks of intra- and inter-familial relationships.

In other words, the prevalent analysis of society has methodologically isolated the organized structures of politics, economics, religion, education and family. It has lost sight of the larger whole of society and the fractions that remain outside of the above analytical categories, that is, 'Civil Society'.

Civil society is therefore that which lies outside and beyond identifiable and established societal structures or institutions, while being in itself an all-pervasive, yet elusive and often invisible category, functioning on the broad fringes of all the established social structures outlined above, yet profoundly influenced by and influencing (as we shall see, for good or for evil) politics, economics, religion, the family and the school. Society (with a capital S) is more than the state; it is more than the market and the churches, more than academia, more than the family, nuclear or extended. 'More than' does not mean 'more important than', 'more powerful than', 'more beneficial than', or indeed 'more pernicious or flawed than' all the formal social institutions outlined. Yet its 'more than' character is essential to an understanding of the concept of civil society and of the role and practices of civil society in Society. This 'more than' character determines the nature of its role and of its practices and of its relationship with the established social institutions of Society.

However, one has to remember that all that has been hitherto stated is in the area of the social, not of the exact, sciences. Moreover, it is in that area of life which is imprecise, uncertain, changing. Hence it is not always possible—in a holistic approach it is not even always and absolutely necessary—to draw a distinction between the organized structures of Society and civil society. In contemporary Sri Lanka, for example, there are the 'four Ys', namely, the Young Men's Christian Association (YMCA) and, taking their lead from the YMCA, which was the first Y in the field, there are the YMBA, YMHA and YMMA for the Buddhists, the Hindus and the Muslims respectively. Are these Ys to be considered and analyzed as part of the organized religious structure of society or do they operate in the much less formalized sector of civil society? The question may be answered either way, or the Ys may be considered as fulfilling functions both in the religious institution of the church and in civil society.

Within civil society there are also non-governmental organizations, some more, some less, formally constituted, with rules and customs and methods of procedure, and often with a written statement of aims and objectives which may be called a constitution. Non-governmental is not a fortunate phrase. The term implies rigidity of organization and this connotes at least some degree of formal establishment, about which some NGOs would be uncomfortable, to say the least. These NGOs believe that flexibility is of the essence. Without flexibility, the NGO cannot react sensitively to the needs of the people for whom it exists and with whom it seeks to establish partnership. The term 'non-governmental' does not capture the originality of the NGO's efforts in discovering needs and responding to them. Neither does it in any way express the rich diversity of the activities of the NGO as it seeks to exercise its mission in its fieldwork areas. Would it not be better therefore to speak of citizens' non-formal, optional organizations for social service and, taking the goals of some NGOs further, for social action and social change. Membership of the State is formal and obligatory: one is obliged to have citizenship in one state (in rare cases, in two or more states), whereas belonging to a non-governmental organization is informal and optional: one can change at will from being a member or a participant to being a non-member or a non-participant. The term 'non-governmental' refers to only this one characteristic of the organization and does not indicate other equally important characteristics.

On the other hand, the term 'non-governmental' may imply too much, insofar as it connotes independence from the government. In reality, the independence is far from complete. Governments may require, as in Sri Lanka, that NGOs be registered officially, have a name and a number. Furthermore, as James Petras (among others) has pointed out:

> In reality, non-governmental organizations are not non-governmental. They receive funds from overseas governments or work as private subcontractors of local governments. Presently they openly collaborate with governmental agencies at home or overseas.[3]

Petras writes in 1997 of NGOs in Latin America. In Sri Lanka the local NGOs do not (yet) receive funds from the government, but their overseas donors do, from their own home governments or from multinational financial institutions.

NGOs function within civil society, but there are hundreds of other organizations in civil society which are not called, and which do not call themselves, NGOs. Such are funeral societies, which fulfil very useful functions in Sri Lankan communities, societies of alcoholics who want to give up the addiction, literary societies, sports clubs, reading clubs. It may indeed be correct to define a non-governmental organization as an organization existing and functioning in civil society which calls itself a non-governmental organization. Those that do not call themselves NGOs or, indeed, anything at all but yet operate outside the formal structures of society, would be civil society organizations or CSOs.

NGO ORIGINS IN SRI LANKA

Vijitha Fernando and J. Henry de Mel seek the origin of the contemporary NGO in Sri Lanka in various late nineteenth-century and pre-1939 forms of social action groups: the temperance movement with its strong anti-colonial, nationalist bent, the beginnings of the movement of organized labour with the first ever industrial strike—that of the printers—in 1893, the beginnings of the cooperative movement in the early twentieth century, the establishment of Christian and Buddhist, and later also of Hindu and Muslim associations to aid young persons, and the formation of Friendly Societies, Provident Societies and Benevolent Associations, the School for the Deaf and Blind (1912), the Ceylon Social League (1914), the Mallika Nivasa Samitiya (1914) and the Sri Lankadara Society (1922). And then there were those linked to international organizations such as the St. John Ambulance Brigade, the Boy Scout and Girl Guides Movements, the Red Cross Society—all of which saw the light of day in the first four decades of the twentieth century.

However, the emergence of the contemporary NGO had to await the inauguration of the modern development era, which was itself the direct result of various factors. It is sometimes stated by western authors that the development era was launched by US President Truman in 1949 and that the term 'development' as it is used (and misused) today became current around this time. But this is to forget the role played by the struggles and the demands for the independence of the colonies and dependencies of the western powers. These acquired irresistible intensity in India—the largest of the dependencies—many years before World War II began. Foremost in this struggle was Mahatma Gandhi in India. He was convinced of two things. First, that the millions of Indians, after long years of colonial rule, needed release from the bondage of deprivation and of subservience and second, that this release would not come from an imitation of the process of development as it had taken place in the West but from the innate energies and resources of the Indian people themselves. Gandhi and other Indian leaders were actively undertaking village development programmes long before Truman was elected President. Once Mahatma Gandhi and Jawaharlal Nehru had wrested independence from Britain, there was to be no respite in the demand for liberation from colonialism and poverty and for development all over the Third World.

The second factor stimulating the call for development was the rapid growth of population leading to the assertion of people's rights and people power. The population of India (when India, Pakistan and Bangladesh were still one country) in 1941 was 319 million, that of Sri Lanka in the last pre-independence census was only 6.7 million. As of 2002, Sri Lanka had a population of 19 million; the population of India exceeds one billion and that of Pakistan and Bangladesh each exceeds 130 million. To cope with the burgeoning population, development in all fields, and especially in the fields of education, health and employment, was required.

The third factor was the internationalization of the world following the end of the War. Development-oriented agencies—the United Nations itself and its allied bodies—were set up. In 1948, the UN issued the famous Universal Declaration of Human Rights. Strongly anchored in the liberal tradition of western political philosophy, Articles 1–21 of the Declaration enunciated the civil and political rights of the citizen. Only in Articles 22–27 who there an enunciation of participatory, social, economic and cultural rights. These rights were probably an afterthought of the framers of the Declaration, but it is clear today—as it was to countries such as Yugoslavia which refused assent to the Declaration—that social and economic rights as well as the rights of whole peoples to development will have to be given pride of place in any future enunciation of universal human rights.

It was in this climate, of the near universal recognition of the interdependence of all countries in the area of development, that the Donor International NGOs were born. However, it needs to be remembered that the earliest agencies—which were probably CARE and Oxfam—began to turn their thoughts to the development of today's Third World only after their tasks of welfare and post-war emergency relief were seen as no longer necessary in Europe.

What then to do with their new-found financial resources and the paid staff engaged to disburse them but to turn towards the countries of the Third World? Following in the footsteps of CARE and Oxfam, and so as to prevent a monopoly in development aid, other agencies came up. By the 1970s their number was in thousands. The Development NGO industry, both in the donor and recipient countries, got into full swing. In the 1970s many donors actually went out touting for takers in the Third World, much of which was still—as Satyodaya was from 1972 to 1975—as innocent as babes in the wood in the matter of private foreign development grant aid. It did not take long, of course, for receivers to open their welcoming arms to donors. Receiver NGOs were born and began to grow.

DEVELOPMENT NGOs IN SRI LANKA

Two pioneering studies appeared in Sri Lanka in 1991, which attempted to chart the origin and growth of development NGOs on the island: *Non-Government Organizations (NGOs) in Sri Lanka: An Introduction*, by Vijitha Fernando and J. Henry de Mel, sponsored by Private Agencies Collaborating Together (PACT), New York and *Development NGOs of Sri Lanka: A Directory*, by Sunimal Fernando and Richard Dias, sponsored by Initiative in Research and Education (IRED). The participants in the two studies do not appear to have been aware of each other's efforts; if they were, Sri Lanka may have had a reliable documentary on the origin and rise of the NGOs in the country. So the findings in the two studies are not final, but tentative.

In all, Fernando and Dias list 65 development NGOs for the period organized before 1970, and 228 for the post-1970 period. To Fernando and de Mel what seems to have been a sufficient criterion for an organization to be called a development NGO is some recognition of socio-economic development by the organization. They look at three factors: some formal recognition of the organization as an organization; some explicit concern for socio-economomc development; and, most significant of all, especially after 1970, linkage of the organization with broadly similar organizations outside the country, the linkage being sealed by foreign funding for at least a part of the developmental activities of the organization. Indeed, foreign funding—total or partial—seems to have been a reason for the origin and growth of Sri Lankan development NGOs after 1970 and, more markedly, after 1977.

A cynical reading of the situation may even be that the availability of foreign funding was not a reason, but the *only* reason for the rise of new NGOs after 1970. Such a reading, however, pays scant respect to the influence of a certain idealism of justice and equality in the founders and the first companions of development NGOs both in the West and in the South. In the West there was a spur to idealism due to a certain sense of guilt over the former vast western colonial empires. In the South, the idealism came from a commitment to socialist humanism and, for those Southern NGOs with Christian connections, there was the influence of the growing radicalism of various Christian churches after the setting up of the World Council of Churches and from the time of the Second Vatican Council. These factors, however, call for further investigation, while such investigation may also shed light on the weakening of the idealism when the 1970s and the 1980s yielded place to the politically unipolar 1990s.

THE IMPORTANCE OF NGOs AND CSOs

The number of civil society organizations or CSOs is legion, and would by their very nature be so in all countries, with the possible exception of totalitarian countries where the State suffers no extra-state organization to exist in society. While it would be virtually impossible to obtain even an approximately accurate count of all CSOs in any country and in the world, it ought to be much easier to obtain a fairly exact count of all NGOs in a country if NGOs are obliged to seek registration in some official body. But not all NGOs have sought registration. In India and Sri Lanka a fair proportion of NGOs are simply not interested in registration because it is felt that such registration brings no noticeable benefits and indeed may lead to interference by state authorities in the affairs of the NGOs. In India some registered NGOs do obtain government aid for their projects on the condition that they submit official narrative and financial reports to the government.

The importance of civil society, composed of both CSOs and NGOs, lies in the capacity of these organizations to address the caring needs and functions of Society. It is now universally accepted that these caring functions are most useful and are even necessary, especially since they are today so threatened by the forces of industrialization, modernization and economic globalization. Social power has shifted from small, caring, human communities to political cabinets distanced from the people and to economic boardrooms of transnational corporations and their local affiliates. Even in religious institutions power tends to be concentrated in a hierarchy to which the so-called common people are not allowed easy access. There is increasingly less personal contact between teacher and pupil in overcrowded classrooms. The nucleated family is often not able to extend the emotional support that individuals in the family seek and need and which were easily obtained in the extended families of the past. The former communities have broken up with the drifting of the young and enterprising to the large, bloated cities where life is not communitarian and sharing but individualist and competitive, no longer a matter of living but of grasping.

However, civil society is not uniformly and during all times and circumstances beneficial to Society, exerting a useful, supportive role in relation to the formal social structures of Society. It may also exercise a pernicious role. In the field of education, CSOs which are somewhat structured, and NGOs established for the purpose, may supplement or complement the work of the formal schools and colleges. So in Sri Lanka, there are NGOs that take on the task of remedial education for school dropouts, establish night schools for illiterate adults, conduct evening classes in mathematics, science and a second language, especially for plantation Tamil students whose schools are ill-equipped for the successful teaching of these subjects. But there are also groups of wealthy parents who in recent years have taken to the setting up of private schools for their children, charging very high fees which only the wealthy can pay. The schools are called international schools in order to attract the children of the affluent expatriate community (some of whom, indeed, belong to NGOs which have come to help the natives); they are established under the (profit-making) Companies Ordinance and so at the time of this writing are legally outside the control of the Ministry of Education; yet they, of course, receive the blessings of the World Bank, the International Monetary Fund and western embassies and high commissions, whose officials are invited to perform ritually at their prize-giving ceremonies and sports meets. It is not difficult to see these schools just as an outgrowth of civil society, but also as seedbeds of unjustifiable privilege, social divisions, jealousy and discontent. In the United States both pro-life and pro-abortion groups function as CSOs; one looks upon the other as pernicious and upon itself as uplifting the moral quality of society. The Ku Klux Klan in the United States, fascist skinhead anti-foreigner groups in European countries, racialist and religious fundamentalist groups in Asia, ethnically exclusive associations in Sri Lanka are examples of CSOs and NGOs that most people would think endanger peace and good neighbourliness in the nation and in the world.

TRUST AND CIVIL SOCIETY

In Sri Lanka there exist in many places among the poor and lower middle classes the *cheettu* groups: a certain number of women and men band together and decide that each one would contribute a fixed sum every month to a fixed pool, maintained by one person in the group whom everyone else recognizes as particularly capable and trustworthy; the entire monthly pool by the drawing of lots is made available each month to one member of the group, until every member has received the pool. The *cheettu* works on trust and the writer has hardly ever heard of a *cheettu* that collapsed midway. What is important for our present purposes is to note that the *cheettu* will not easily be accommodated by the formal economic structure of Society but is eagerly embraced by civil society. The banks and even registered cooperative societies may consider the *cheettu* system to be an unauthorized and unsafe intruder into their territory, but the *cheettu* members continue regardless, proud of the fact that the system works on mutual trust, which has little place in formal financial institutions. The latter look for collateral, and say no to trust.

Yet, trust is of immense importance for the moral and mental health of human society. It is the foundation of true community among human beings in any social unit, small or large. Where there is no trust, there may be aggregation, association, *gesellschaft*, but it is only trust that makes possible the union of minds and hearts, community, *gemeinschaft*. But how then do humans live together in modern industrialized societies? They live in association but not in community. Such societies will be viable and avoid explosion or implosion only to the extent that something is found to refashion and extend trust.

Civil society provides the opportunity for building trust in a way not available to the formal structures of society. It is in democratic developing countries which have an inter-ethnic population and face complex inter-ethnic socio-political situations that civil society is able to play an important role by calling into action the pressures of trust. In Sri Lanka it has been the case since universal franchise was introduced in 1931 that the majority ethnic group has always controlled the political processes of society. Though to a lesser extent, it is the majority ethnic group that has exercised power in the other formal social structures as well. The result has been social distrust in the body politic as a whole. If two candidates apply for the same post, one Sinhalese and the other Tamil, and if the Sinhalese is chosen for no other reason than that of better qualifications, the Tamil nearly always suspects that ethnic discrimination has determined the choice. Similarly, if the Tamil is selected, there is often inter-ethnic rancour and dissatisfaction. It is the organization of civil society that can avoid these inter-ethnic tensions by ensuring that the positions of control within the organization are shared equitably by the various ethnic groups in the country. With trust there follows social cohesion, which is indispensable for the social well-being of the entire country.

Civil Society and the State

Existing theory begins with a distinction between a strong state and a weak state. The former has well-organized and efficient service delivery systems; the latter lacks these, not entirely, but in important parts. Civil society exists in both strong and weak states but its role, and the expectations citizens have of it, are different as between the two States.

In a weak state, the NGOs of civil society were obliged to do, and did, so far as they could, nearly everything that the State had to do. This is so because in the weak state the service delivery systems are either non-existent or incapable and weak. The space occupied by the formal structures has yawning gaps and these are filled in as so far as possible by the CSOs and the NGOs.

These latter move in to provide homes and services for the aged and the disabled, free healthcare for the poor, extra tuition classes for children attending poorly staffed and inadequately equipped schools, various self-help community economic activities to compensate for low income and lack of full employment, recreation centres for poor families, and the like, all of which in the strong state are catered to by state institutions. A young Asian immigrant in Australia when asked why he no longer prayed to God as he did in his country of birth replied: 'God? But here in Australia Social Security is my God.'

Within weak states there is the very real danger that some organizations of civil society become so powerful and are so well funded that they may usurp the power of the State. James Petras, investigating the role of the NGOs vis-à-vis the State is trenchant in his criticism of the NGOs:

> By the early 1990s the more perceptive sectors of the neoliberal ruling classes realized that their policies were polarizing the society and provoking large-scale social discontent. Neoliberal politicians began to finance and promote a parallel strategy 'from below', 'grassroots' organizations with an anti-statist ideology ... to create a 'social cushion'. These organizations were financially dependent on neoliberal sources and were directly involved in competing with sociopolitical movements for the allegiance of local leaders and activist communities. By the 1990s these organizations, described as 'nongovernmental', numbered in the thousands and were receiving close to four billion dollars worldwide.[4]

The World Bank and the International Monetary Fund, often acting at the behest of the United States Treasury, are at no pains to conceal the fact that their goal is to promote a private enterprise-led, economically liberal, non-interventionist state and that they will cope with the problems of poverty, including the poverty created by their own structural adjustment and other programmes and projects, by the creation of safety nets. What better agencies to hold up the nets than the NGOs, both the donor NGOs of the north and the receiver NGOs of the south. Hence they have begun to invite these NGOs to be their 'partners in progress'. It is easy therefore to understand that any neo-liberal state whether in the north or in the south will welcome such NGOs. On the other hand, any state (though, outside Cuba, increasingly difficult to find) which has a socialist social order as its goal, will be wary of these NGOs and seek to control them.

The 'safety net' upheld by many well-funded NGOs all over the world is not the answer to problems of poverty and social deprivation. In fact their programmes of 'poverty alleviation' can only delay poverty eradication. So Pasha writes:

> Once the critical, if not primary, goal of economic development, the eradication of poverty now appears as a distant aspiration ... (As) the state internationalizes, the burden of poverty alleviation is increasingly placed on civil society, the latter being equated with the domain and activity of non-governmental organizations (NGOs). The emergence of the 'new poor' under structural adjustment has given NGOs a more legitimate role in a climate of public retrenchment ... (Yet) the stress on agents in civil society, notably NGOs, fails to tackle the question of structural inequality; the latter lies at the root of poverty.[5]

THE STATE, POLITICAL PARTIES AND CIVIL SOCIETY IN SRI LANKA

In Sri Lanka the relationship between the State and civil society changed with the formation of the development NGOs around 1970. Development—including human rights, women's rights, the creation of social and political awareness in the quest for employment and income—began to be pursued by NGOs in an organized manner after 1974. Some Sri Lankan NGOs began to forge links with donor NGOs in the West.

The development NGOs gradually came to be a force to reckon with. The State responded with Act No. 31, entitled the Voluntary Social Service Organizations (Registration and Supervision) Act. The Civil Rights Movement (Sri Lanka) had warned the Government against enactment of the law when the bill was proposed early in 1980 on the grounds that it was a 'gross and unprecedented violation of freedom of association'. Probably because of the criticism to which the bill (and later the act) was subjected, the government delayed the date of implementation of the act to 1 February 1982. What followed was that several NGOs obtained registration under the act, as much because of the stipulations of the act as because the donor NGOs increasingly required state recognition of the NGOs seeking assistance. In 1991, the Government went a step further by appointing a Presidential NGO Commission, empowered to investigate the role of all NGOs in the island, but dictated, so it was said, by the desire to harass the leader of one large development NGO (Sarvodaya), probably the largest in Asia. NGOs were ordered to submit the detailed Annual Accounts of the preceding three years, Annual Reports, Certificates of Registration, etc. However, the President of the Republic was assassinated on 1 May 1993 and no more was heard of the Commission.

RELATIONS BETWEEN DONOR NGOs AND RECEIVING NGOs

Many writers have laudably begun to be critical of the donor–receiver relationship. Riddell and Bebbington issued their report in 1995 on the subject of the relations between British donors and their southern partners.[6] The important aspects of the relationship that they then highlighted are today still open to question: the pitfalls of the relation for both donor and receiver, the 'reverse agenda' or the lessons that receivers can teach donors, and the constant tensions of the relationship. Michael Taylor, director of a large British NGO, gave his 1997 University of Bradford lecture on the relationship with the provocative title, 'Past their sell-by Date?'.[7] Taylor fears that the day of the donor NGO is gone, or is going. In place of the Rich Donor–Poor Receiver relationship he argues for international organization among equal players. Donor aid will disappear from the agenda and its place will be taken by actively promoted cooperation and solidarity among the peoples of the world. The rich countries need peaceful, plague- and famine-free, non–environmentally destructive, non-disruptive states throughout the world if they are going to continue to enjoy their riches. The makings of a common agenda require cooperation if the agenda is to be realized.

To a writer in the Third World, it is necessary to insist that even international cooperation needs to be carefully and truthfully calibrated in order for it to be what it says it is: cooperation among all nations, all of which have a stake in entering into and sustaining a cooperative relationship. Failing this, it will merely bring back the former unequal and unfair donor–recipient relationship in a thinly disguised form. And if genuine international cooperation is simply a pipe dream in an unjust world order, is it not action to change the world order that is the need of hour?

There follows what the writer wrote in 1996 as a background paper for a Consultation of Satyodaya's Donor-Partners with Satyodaya.

> The times are crucial. Southern NGOs have to decide whether they are going to be civil or political status quo promoting societies, as the growing NGO culture promoted by the World Bank is beginning to try to make them to be, or whether they are to be the catalysts of change in the national and international social order. Donor-Partners have to decide whether they are really ready to partner us in this great work both in their countries and in our own.
>
> I would indeed define Partnership as the joining together of Donor-Partners and Receiver-Partners with the objective of helping each other in the task of creating the New World Order in their own countries and worldwide.
>
> I am aware that, when the New World Order becomes a reality, both Donor-Partners and Receiver-Partners will be out of business. My answer to that is, let the NWO come, and then we shall see into what directions the partnership between South and North could go. In the partnership the Donor-Partners give funds. There is not the slightest doubt that Satyodaya can do its work because Donor-Partner funds are available.
>
> Yet, what I told Christian Aid at its annual Consultation in 1987 is, I think, still valid: 'History has much evidence to lead us to suspect that foreign aid is not indispensable for a whole people to rise. But the right kind of assistance at the right time may make the wheels of history turn earlier and faster.'

Hence, if we ask, 'Do the people need Satyodaya?' the answer would be an absolute 'No'. But relatively, that is, relative to their needs and their sufferings, 'Yes'. Similarly if we ask, 'Does Satyodaya need Helvetas or Norad or Oxfam?' The answer would be an absolute 'No'. But, relatively, that is, relative to the tasks it has and its vision of their fulfilment, relative also to the existing world order, then 'Yes', a thousand times 'Yes'.

The Donor–Receiver partnership is—let us live with it—an unequal relationship. Receivers have to submit their financial accounts to the Donor. The Donors do not reciprocate. Receivers have to submit proposals upon proposals to Donors in order to get donor-funds. Donors do not submit Proposals to Receivers, asking for the privilege of partnership. Yet it is a privilege, isn't it, for Donors to join Receivers in the great task of creating a new and just world? Certainly the relationship is both unequal and asymmetrical. Yet both need each other to carry out the larger task of building a better world. What should be done to make an unequal but complimentary relationship a genuine partnership?

As I said at the Helvetas Consultation in Zurich in 1993

> If in the first years of its field work, Satyodaya asked, 'What can Satyodaya do *for* the People?' the question soon changed to, 'What can Satyodaya do *with* the People?' But now Satyodaya asks, 'What can the *People do together* with Satyodaya?'

These transformed questions mark a major charge in thinking about Donor-Partner relations. So today, I submit, the Donor-Partners must ask themselves three questions:

> 'What can the Donor-Partner do *for* Satyodaya?'
> 'What can the Donor-Partner do *with* Satyodaya?'

But only when they ask, 'What can *Satyodaya do together* with the Donor-Partner?' will the words 'Donor' and 'Receiver' be replaced with the word 'Partnership'.

NOTES

1. Michael Edwards, 'The Rise of Civil Society', *Developments: The International Development Magazine,* Vol. 14, Second Quarter, 2001, p. 5.
2. Ibid., p. 6.
3. James Petras, 'Imperialism and NGOs in Latin America', *Monthly Review: An Independent Socialist Magazine,* Vol. 49, No. 7, 1997, p. 13.

4. Ibid., p. 10.
5. Mustapha Kamal Pasha, 'Globalization and Poverty in South Asia', *Millenium Journal of International Studies,* Vol. 25, No. 3, 1996, pp. 637–39.
6. Roger C. Riddell and Anthony J. Bebbington, *Developing Countries NGOs and Donor Governments,* London: Overseas Development Institute, 1995.
7. Michael Taylor, 'Past Their Sell-by Date? NGOs and Their Future in Development', Seventh Bradford Development Lecture, University of Bradford, 1997.

IV

Building a Better Society? Large Problems with Weakened Capacity

The contests over government, the distribution of power and other issues within the society are being joined on the agenda of policy makers by the practical problems of reducing violence, finding a place for thousands of displaced people, coping with an aging population and a host of other problems. For the Sri Lankan government, many of these are unprecedented problems, as they are for many governments. There is no experience to draw upon.

Who knows what to do? Where can the much-needed information be found? How can the resources be mobilized? What agencies can undertake to implement which policies? To whom will they be held accountable?

Implicitly and explicitly, Hasbullah, Waxler-Morrison and Pinnawala point to the need to join together the grounded experience of the 'subjects', those experiencing the problem, with the knowledge and resources of local and international NGOs and with the organizational and delivery skills of the relevant public and private corporations, in an arena for mediating conflict and generating cooperative action. Such policy-specific arenas have been formed and are successfully functioning in other countries.

11

Justice for the Dispossessed: The Case of a Forgotten Minority in Sri Lanka's Ethnic Conflict

S.H. HASBULLAH

The last two decades have witnessed unspeakable hardship and suffering for the peoples of all communities in Sri Lanka. The ethnic conflict and the ensuing protracted civil war have been responsible for this disastrous development. More than 60,000 people have lost their lives and more than three million have been displaced.[1] In the midst of this sad state of affairs, the people yearn for an end to that crisis and hope for an honourable solution that will satisfactorily address the fears and aspirations of all communities.

Hopeless suffering has been inflicted upon the weakest segments of the communities. Victims of the war and the ethnic conflict are commonly found among minorities or minorities within minorities and economically and politically less powerful people. This chapter is about a minority community that has been caught in the middle of the ethnic conflict in Sri Lanka. Muslims, who have lived in the Tamil majority Northern Province as a minority for generations, were evicted by an armed militant group fighting for the rights of Tamils of Sri Lanka. This expulsion brings up, more sharply than any other issue of the ethnic conflict, the crisis besetting the foundational structures of the nation-state and of ethno-nationalism. Majority–minority politics have dominated the Sri Lankan scene since independence. The rigidity of the modern nation-state formation and structure has resulted in creating majority-centred politics and majority–minority dichotomies. This is one of the major causes of not only majority–minority conflicts but also of conflict between minorities. This is clearly evident in the way the minority nationalism of the Tamils turned chauvinist and targeted a smaller minority in its bid to purify the northern territory. This attempt at ethnic cleansing was based on the majoritarian claims of an extreme version of ethno-nationalism.

Using Sri Lanka as a case study, the major objective of this chapter is to highlight the negative impacts of ethno-nationalism, which has been destabilizing the Third World democracies in recent years. This paper reviews the recent experience of the northern Tamil-speaking Muslims. By bringing out into the open the question of the affected people's political and human rights and their right to live in their homeland in the north or anywhere else, their right to their property and to continue with their established ways of conducting their lives, this paper hopes to force the question of the Muslims onto the political agenda. It is my express hope and optimism that the problems of the Muslim refugees will be solved amicably, paving the way for the restoration of coexistence and ethnic harmony among the different communities in the country.[2]

The data for this chapter come from various sources. I have been engaged in a study of Internally Displaced Persons in Sri Lanka from the time large-scale displacement of people took place in Sri Lanka in 1990. I conducted a refugee survey of the study population in 1991 and that is the source for most of the data on the economic losses of the study population. Since then, I have been a constant observer of the changes that took place within this particular ethnic group. In 1999, I conducted another survey of the present conditions and future prospects of the displaced people in Puttalam district. This chapter uses many of the findings of that survey as well.

The Muslim Minority

Muslims constitute about 8 per cent of the total population and are recognized as a distinct religio-ethnic category in Sri Lanka. They have lived interspersed among the Sinhalese as well as the Tamils for a long time, having enjoyed peaceful coexistence with other cultures and communities.[3] Economically, most Muslims are engaged in secondary and tertiary occupations, petty trade and are employed in small sales centres in many regions of the country. In certain parts of Sri Lanka, however, notably in the lowlands of the east and the north-west, subsistence agriculture and fishing are important as their sources of livelihood. The bilingual proficiency (Sinhala and Tamil) of the Muslims helps them to interact with other linguistic and cultural communities without hesitation and to establish stable relationship with all. There have been no major outbreaks of violence against Muslims in the recent past except a few isolated incidents here and there.

Until recently, Muslims have aligned themselves with 'national' political parties. Where the current Sinhala–Tamil conflict is concerned, they have chosen to remain neutral. This can be attributed to several factors. Muslims did not clamour for facilities in higher education, white-collar jobs and the distribution of state lands, the issues that have exacerbated the Sinhala–Tamil conflict. At the same time, their leaders have begun to emphasize that the resolution to the ethnic conflict must take into account the aspirations of Muslim minorities as well.

The Northern Province is a predominantly Tamil area where the Muslims formed a distinct and the largest minority community. As in the rest of country, they were scattered all over the province. However, there were large concentrations in parts of Mannar district, Jaffna city and Mullaitivu town. Agriculture, fishing and business were the main occupations of the Muslims. The northern Muslims married within their own community and had strong religious and cultural ties with the Muslims of other villages of the Northern Province. Muslims lived within the dominant socio-cultural milieu of the Tamil people. They had been living in this manner for centuries. It should also be stressed that while Muslims maintained their distinctive religio-cultural identity, different communities had coexisted peacefully in the entire Northern Province.

ETHNIC CONFLICT AND THE MUSLIMS

Ethnic tensions became increasingly visible in Sri Lanka from the time of independence in 1948. Scarcity of land and other resources, in the absence of technological alternatives, coupled with a sharp population increase, contributed to disparities in the economic and social welfare of minority communities, leading to ethnic strife. This was the beginning of the present situation. Social and economic issues were exploited by politicians seeking electoral benefits. Consequently, political affiliation has become largely polarized along ethnic lines.[4]

The conflict was initially seen as one between the Sinhalese majority and the Tamil minority. It began over issues such as the use of language, shares in state land, educational and employment opportunities, and culminated in the demand for greater autonomy for the regions where Tamils formed the majority. Tamils have been expressing their grievances politically for several decades and in recent years through armed struggle.

Muslims, who form the second largest minority in the country, are numerically second to the Tamils in the regions where Tamils are seeking regional autonomy, namely the Northern and the Eastern provinces. Muslim concentration was higher in the Eastern Province in comparison to that of the Northern Province. Muslims in these two provinces spoke Tamil at home and were also educated in Tamil medium. However, they claimed to be a separate community as their culture and way of life were quite distinct from that of the Tamils.[5] Politically too, they differed. In the late 1980s, the emergence of an exclusive political party for the Muslims in the Eastern Province reflected this line of thinking.[6]

The Sri Lankan ethnic conflict has gone through several phases. During the last 15 years or so, there has been an escalation in the intensity of the conflict, accompanied by the deterioration of ethnic relations. Armed Tamil militants have been fighting against the state of the 'Sinhala majority' for more than a decade now. In early 1990, the Liberation Tigers of Tamil Eelam (LTTE) became the most powerful militant group among the Tamils. The withdrawal of the Indian Peace Keeping Force (IPKF) from Sri Lanka gave them the opportunity to take control of many areas in the north and the east.[7] The power vacuum created by the withdrawal of the IPKF from the area during this period was largely responsible for strained Tamil–Muslim relations. The Sri Lankan armed forces, the LTTE and other small Tamil and Muslim armed groups tried to fill in the vacuum. As a result, the struggle for domination by these armed groups and by the armed forces spilled over into the normal life of the people and created ethnic tensions between Tamils and the Muslims in the East.[8]

The political activism of Tamils interfered with the affairs of the Muslim population in the north and the east. But Muslims have not considered Tamil activism a threat to their day-to-day life, culture and identity. It also is true that a few Muslims felt that the cause of the Tamils was theirs too. However, in early 1990 a decisive change in Tamil–Muslims relations occurred, particularly in the eastern province.[9] Tamils and the Muslims became increasingly suspicious of each other during this period. Both communities alleged that they had been victimized by the other.[10] The massacres of Muslims in Kathankudy and Eravur by Tamil militants shook the Muslims and aggravated their growing distrust of their Tamil brethren. Naturally, Muslims felt insecure in the region. This unfortunate situation of ethnic rift between the two communities was well exploited by groups that had vested interests in the conflict.[11]

EVICTION OF MUSLIMS FROM THE NORTHERN PROVINCE

The Muslims of the Northern Province were forced to leave their homes in the third week of October 1990. The LTTE announced over the loudspeaker through the streets of Muslim areas in the Northern Province that the Muslims must leave their homes, their villages and towns, leaving behind all their valuables, or face death at the hands of the LTTE. The ultimatum in many places was that Muslims should leave this region within 48 hours, but the 15,000 Muslims of Jaffna were given only two hours to leave.[12]

Most of the Muslims of the Mannar district fled by sea in small boats and arrived at the Puttalam and Kalpitiya coasts, while others crossed the Vilpattu and Madhu jungle by trekking several miles and arrived at Medawachchiya, Horowupotana, Gambrigaswewa and other settlements in the Anuradhapura district. At the same time, Muslims of Jaffna and Killinochchi districts crossed a long stretch of no-man's-land from Kerativu to Thandikulam and reached Vavuniya town. Mullaitivu Muslims crossed a jungle and reached Vavuniya town safely.

For several years the LTTE did not even acknowledge that they had ordered the Muslims to leave. Nor did they reveal why they expelled the Muslims from their homes. One assumption was that the LTTE had to resort to this forcible eviction in view of the new developments in ethnic relations in the Eastern Province between the Tamils and Muslims. Satyendra, an LTTE sympathizer, gives three possible reasons for the eviction. First, that the

Muslims claimed to be a separate ethnic group and thereby distanced themselves from the Tamils. Second, that the Sinhala government exploited this claim of the Muslims and deployed them against the Tamils in the Eastern Province prior to and during the 'Eelam War II'. Finally, that the Sri Lankan Government wanted to exploit the Muslim community's claim to a separate identity to quell the Tamil resistance and the LTTE movement. Citing these reasons he says: '... there was a "substantial basis" for the action taken by the LTTE to evacuate the Muslims from Jaffna'.[13] Satyendra further substantiates this by saying that such incidents were nothing new in war situations, citing similar instances during World War II in the USA.[14]

Were the reasons given by the LTTE for the eviction of Muslims from the north plausible? It is true that the Muslims did want to maintain a separate ethnic identity based on their religio-cultural foundation in Sri Lanka. But at the same time, it has not been established anywhere that the Muslims as a community were associated with the government forces against the Tamils in the Eastern Province. It was indicated that innocent Muslims were also the victims of increasing ethnic tension and they were feeling insecure in the Eastern Province during the intense war between the armed forces and the Tamil militants.

As to the question of whether there was any possible link between worsening Tamil–Muslim relations in the Eastern Province and the northern situation, it should be mentioned that such possibilities were remote in the context of the changing scenario of war and ethnic relations in the north and east at the time. For example, Muslim concentrations in the Northern Province were physically separated from the Muslim concentrations in the east by a significant distance, thus reducing the possibility of mutual ethnic hatred spreading from one region to the other. According to John Richardson, there was no serious incidence of Tamil–Muslim related violence reported during this period.[15] Contrary to this, until the proclamation of the expulsion order by the LTTE, ethnic relations between the Tamils and Muslims were harmonious in the Northern Province. This could be established by the poignant expression of the grief of Tamils in general at the ordeal suffered by the Muslims when expelled from their homes. Further, there was no evidence to say that Muslims as individuals or as a community engaged in any sort of espionage activities against the

Tamil cause. It was not only the Muslims of Jaffna who were expelled, as Satyendra says, but the entire innocent Muslim population living scattered over the five districts in the Northern Province that was expelled in an organized fashion. The overall war strategy of the LTTE at the time may have been an acceptable excuse for them to evict the Muslims from the Northern Province. We must ask today why the minority Muslim community of 5 per cent of the total population who had always maintained healthy relations with the majority (Tamils) was singled out and targeted by the LTTE. There can be no justification for this damning act of betrayal and injustice.

THE ECONOMIC LOSSES FOLLOWING EXPULSION

The impact of the forcible expulsion has many facets. I have attempted to estimate the economic losses of the forcible expulsion. The estimates of the economic losses have been broken down into four major categories. First is the losses of village institutions. A number of religious institutions along with government and non-government institutions located within the Muslim settlements were serving the population. It was estimated that at the time of expulsion of Muslims, there were 128 mosques, 26 shrines and 189 madrasas (Quran Schools) run by the mosques and individual Quran teachers and of course 65 government schools. Besides these, there were several other Muslim associations and clubs. Most of the village religious institutions (e.g., mosques) owned income-generating paddy fields, coconut estates, etc. They also possessed buildings, vehicles and so on. Besides these assets, they also represented a sentimental and cultural value. The financial value alone of the properties would run into millions of rupees.

Those expelled were the owners of thousands of acres of fertile agricultural land. They were engaged in coconut, palmyra and cashew cultivation. The total extent of the land area under cultivation by the Muslims is not known at the moment. However, it has been found that the 9,025 families surveyed by the author owned a total of 13,978 acres of paddy land and 18,907 acres of coconut and highlands. The loss of agricultural land led to the loss of regular income for the owner families. Further, the agricultural equipment and implements, such as tractors, water pumps and sprayers left behind by the Muslims were plundered. The cost of these items amounts to millions of rupees. In the meantime, a significant number of Muslims in the north were engaged in fishing and related occupations. The fishermen in these areas owned fishing boats and valuable fishing gear that included millions of rupees worth of fishing nets. These were all lost during the chaos of eviction and displacement.

There was a high proportion of Muslims in business as compared to other communities in the region. Muslim businessmen lived in the major towns as well as the small towns of the north. The expelled population had a high proportion of ownership of business and property in many major towns of the Northern Province such as Mannar, Vavuniya and Jaffna. It must be noted that some villages of exclusive Tamil population typically had Muslim-owned groceries and tea boutiques. According to this information, Muslims owned a total of 2,395 commercial and industrial establishments. The monetary value of each establishment varies according to its significance, size and location. What is to be noted here is that the Muslims had to leave behind their business and industrial property when they were forced to leave the province at very short notice.

The values of the houses vary according to type, location, size and furnishings. Houses and house yards in urban areas are much more valuable in terms of price than those in rural areas. Naturally, people living in the urban areas possessed expensive electrical and electronic equipment and household items such as TVs, radios, refrigerators and furniture. More than 50 per cent of the Muslims in the north lived in urban (Jaffna, Mannar, Vavuniya, etc.) and semi-urban (Erukkalampiddy, Tharapuram, Chilawathury, etc.) areas. Their rural counterparts too led a contented life, possessing their own houses and essential household items relevant to the rural environment. They were forced to leave all their possessions, as the LTTE did not allow them to take along anything but the clothes they were wearing, while their houses and household articles were destroyed or were damaged beyond use. In short, they lost everything but their lives.

Grain and animals constitute a vital part of the wealth of rural people. Muslims owned thousands of heads of livestock and poultry. Among the reported 9,025 families there were a total of 59,646 cattle, 45,369 goats and 83,452 poultry. The Muslims in the agricultural areas had stored stocks of grain worth millions of rupees at the time of eviction, which too they had to forgo. The estimated total value would exceed the colossal sum of Rs 11,000 million at 1990 price level.

THE PLIGHT OF THE REFUGEES

Most Muslim refugees continue to live in abject conditions outside the north. Contrary to many other situations of displacement in the country, the majority of the displaced Muslims have not been able to go back to their places of birth in the north as the LTTE continues to have a stranglehold on the affairs of most areas of the province.

The northern Muslims have continued as refugees in large numbers for more than a decade, without the possibility of any productive resolution to their problems in sight. It is sad to see that the responsible parties are largely unconcerned about their plight. Desperate appeals by Muslims have fallen on deaf ears. The majority of northern Muslims are living as displaced people in various parts of the southern provinces. At present, there are about 65,000 Muslim refugees living in the north-western coastal region in the Puttalam district. The rest of the Muslim refugees are scattered in the districts of Anuradhapura and Kurunegala and in cities such as Colombo, Negombo, Panandura and others. So far, no constructive attempts have been made to find a durable solution to the problems of these displaced people.

In 1999, our team conducted an exhaustive study to assess the present conditions of the refugees who have ended up in Puttalam. The study was appropriately named *Puttalam Refugee Research.*[16] The study discovered that about 80 per cent of the displaced people in Puttalam were living in cadjan-thatched huts. These huts are found in the precincts of the refugee camps (also called welfare centres), in relocation camps and in refugee self-settlements dubbed by the government as 'resettlement villages'.[17]

Another 15 per cent of Puttalam's Internally Displaced Persons (IDP) are living in uncompleted permanent houses. Some of these houses are in the process of being built with state assistance while still others are being built with their own sources of income. More than 75 per cent of the types of huts and houses mentioned above are located on land that is inundated during the rainy seasons or on land that experiences continuous dust deposits from the nearby cement factory.[18]

It is not possible for the refugees to stand on their own feet in the resource-poor north-western coast of the Puttalam district.[19] More than 90 per cent of these displaced people are still dependent on dry rations issued by the State and the World Food Program. As dry rations are issued only in the form of commodities, refugees are desperately in need of cash for medication, transport and schooling of their children and for other essentials. They are prepared to grab any opportunity for any kind of menial job available to them in order to keep the home-hearth burning. Large-scale vegetable cultivation in the Kalpitiya peninsula provides part-time employment to women. Some of the refugee women and girls have taken up these jobs.[20] The employment opportunities available to refugees in other areas of Puttalam district are worse than those available in the Kalpitiya Peninsula.

The refugees who have continued to live in the camps and relocated camps in Puttalam are faced with the problem of deteriorating living conditions. This is because the government has terminated its assistance to refugee camps and relocation camps following the introduction of resettlement programmes in Puttalam in order to encourage the refugees to accept 'their' (government's) resettlement package.[21] The inadequate quantities of food items and their improper distribution have seriously affected the daily food intake of the displaced people, resulting in malnutrition.[22] Educational and health aspects of the refugees are the immediate areas of concern.

Socially as well as psychologically, a large majority of the displaced families feel insecure and vulnerable. Continued displacement is a traumatic experience, which can destroy people both physically and psychologically. These people are uncertain and insecure about their future; there is no stability in their lives. They feel that they have no control over their lives and fate.

UNCERTAINTIES ENCOUNTERED BY RETURNING MUSLIMS

Muslims started returning to their homes in handfuls in 1991—about a year after their expulsion. The Muslims who were residents of border towns and villages of Vavuniya and Mannar Island were the first to return. However, the Muslims returned only to the areas cleared by Government forces at that time. In 1992, about 5 to 7 percent of the northern Muslims opted to return to their homes on Mannar Island and in the Vavuniya district.

The number of returning Muslims gradually increased and was taking place at a more rapid pace during the peace talks between the government and the LTTE in 1994. The collapse of the peace talks was a blow to the hope of the Muslims. The government's military reoccupation of parts of Vanni and the Jaffna Peninsula in 1995 encouraged many Tamils to return to their original places in the north. Some displaced Muslims too, especially of Vavuniya district, Mannar Island and Jaffna town, made use of this opportunity and returned to their homes.

Altogether about 10 to 15 per cent of displaced Muslims have returned north so far. The largest number returned to the Muslim villages located in the southern part of the Vavuniya district. According to our study, 1,900 families have returned to a total of 24 villages in Vavuniya district. In fact, 60 per cent of the Vavuniya Muslims have returned to their homes, which is a great relief and achievement considering the arduous process and uncertainty of return of expelled Muslims. On Mannar Island, most of the former Muslim communities are back to life with Muslim returnees. It must also be mentioned that in 1998 a small number of Muslims returned to Jaffna town. But the percentage of returning refugees is small. Even today, the total number of Muslim returnees to Jaffna town is less than 100 families.

Obviously, Muslim returnees do face many problems, as they are restricted to certain economic activities, religious observances, etc., while they suffer due to lack of food supplies, medical facilities and schooling for the children. These problems are faced by most residents of war zones. Apart from these, problems specific to the Muslim returnees must be faced. Security restrictions are the most serious ones in certain areas, particularly Vavuniya district. Another is that they feel insecure and vulnerable because of the small number of returnees compared to the number of Muslims who lived there prior to the expulsion. Meanwhile, the ownership of property of the Jaffna Muslims is under threat.

PROPERTY RIGHTS

There are justifiable apprehensions in the minds of the displaced Muslims about their legal rights regarding their assets and the property they left behind at the time of their expulsion. Legal experts indicate that the displaced Muslims face the threat of losing ownership of property through the application of the Law of Prescription which gives ownership of a private property to a person if he or she has occupied it for a period of 10 years.[23]

Muslims have now lived away from their homes and other immovable property they owned in addition to their dwelling houses for more than 10 years. As long as these displaced people live away from their original abodes because of threats to their life on return, the chances of reclaiming their property later are legally difficult. This will be possible only if the new occupants voluntarily give up the land and property that had come into their possession after the expulsion of the Muslims.

At the same time, unfortunately, some of the displaced Muslims have been transferring their property to others for a song, as they have lost all hope of returning home. A group of Muslims who visited Musali in the Mannar district in 1998 found no traces of their houses and of other permanent structures used by them before their expulsion. This is a result of natural causes and lack of maintenance. It is presumed that this will be the condition of much of the rest of the property belonging to Muslims of the rural areas of Mullaitivu, Killinochchi, Manthai, Nanaddan and Vavuniya as well. Many attempts have been made in the past—through legal and other means by concerned individuals and organizations of displaced people—to change the terms of legal restrictions pertaining to the period of ownership. Sadly, they have been unable to make any progress towards this change.

At this juncture, it is reasonable to suggest that the right to retrieve the movable and immovable property of the displaced Muslims be asserted by legal methods and through a humane and conscientious approach. An independent arbitration commission should be appointed to look into the undoubtedly legitimate claims of the expelled Muslims as regards the restoration of ownership of both movable and immovable property. The commission should be given the power and mandate to resolve the disputes between the Muslims and the non-Muslims arising out of competing claims of ownership along the same lines as those that were successfully executed in the case of Bosnian Muslims.

RETURN

Muslim refugees came to the south not of their own volition. The majority of the refugees chose the north-western part of Puttalam because it was the most convenient location that could be reached with relative ease from some of the important northern Muslim concentrations. Once they reached their destined place, they were compelled to live in camps, as they had nowhere else to live. Needless to say, living in camps in squalid conditions is difficult and unendurable. Justifiably therefore, the refugees living in the disorganized camps do want to return to their homes to restore normalcy to their lives.

The northern Muslim refugees hoped that the LTTE who evicted them would call them voluntarily, asking them to return to their houses.[24] They also hoped that the situation in the north would improve through negotiations facilitating their return. The cordial and healthy relationship that existed between the Muslim minority and the Tamil majority in the Northern Province earlier was yet another factor that helped them hope and look forward to returning.

There were a few occasions—like the attempts at national level peace talks—which held out some hope to the refugees wanting to return. One such attempt was the failed State—LTTE dialogue in 1994 and 1995. Such positive attempts encouraged the Muslims and enabled them to accept the conditions in refugee camps; they took their displacement only as temporary and hoped for early relief. There was no place of refuge as an alternative to the camps.

Unfortunately, all past attempts to bring about peace have been negative. The failure of the 1995 peace talks has particularly weakened, or rather, erased the Muslim refugees' hopes of an immediate return. In 1995, the Muslim refugees in Puttalam and other areas completed five full years of life in refugee camps. During this period the refugees have desperately looked for some meaningful alternative to their miserable lives. At this state of affairs, the government came up with a new suggestion for the return of the refugees. The re-enacted state policy on 'resettlement' in 1995 declares, 'The problem of displaced persons will not be tied up to the ongoing war. The displaced persons who cannot resettle in their original places of residence and where the prospects of resettlement are bleak in the near future will be helped by the provision of a piece of land and assistance for resettlement'.[25]

The refugees did not want to settle permanently in Puttalam. But of course they preferred this alternative to camp life. They knew that a return to the north would take a while. At the same time, they could not continue to put up with the appalling conditions in the camps either. In early 1996, Muslim refugees said that they 'agreed that the resettlement as an interim arrangement would make them prepare for their ultimate return to the north'.[26] Along this line of thinking, they used the first instalment of the resettlement allowance of Rs 10,000 (equal to $110) to invest in a piece of land in Puttalam and to put up their own individual huts, in order to get away from the deteriorating conditions at the refugee camps. Despite the limited facilities their new location provided, they enjoyed independence as the atmosphere gave them dignity and a certain degree of privacy for their families.

At present, refugees are concentrated in four coastal Divisional Secretariat Divisions in the Puttalam district. The total population of this region doubled with the arrival of Muslim refugees in 1990. These four coastal regions are among the most underdeveloped areas in the country. Traditionally, fishing was the major economic activity and the fisher-folk are usually engaged in fishing only during those six months when favourable wind conditions prevailed in the areas. They used to move to the north-eastern coastal areas (Mullaitivu and Trincomalee) for fishing during the other seasons. However, the war in the north and east prevented the fishermen from moving to those areas. At the same time, *The Land Use Map of Puttalam* (Survey Department, 1985) clearly shows that large tracts of land in the four coastal regions are suitable neither for cultivation nor for settlement. The majority of refugee resettlements are located in the lands categorized as unsuitable for cultivation or for settlement. In short, the refugees had no choice other than to decide to live in Puttalam where the people already face tremendous economic and social problems. The refugees do not possess anything larger than the 10 perches of land (one-tenth of an acre) they managed to buy using their resettlement allowance. Since employment opportunities are very scarce in the areas where the refugees are concentrated, they are forced to rely on food assistance to help them survive. Facing these conditions in Puttalam, the refugees have attempted several times in the past to get back to their own homes. But as the LTTE remains in control of most of the areas, the refugees cannot even think of returning to the north without any encouraging signs from the LTTE. In this kind of situation, the guaranteeing of their security is far more essential than anything else.

Second, as no one lives or uses their premises in many of the Muslim villages in the north now, it is unthinkable for an individual or a single family of Muslim refugees to take a unilateral decision to return to their respective areas alone. In the case of the non-Muslim Tamil returnees, the situation is different because their settlements are not totally abandoned and are completely intact. In view of these reasons, the refugees want to return in groups, and not as individuals. In addition, it must be remembered that Muslim refugees have been away from their homes for a very long period of time. The current living and economic environment in their original settlements presents a completely different picture from that which existed when they left their homes more than a decade ago. Under these circumstances, it is justifiable on the part of the refugees to have reservations about returning until such time as it is possible to guarantee the social and economic sustainability of their return.

The new development on the war front in 1997 encouraged some Muslim refugees from Musali region of the northern province to return to their homes. They expressed their willingness to return to their original places. They were however naturally concerned about the 'liveability' and 'sustainability' of their return. They brought their apparent perceptions to the notice of the 'concerned' parties of the conflict—the state and the LTTE.[27] Briefly speaking, what they said at that time was that they wished to live in their original places with the same facilities normally enjoyed by other people. The refugees needed a definite assurance from the state, the LTTE as well as the international community to that effect before committing themselves to return. They considered their security and liveability as essential pre-conditions for returning to their places of origin. In 1997, when there was a change of complexion in the war situation in the north, they correctly sensed that their return would be hazardous unless they got a clear signal and assurance from the LTTE. Unfortunately, none of the above concerns of the refugees were taken into serious consideration by the parties involved—the state, the LTTE or the international community.

Future Prospects

The forced displacement of the entire Muslim community of the Northern Province is different and distinct in many respects from other situations of displacement in the country. The northern Muslims are a special category of refugees in Sri Lanka because of the way they were displaced and the types of problems they encounter. Therefore, people who are in such a dilemma require special safeguards to protect their interests as a whole because of their legitimate status as a distinct community not only during their period of displacement but also after they return to normal life.

There are examples from other parts of the world, where people who have experienced similar problems have been given special protection through international conventions. For example, Muslims in Bosnia experienced forced expulsion or rather ethnic cleansing during the recent spells of civil war from 1992 to 1995. It was estimated that about 55 to 62 per cent of Bosnia's population were made refugees and internally displaced people as a result of this civil war. Nevertheless, measures have been taken by the international community to improve the situation for the Bosnian Muslims. International mediation and conventions have attempted to resolve many of the problems of the forcibly evicted people of Bosnia. The Dayton Agreement is one such well-known contract. This agreement assured protection to those returning and security for the displaced people and also proper measures of rehabilitation and reconstruction.

Unfortunately, such efforts in the case of the forcibly expelled northern Muslims have not been taken, nor has there been any planning for it. Instead, they are fast becoming a forgotten lot. Knowing the complexity of the problems of Muslim refugees, some suggestions have been made in the following section for the special protection and safeguards for the return of the refugees.

Conclusion

It is obvious that although 10 years have passed since the forced eviction, the Muslims are still unable to reoccupy the land of their birth. To date, no arrangements have been made for their safe return by the parties responsible, neither by the government nor the Tamil militants. Even international humanitarian agencies are unable to help. The displaced persons are still categorized as refugees or Internally Displaced Persons living in the Southern provinces. They lead a precarious life with a deep sense of insecurity about their future. Their suffering cannot be gauged in words. Regrettably, no constructive attempts have been made so far to find a durable solution. The magnitude and the nature of the problems faced by the displaced Muslims warrant serious national attention.

Seeking social justice for people affected in similar situations is nothing new. It has happened in many other parts of the world. The objective of the Assets and Property Rights section of the Dayton Agreement which was brought in as one of the solutions to the Bosnian ethnic crisis was to give justice to those people who were expelled by force during the ethnic war.[28] The forcibly evicted Muslims from the Northern Province justifiably qualify for such a right to compensation on identical grounds.

The return of the Muslims will not be viable and secure unless accompanied by a lasting solution to the ethnic conflict. To achieve this, all of us concerned about it must reassess the situation in both practical and theoretical terms. A reformed structure of the state and of the nation becomes paramount in this regard. One must historically analyze the exclusions that have taken place in the name of the monolithic nation. We can no longer continue to seek homogeneity within the nation-state structure. Homogeneity is not a healthy environment for any nationality or state structure. The historical developments that led to the formation of Sri Lanka demonstrate the richness of the multi-cultural community, which depends on the complementary nature of the heterogeneity. Without this sense of diversity and plurality we cannot survive and evolve as the peoples of this country. Pluralist societies are a must and contribute to the survival not only of minority communities but that of the dominant ones too. The displaced Muslims from the north long to return to their original homes. They long for that multi-cultural space. Let us all dream along with them. Let us work toward a composite solution to the problem. Let us look at the issue of the displaced as one of crucial importance to the solution of the ethnic conflict.

NOTES

1. Correct and systematic statistical figures of the number of people affected by the ethnic conflict are not available. It is generally stated that about 55,000 people have died as a result of ethnic conflict since 1983. Further, when the ceasefire agreement was signed in February 2002, the number of people who were considered internally displaced according to the government definition was 800,000. There is certainly a degree of underestimation in this source of information.
2. As this chapter is being prepared, there are positive signs emerging that the main players in the conflict are willing to enter negotiations for a durable solution to the ethnic conflict. The LTTE has now acknowledged responsibility for the expulsion of the Muslims. It accepts that it was a mistake and a political blunder on its part and is prepared to compensate for any harm done to the Muslims of the Northern Province. This is a welcome sign, especially at a time when the LTTE is participating in negotiations to end the ethnic conflict. The invitation of the LTTE to the Muslims to return has not been responded to on the same scale as the other displaced Tamils from the north, where nearly a third returned in the eight months following the ceasefire agreement. It indicates that the Muslims expect greater assurances for their safety and living conditions in their former home communities to emerge from the ongoing peace talks before returning on a large scale.
3. Read more about the Muslim–Sinhala relationship in L.S. Dewaraja. *The Kandyan Kingdom of Ceylon, 1702–1760*, Colombo: Lake House, 1972. Also, see Tamil–Muslim relationship in D.B. McGilvray, 'Tamils and Muslims in the Shadow of War: Schism of Continuity?' in Siri Gamage and I.B. Watson (Eds), *Conflict and Community in Contemporary Sri Lanka: 'Pearl of the East' or the 'Island of Tears'?*, New Delhi: Sage Publications, 1999, pp. 217–28.
4. See for example Mick Moore, *The State and the Peasantry in Sri Lanka*, Unpublished Ph.D. Thesis, University of Sussex, 1981.
5. The formation of the Muslim ethnic identity on the basis of religion has been a subject of academic discussion in recent years. See for example Q. Ismail, 'Unmooring Identity: The Antinomies of Elite Muslim Self Representation in Modern Sri Lanka', in Pradeep Jaganathan and Qadri Ismail (Eds), *Unmaking the Nation: The Politics of Identity and History in Modern Sri Lanka*, Colombo: Social Scientists Association, 1995.
6. Sri Lanka Muslim Congress (SLMC) was registered as a political party in 1989. It contested in the 1989 General Election on the issue of an independent political voice for Muslims in the resolution to the ethnic conflict. SLMC won most of the Muslim constituencies in the elections and claimed that it had been mandated to speak for Muslims of not only the Northern and Eastern provinces but also of the other areas of the country as well. The SLMC was able to maintain its popular political support base among Muslims, as was evident from the results of subsequent elections.
7. A unit of the Indian armed forces was stationed in the Northern and Eastern provinces from the early part of 1987 to the latter part of 1989. It was called the Indian Peace Keeping Force or IPKF. The IPKF personnel,

numbering about 100,000 were brought to the Island under the Indo-Lanka accord signed by the Governments of India and Sri Lanka in order to end the ethnic and armed conflict. It was expected that the presence of the IPKF would ensure smooth implementation of the Accord. At the end of 1989, the Sri Lankan government asked the IPKF to leave the Island, as the then government and the LTTE felt that the presence of Indian forces on the Island was no longer needed.

8. In conflict areas in the north and east, individuals and families of different ethnicity interacted and maintained the bond with each other even during the height of intense 'ethnic tension'. Most of them (families and individuals) were interdependent, economically and otherwise.
9. Violent incidents of Tamil–Muslim conflicts had begun by 1985 in a sporadic and selective manner, especially in the Eastern Province. For more information see John Richardson, *Sri Lanka Violence Data 1948–1988*, Washington D.C.: School of Internal Service, The American University, 1990.
10. McGilvray (n. 3) discusses Tamil–Muslim relations in the context of increasing ethnic tensions between the two groups in the Eastern Province after 1990.
11. The groups with vested interests referred to are the Sri Lankan armed forces, the LTTE, Tamil and Muslim armed groups and the politicians of all communities and parties.
12. The event of forced expulsion was reported in several documents. For example, a seven-volume book series authored by me gives a detailed account. See S.H. Hasbullah, *Ethnic Conflict in Sri Lanka and the Forcibly Evicted Muslims of the Northern Province: Mullaitivu Muslims* (In Tamil), Colombo: The Northern Muslims' Rights Organization, 1997. See also S.H. Hasbullah, *Muslim Refugees: The Forgotten People in Sri Lanka's Ethnic Conflict*, Nuraicholai: Research and Action Forum for Social Development, 2001.
13. Satyendra's writing is available at *http://www.sangam.org/ANALYSIS/MuslimFactor.htm*.
14. Satyendra says, 'In early 1942, the United States was at war with Japan. Out of fear of espionage by the Japanese in the United States, the U.S. government imposed severe restrictions on the rights of people belonging to Japanese ancestry during the World War II.' *www.sangam.org/ANALYSIS/MuslimFactor.htm*. Accessed October 2002.
15. See Richardson (n. 9).
16. Several publications have been brought out using the findings of this research. For example, see S.H. Hasbullah, S.H.M. Rizni and A.G. Anees, *Preliminary Findings on the Living Conditions of the IDPs in Puttalam District*, 1999, Mimeo. In addition, these findings were presented and discussed among the representatives of displaced people, NGOs and government officials at a workshop titled 'the Present Conditions and Future Prospects of Displaced People in Puttalam District' held in Puttalam on 9 April 2000.
17. Displaced people in Puttalam live in nearly 200 different locations. They are called Welfare Centres, Relocated Camps and Resettlement Villages according to government terminology. Of the abovementioned refugee settlements, 86 locations are resettlement villages, 94 are welfare centres and 9 are relocated camps according to our survey in 1999. As far as basic living facilities are concerned, there isn't much difference among the various refugee settlements as categorized by the government.

18. For example, the south of Puttalam town, called Thillayadi, is a marshy area where floodwater reaches the sea. Malaria is common in this area. Until recently, local residents of Puttalam made no attempt to settle here. Now it has been densely populated by refugees.
19. Puttalam district is one of the least developed districts of Sri Lanka. At the same time, the development of the north-western part of Puttalam where the refugees are concentrated has been neglected for a long time and has very low socio-economic indicators.
20. Involvement of women in low-paid employment such as working in vegetable gardens has created many social problems for refugee families. At the same time, it has also increased the number of female dropouts from the school. A study that I conducted in Kalpitiya peninsula on this aspect confirms this. See S.H. Hasbullah, *The Present Conditions of Refugees: Four Issues*, Nuraicholai: RAAF, 2000.
21. The state introduced a resettlement programme in Puttalam without proper assessment of the area's socio-economic and ethnic conditions. In a way, the resettlement programme introduced in Puttalam district for Muslim refugees was politically motivated. As a result, the long-term impact of making a permanent home for nearly 75,000 refugees in a resource-poor and ethnically sensitive region has not been planned properly.
22. It should be acknowledged that the impact of NGO activities from the early part of the arrival of refugees to Puttalam district had helped refugees to overcome extreme poverty, starvation and serious health problems. But at the same time, NGOs and state activities were ad hoc in nature and not aimed at having any long-term impact on the life of the IDPs, as is evident in the recent research. See Hasbullah, Rizni and Anees, n. 16.
23. The land legislation pertaining to prescription on state land declares, 'Proof of the undisturbed and uninterrupted possession by a defendant in any action, or by those under whom he claims, of lands or immovable property, by a title adverse to or independent of that of the claimant or plaintiff in such action ... for ten years previous to the bringing of such action, shall entitle the defendant to a degree in his favour with cost.' (Constitution, Chapter 81: IV, 70)
24. It was reported by many northern Muslims that the LTTE cadres, when they forced Muslims to leave their homes, said in many Muslim villages in the Northern Province that they would be invited by the LTTE to come back once the situation in the north got back to normal.
25. Ministry of Shipping, Ports, Rehabilitation and Reconstruction, 1995/96.
26. See S.H. Hasbullah, *Refugees are People: Proceedings of the Workshop on the Resettlement Program for the Forcibly Evicted Muslims of the Northern Province*, Colombo: NMRO, 1996.
27. See Hasbullah, n. 12.
28. The agreement reached between the warring factions in Bosnia on 21 November 1995 is called the 'Dayton Agreement'. This is a general framework agreement for peace in Bosnia Herzegovina signed by the Republic of Bosnia Herzegovina, the Republic of Croatia and the Federal Republic of Yugoslavia. For more details, see *Dayton Agreement. http://www.soros.org/fmp2/html/dayton_accords_summary.html.*

12

Who Will Care for Those Left at Home? The Effect of New Opportunities for Work on Families in Sri Lanka

NANCY WAXLER-MORRISON

Talk about 'globalization' often sounds very impersonal, as if it involves only electronic signals bounced off of satellites or decisions in distant boardrooms to shift assets from country to country. Yet if one traces these 'impersonal' events down to the ground it is clear that individuals and their families are almost always directly affected, sometimes positively, through increased income and new opportunities but often very negatively, due to job losses, and the breakdown of families and family support. The ultimate results of such changes for families may well be new social structures and new cohesive bonds but the pathway to change is often stressful.

Sri Lanka provides good examples of these processes. It has been drawn into the global economic network in many ways that affect families. One major economic development is the Free Trade Zone established outside Colombo in 1979, which provides jobs in foreign-owned textile factories to an increasingly large number of young Sri Lankan women.[1] The second development is linked to a decision by OPEC to increase oil prices in 1973, which led to new opportunities for Sri Lankan women to find employment as housemaids in Middle-Eastern countries. These and other economic opportunities, internally and abroad, have led to increased migration and, in particular, have meant that women have left their families, which must then find ways to take over the women's responsibilities.

Increased migration has occurred in the context of the kinds of 'modernization' common to many developing countries. In past decades Sri Lanka has completed the demographic transition, that is the shift to long life expectancy (see Table 12.1) and a low birth rate. For the family, this means there are fewer children available to care for more elderly members. The combination of demographic change and new economic opportunities leading to migration create new and ongoing issues for policy makers, service providers and, of course, for families.

Table 12.1

Life Expectancy since 1946

	1946	*1953*	*1962*	*1967*	*1971*	*2000*
Males	44	59	62	65	64	70
Females	42	57	61	67	67	75

Sources: Data for 1946 through 1971: Statistical Pocket Book of Sri Lanka, 1977. Data for 2000: Asian Development Bank. Basic Statistics, April 2000.

I will look at some of the ways in which globalization and modernization have created new stresses and problems for families by referring to two kinds of data, published reports by others and data which we collected in our research on the quality of life in Sri Lanka.[2] In 1980 we began with a study of 12 communities drawn from Galle, Nuwara Eliya and Batticaloa districts. In each community we interviewed the heads of 40 randomly selected households, thus 480 households in total. In 1994–96 we re-studied eight of these communities in Galle and Nuwara Eliya, again interviewing 40 households in each, producing 320 interviews.

A look at the family stories we have heard will make it very clear that entrance into the global economic system in the context of demographic changes has created new issues that policy makers and service providers must tackle. These changes cause often stressful problems that Sri Lankan families must solve. Who will care for the elderly? Who can substitute for the missing women? And are the new strategies predictive of more permanent changes in Sri Lankan society? These are some of the questions I ask here.

Migration in Search of Work

While Sri Lanka has long had links to other parts of the world, first through early traders and later through Portuguese, Dutch and British colonial connections, movement within and out of the country did not occur in large numbers until after World War II when professionals—doctors, accountants, university professors—began to leave the country in search of better opportunities. Out-migration increased in the early 1970s as new political policies affected English-speaking Burghers as well as upper middle-class professionals. Many chose to go to Australia, UK, USA and Canada. Therefore, migration for economic opportunities and the resulting problems for those left behind are not new to Sri Lanka. But post-1970 migration has not only been more extensive, it also involves quite different people, many of them women, and it is both internal to the country and overseas.

Migration to the Middle East and Its Implications for the Family

In the mid-1970s, when the Middle-Eastern economy expanded due to high oil prices, a few Sri Lankan men migrated and worked as labourers and skilled workers—masons, electricians, etc. The Sri Lankan government quickly saw the advantage not only of their remittances but also of using migration as a strategy to relieve unemployment. Men who are skilled labourers, technicians, managers, etc., continue to take these jobs and are often away for as long as 15 years.

As the households of Middle-Eastern migrants became more affluent, more and more housewives could emulate the rich by turning over cooking, cleaning, and childcare to others. And, in Sri Lanka, in the context of high unemployment and increased cost of living, it became acceptable for married women to leave home to improve their families' economic positions even though the jobs they were paid for abroad, as servants, have never been acceptable to them at home.

Therefore, by the end of the 1970s, women joined the expanding group of migrants to become housemaids in Middle-Eastern homes. Currently approximately 130,000 persons leave Sri Lanka each year for temporary employment abroad and 83 per cent of those are women.[3]

Who are they? The majority are aged between 26 and 35, almost 80 per cent are married, and 80 per cent of the children they leave behind are aged 15 or younger. While initially they were from urban and semi-urban areas, now women from most parts of the country and from rural families predominate. Poverty is their main motivator. Women want to pay off debts, buy land, improve their homes and provide for their children's education. Some choose to leave home to escape from intolerable situations such as spouse abuse and a few are curious about other parts of the world. But the main goal for most is to earn money for their families. Many return home for holidays but continue to extend their housemaid contracts. Thus, wives/mothers are absent for long periods of time.

What happens to their families while they are away? Husbands are normally left in charge and it is often the husbands who receive remittances. Our studies reveal that almost half of these rural homes have an elderly parent, an unmarried sister or some other woman who becomes the cook and child-minder. The husband, faced with the fact that his wife is earning very large sums of money while he may be struggling to earn or even to find work, feels that his earlier position as 'family head' is threatened. One common response by the husband is to 'become voluntarily unemployed' as Gamburd describes it, to use his wife's remittances for daily family expenses and, in emulation of richer men, for drink, betting on races and 'loans' to family and friends.[4] Often, choosing not to work is explained by 'having to stay home to supervise the building of a new house'.

In one family Gamburd interviewed, the wife knew enough of her husband not to send money from abroad since the fact that he drank and gambled was one reason for her migration. Upon her return money-lenders and credit given by shops had to be repaid; there was nothing left from her earnings to buy land or build a house, her original goals. Therefore she decided to return to the Middle East 'no matter how', to escape and earn more. While variations of this scenario are very common, some husbands do manage family and funds effectively and improve their status permanently, especially by 'contributing lavishly to community projects'.[5] But often, as many villagers understand, the cycle of poverty is not broken.

What about the children? A grandparent, at home or in the neighbourhood, may help with household tasks and childcare but health problems and other responsibilities sometimes prevent it. Mother substitutes, no matter how well intentioned, have found they cannot always take the central role of the real mother. As a result, children may not go to school, some have become involved in illegal activities such as drug use and, especially in communities close to tourist centres, in child prostitution.

We saw the results of these problems in a family we interviewed very soon after the mother had returned from Kuwait. While she was away her husband found work as a labourer in Colombo and her parents next door took charge of their three sons. Upon her return she found a partly constructed house of piled-up building blocks, fertilizer bags and sheets of tin. Her parents had sold their house and departed. Her husband came home only twice a month, sometimes bringing money, and her 16-year-old son, having got into trouble with the law, was in a school for delinquent boys. She was left with very little support to care for her two younger sons. These are some of the more extreme examples of failed attempts to improve families' lives. Not all women have these experiences. We visited a Muslim woman who had worked in Saudi Arabia for 8 or 10 years, sending her earnings back to her husband, a labourer in the Cement Corporation. These funds had been used for a small house with polished floors, a modern kitchen including refrigerator, sink, built-in cabinets, etc. Their son continued in school throughout her absence.

While women are away it is clear that families sometimes suffer and some problems created in that time are likely to continue into the future. For some women goals are met; they have a new house, perhaps some land or even a thriving business that has been established and the family's position in the community has improved.

But does the opportunity for temporary migration improve the long-term position of women? When migration began in the 1970s there were expectations that women's status in the family would rise, given that they were earning their own money and perhaps becoming more self-confident and independent. One person predicted that women would want opportunities outside the family, too, for 'participation in the social and economic process'.[6]

In fact, women usually return from the Middle East to take up the same roles they had before, not attempting to challenge the authority of their spouses or older family members. Since their work experience—housework—does not give them special qualifications for other Sri Lankan jobs, they do not strike out on their own. If they do participate in the community it is likely to be in the form of gifts of money such as donations for temple events. The benefit to the country of this kind of migration is the remittances which, in 1994, were second only to the garment industry in foreign exchange earnings.[7] Whether money is spent on construction, gifts or alcohol, it is spent. But for the women and their families benefits may be mixed and for some, the result of migration is a family situation no better and sometimes much worse than the one they left.

MIGRATION AND ITS IMPLICATIONS FOR THE ELDERLY

Ideally, Sri Lankan families expect to care for elderly parents in their own homes and, generally, this is still the practice, both in rural and urban areas. But temporary and permanent migration is beginning to threaten the ideal. Married women are abroad for long periods, professionals leave Sri Lanka for good, and many, especially men, have moved far from home. It is the elderly who are left behind.

The 'brain drain' of Sri Lankan professionals began after World War II and has recently increased. Most leave for economic benefits and to improve prospects for their children. In 1997, of the total number of Sri Lankans leaving for foreign employment 11 per cent were professionals.[8] Earlier these were mainly doctors, accountants, engineers, and university professors, that is, those whose Sri Lankan training was recognized internationally. By virtue of their education they belonged to the global community. Many of these migrants had international connections through graduate training in the West and links with the United Nations and aid agencies. These connections were, and still are, used to arrange jobs in Western and Commonwealth countries. More recently other professionals and managers have benefited from newer global links and used these to move out of Sri Lanka to countries where they feel their future will be more comfortable. For example, the Free Trade Zone (FTZ) textile factories have provided managerial experience as well as foreign contacts for some who have subsequently moved abroad. In contrast to the Middle-East migrants, professionals leave Sri Lanka permanently.

Migration within Sri Lanka has steadily increased as the rural population exceeds the amount of land available and as work opportunities open up, many of them stimulated by linkages to international business and tourism.

The FTZ established in 1979 attracts young unmarried women, mostly between the ages of 18 and 25, to work in textile factories, most of them in and around Colombo. The prospect of their own money, some stylish clothes, the excitement of living away from home, and the opportunity to help their families financially are strong motivators. But the work requires long hours, and with little chance for advancement most young women save what they can for a dowry and eventually return home to marry. In our studies parents often report that once their daughters have paid for room and board near the factory they have very little left to contribute to those at home.

While the FTZ workers have received a great deal of attention from researchers, other kinds of internal migration are much more common. For example, in 1971, 16 per cent of those resident in Colombo district were born elsewhere; by 1981 migrants to Colombo comprised 20 per cent of its population. By 1981 one in every seven Sri Lankans had moved away from their original district.[9] Add to these permanent migrants those who are away from home for substantial periods of time and it is apparent that their absence will have implications for the family left behind.

Internal migrants are mainly but not entirely male and of all ages and social classes. In our research these range from an 18-year-old boy raised on a Nuwara Eliya tea estate who was sent to a Colombo relative to help sell textiles on the street. Or a 45-year-old husband/father from Galle, the only bread-winner in the family, who is a peon in a private Colombo company but travels home each weekend. Some are like the 33-year-old unmarried son from a fairly remote Galle district village who works in a bakery in Colombo and comes home only once a year. Others, both male and female, are adults with sufficient education to be placed as teachers, post office employees, bus drivers, etc., far from their original family homes. Finally, most recently, many men who have joined the army are absent for long periods of time.

Increasing opportunities for work away from home interact with the demographic changes that accompany 'modernization' in Sri Lanka. Together they threaten the expectation that elderly parents will be cared for by their children. Increased life expectancy and low birth rates mean that the proportion of the population over age 60 has increased steadily. It is now 9.9 per cent of the population and within the next 40 years it is expected to rise to 28 per cent.[10] The dependency ratio reveals that the labour force is shrinking relative to the large proportion of elderly and a decreasing proportion of children. By the mid-twenty-first century about 25 per cent of the population must care for the remaining 75 per cent, two-thirds of whom are elderly. And the elderly are getting older. As in the West there are increasing numbers of 'old old' persons. Currently about 24 per cent of those over 60 are aged 75 or older. In 40 years Sri Lanka expects that one-third of the elderly will be over 75, certainly some of whom will require daily care.[11] With a maximum of two or three children available to care for parents both the temporary and permanent migration of children threatens the traditional pattern of care.

INTERNAL MIGRATION AND CARE OF THE ELDERLY

Our research in the mid-1990s was in rural and suburban communities who produced migrants but did not often receive them. Even given extensive migration the large majority of elderly were living with a married child, either a son or daughter. The same is true in a 1995 urban sample from Kandy town where 80 per cent of persons over 60 were living with a child.[12]

However we found many fragmented families, a pattern which suggests that problems for the elderly have already begun and will undoubtedly increase in the future. Typical of these is one household in a highland village of Galle district where we met a 42-year-old unmarried daughter living with her father, aged 86, her mother, who was 76 and a 10-year-old niece sent to go to school and help in the house. The daughter's elderly father was senile and her mother well but not able to take responsibility for their home. Other siblings were not readily available since the closest of three married children lived five miles away. The sole income for their household came from this daughter's occasional work teaching sewing at an evening school and from the sale of clothing that she made.

A similar family in a Sinhalese village in Nuwara Eliya district consisted of three unmarried daughters, aged 48, 47 and 42, of an 83-year-old widow. Two daughters support the household, one as a teacher and the other by commuting daily to Kandy for a government job; the third cares for her mother and does the housework. Six other siblings including a teacher, bus driver, hospital attendant, and army officer—live in other districts.

In one family everyone had gone, leaving behind an ancient woman, aged 91, and her 70-year-old daughter who earned a bit of income weaving mats. This work supplemented the money that a 34-year-old unmarried daughter brought once each month from her work in a Colombo garment factory and the small gifts brought by a son on his monthly visit. No family member lived nearby and thus it was the neighbours who watched over these two elderly women.

These are three examples of what appears to be a growing trend among the families we interviewed. As children become educated and find better economic opportunities elsewhere, especially the men, they leave one sister at home. This is not likely to be a 'planned' strategy but instead the result of many discrete decisions by siblings. At first these women may be 'waiting to be married' but many wait too long, become unmarriageable and then settle into spinsterhood. This is a new demographic pattern in Sri Lanka. In 1971 only 4.6 per cent of women aged 40–44 had not married, by 1981 that proportion had increased to 5.9 per cent.[13] The 1991 census is likely to show an even greater increase. What will happen to these spinsters when they grow old? Smaller families, therefore fewer siblings to help, combined with migration, will undoubtedly mean that many of these women who have cared for their parents have no one to care for them.

A few have already foreseen this problem and found ways to deal with it. In a suburb of Galle town we visited one 72-year-old unmarried lady, a school teacher, who had cared for her parents at home until their deaths. Then, she took in a female medical student as a boarder, for 'company' in the house. When the student got married, the couple, now with a baby, continued to share her home and provide help. Essentially she has 'adopted' an unrelated couple to care for her in the future and, probably, to inherit her home.

INTERNATIONAL MIGRATION AND CARE OF THE ELDERLY

Those who leave Sri Lanka for employment overseas generally take their families with them and do not return except for holidays. Most are in the middle of their professional careers and already have older parents who prefer to remain in Sri Lanka rather than accompany their children abroad. In some families several or all of the siblings have permanently migrated. The problems for elderly parents of middle-class permanent migrants are somewhat different than those I have already described. In contrast to most rural families more parents have their own income, sometimes from a government or private pension, sometimes from land, and thus day-to-day financial support from their children is not always crucial. Some children living abroad can afford to send money although often their foreign incomes, which appear to be huge from a Sri Lankan perspective, must be used entirely for living expenses in the new country.

Instead, much more central, are problems of care. Who will help when a parent needs to be taken to a hospital? Who can take over management of their financial affairs when parents can no longer cope? Some may remain in their own home with a servant, or with a relative 'sent' to provide companionship and practical help; in these cases day-to-day needs may be met but more subtle problems may be ignored and major decisions not made.

Currently, probably the most common experience in these families is like this one. Two professionally trained sons have migrated permanently, one to Australia and the other to the USA. Their elderly mother lives with one of her married daughters who, with the help of a servant, can provide for her needs and manage her affairs. An informal agreement among all the children is that the daughter will take charge but when there are unusual medical bills the sons abroad will send money.

But other family experiences, while relatively unusual now, are likely to be common in the future since families are becoming smaller and opportunities for employment abroad are increasing. One Colombo family consists of an elderly widow and her only son who left Sri Lanka permanently many years ago. Because his mother had a relatively large income she lived alone comfortably in her large home with the help of three servants. But increasing age has brought both chronic illness and a series of medical emergencies that have required immediate decisions and action that a servant alone cannot take. As a result the brother of the son's wife oversees her care and takes charge in emergencies.

In another urban family all three children have permanently left the country, two for Australia and one for England. Their elderly parents continue to live in Colombo where they have a servant who comes daily to cook and clean. In addition, they have given free rooms to the servant's son and daughter both of whom work elsewhere but are in the house at night in case of an emergency. However, when one parent was badly injured in a fall at home it was the neighbours who initially arranged for care until one daughter could fly from Australia to take charge.

Other elderly people left without the help of children take in a distant relative as a companion and helper in exchange for free room and board. Some choose to move in with relatives. One elderly widow, whose only child left for New Zealand, moved into an independent apartment in the home of her daughter-in-law's family who could then provide emergency care if she needed it.

It is clear that when middle-class elderly parents find that all of their children have left Sri Lanka permanently they tend to rely on servants and/or on distant relatives or relatives of relatives who, normally, would not take such responsibility. These arrangements commonly require money to pay servants, often to feed servants' families and money to maintain a household suitable for extra helpers. Therefore a shift from the ideal that children should care for their parents to a practice in which parents pay for their own care has probably already begun among middle-class urban families affected by increasing permanent migration.

Conclusion

I have looked at only one example of the ways globalization and modernization affect Sri Lankan families. Here the focus has been on the movement of people away from the family home to take work, both inside and outside the country, which may improve their economic status. It is clear that these relatively new kinds of migration affect family members left at home, often in a negative way.

I could have looked, as well, at similar kinds of problems for the family that arise from another product of globalization, that is, the development of the tourist industry, which attracts a large numbers of visitors from Europe and Asia. Some Sri Lankans have been drawn into the illegal drug business and children into prostitution, often centred in tourist areas, which may lead to sexually transmitted diseases and trouble with the law, problems that the whole family must then deal with.

I have raised two specific issues for the family in this chapter. One is the stress on nuclear families when a central person, the mother, is away for years at a time. While the economic and social position of the family sometimes permanently improves, often the negative impacts on children, husband and income outweigh the benefits. In the long run the status of these women seems to change very little. The major benefit of these employment opportunities seems to go to the Sri Lankan economy as a whole in the form of remittances that are spent by the family.

Opportunities for women to work abroad are linked closely to political and economic conditions outside Sri Lanka. They may disappear as quickly as they appeared and new kinds of overseas employment appealing to others, for example, young men or trained teachers, may arise just as quickly. Therefore families, and those organizations providing services to families, can expect further, largely unpredictable, problems that have been generated by global politics and economics over which Sri Lanka has little control.

The second issue raised by migration for employment concerns the care of the elderly who are often left behind. And in contrast to problems caused by the temporary migration of women, this one is probably permanent. Currently, as more children move far from home, unmarried daughters, neighbours, or servants, often take charge. But in the long run, given that there will be smaller families and therefore fewer siblings to help parents plus more women working and even more migration far from home one should expect to see a major shift in sources of support for the elderly similar to those in the West.

Instead of help in kind from children, elderly parents may require health insurance, new kinds of housing, institutional care such as nursing homes, and social and personal services, all of which must be paid for, either personally or by the government. A few nursing homes for elderly parents who cannot be managed at home and retirement homes with several levels of care similar to those in the West are already available. Therefore the shift from family to formal institutional support has already begun and the process is likely to create conflict and harm to families before functional institutions are readily available to take over.

NOTES

1. Women and Development III, *Economic Review*, January 1986, p. 8.
2. N.E. Waxler, B. Morrison, S. Pinnaduwage and W.M. Sirisena, 'Infant mortality in Sri Lankan households: A causal model', *Social Science and Medicine*,

Vol. 20, No. 4, 1985, pp. 381–92. See also B. Morrison, 'The Transcendence of Locality and the Persistence of Community in Sri Lanka, 1980–1995', *Journal of Asian and African Studies*, Vol. 33, No. 2, 1998, pp. 205–22.

3. L.K. Ruhunage, 'Sri Lankan Labour Migration: Trends and Threats', *Economic Review*, January 1996, Table, p. 4.
4. M.R. Gamburd, 'Women's Work, Women's Wages: Sri Lankan Labor Migration and the Microprocesses of Gender Transformation', 5th Sri Lanka Conference, Durham, New Hampshire, August 1995.
5. Ibid., p. 16.
6. R.B.M. Korale, 'Migration for Employment to the Middle-East: Its Demographic and Socio-economic Effects in Sri Lanka', Colombo: Ministry of Plan Implementation, 1983, p. 23 (Quoted by Gamburd, n. 4).
7. M. Jinadasa, 'Private Remittances', *Economic Review*, August/October 1999.
8. Ruhunage, n. 3, p. 6, Table 8.
9. R. Kearney and B.D. Miller, *Internal Migration in Sri Lanka and its Social Consequences*, Boulder: Westview Press, 1987, Table 1.6, p. 15.
10. I. de Silva and D. Samarasekera, 'Population Ageing: Emerging Issues in Sri Lanka', *Economic Review*, April/May 1999, Table 1, p. 3.
11. Ibid., Table 5, p. 5.
12. D.B. Nugegoda and S. Balasuriya, 'Health and Social Status of an Elderly Urban Population in Sri Lanka', *Social Science and Medicine*, Vol. 4, No. 4, 1995, pp. 437–42.
13. *Statistical Pocket Book of Sri Lanka (Ceylon) 1977*, Data derived from Table 17, pp. 19–20. Also see, *Statistical Pocket Book of the Democratic Socialist Republic of Sri Lanka*, 1981, Table 19, pp. 24–25. Both published at Colombo by Department of Census and Statistics.

13

Damming the Flood of Violence and Shoring Up Civil Society in an Era of Globalization

SISIRA PINNAWALA

Sri Lanka, which was once a model democracy and one of the few peaceful countries of the Third World, is better known today for its violent politics. Politics marked by a civil war that has been going on for two decades and the two insurgencies that the country experienced in 1971 and in 1987–90. There is also an emerging new form of politically motivated and organized violence sponsored by the regime in power against the opposition political forces in the conduct of mainstream politics. General intimidation of opposition groups by the ruling party politicians, especially during elections, is a part of this spreading violence. Even more extreme violence is being used by the LTTE against the groups and individuals who oppose their hegemony in the north and east.[1] The role that violence has begun to play in all aspects of life of Sri Lankan society not only indicates a general breakdown of law and order and deterioration of democratic institutions but also a crisis of civil society. The democratic institutions of the country have been either made ineffective or highly compromised as a result of these developments.

Though incidents of organized political violence have been on the rise, both in civil war areas as well as in the south, it is not only the numbers that are important to understand this emerging culture of violence. Violence has increased in 'quality' and in 'organization' as well. Torture and mass killing, for example, have become part of the methods employed by the perpetrators of violence. Further even common criminal activities have become politicized, a development that is clearly manifested by the domination of the crime scene by organized networks of the underworld, which are in a mutually beneficial relationships with politicians. It is well known that the regime actors who sponsor violence against their opponents mobilize underworld links.[2] It is also known that underworld links are a resource mobilized by the LTTE, especially when it operates in the south. The second JVP (Janatha Vimukthi Peramuna) insurrection from 1987–90 had very strong links with the underworld before they renounced violence and entered the democratic arena.[3] The result of these developments is the elevation of ordinary crime onto a new plane where crime and violence become part of the political process. Not only has crime become politicized, politics too has become criminalized.

UNDERSTANDING ORGANIZED VIOLENCE

Today violence has taken on a new form and a new meaning. In addition to the society-focused violence that is organized, such as wars, we also have a form of organized violence that focuses on individuals and groups. The perpetrators of violence are not concerned with the general benefit of society but the benefit of a group or an individual. This is where the question of the legitimacy of violence arises. States can use violence in an organized form in the legitimate execution of power but only as long as it is used fairly and for the protection and well-being of citizens. When the use of violence by the state crosses the boundary of fairness it is no longer sanctioned, at least not morally. State violence can be illegitimate when it targets specific political, ethnic, or religious groups or those from specific socio-economic sectors. This occurs when arbitrariness replaces political consensus and social dialogue. When this happens, even state-sponsored violence can be illegitimate. A similar situation of legitimacy can be seen in relation to violence sponsored by non-state political actors. Unlike the state, they do not have the legal right to use violence in their political conduct. But they may have a moral right if their aim is to protect people from the use of violence by the state or other actors. The question of the legitimacy of violence becomes a complex issue when organized violence is thought about in this way (see Table 13.1).

Table 13.1
The Right to Use Violence

Actor	*Legal*	*Moral*
State	+	–/+
Non-state	–	–/+

States lose moral legitimacy when violence is not meant for the general well-being of the subjects. This happens when the state machinery is used by the regime in power to violate the rights of the citizens. On the other hand, violence by non-state actors has no legitimacy, either legal or moral, when they are fighting against a legitimate state. If the state loses legitimacy by using violence for the benefit of the regime only, then on moral grounds, organized violence by non-state actors may become legitimate. Therefore, it is important to understand on what grounds and when organized violence by non-state actors receives legitimacy and how and from where it is derived.

The social perception of violence changes with the context, both historical and social, and hence it is susceptible to the influence of globalization. This influence leads to a redefinition and re-evaluation of values as different cultures interact and a global consciousness emerges. Though globalization implies an acceptance of cultural diversity, there is cultural domination as well. In practice, globalization has led to the cultural hegemony of the west. Though there is some room for values of peripheral cultures to enter into the emerging global value system, the changes of values under globalization tends towards the acceptance of western values in the conduct of public activities, i.e., politics and economics. Value hegemony is one of the ways in which globalization influences our assessment of the legitimacy of organized violence.

The above discussion shows that organized violence derives legitimacy from two different directions. There can be either a politico-legal legitimacy, which is the state-centred way of defining organized violence, or a moral legitimacy, which is a more social definition. Both can and will change with the changing context.

GLOBALIZATION AND ITS IMPLICATIONS FOR UNDERSTANDING THE LOCAL

The multiplicity of linkages and interconnectedness, which make up the modern world system, is a major feature of globalization. Those who consider globalization as a structural phenomenon see global interconnectedness mainly as an economic and political relationship. These interconnections are leading to centre-periphery dependency among states, which accepts that the state is still important. However, the majority of globalization explanations do not see the world relations in terms of global geopolitical connections based on discrete political units, i.e., states. They are concerned with the transnational nature of globalization, which is described as the de-territorialization of the state and sovereignty. The emergence of transnational actors and structures is the most important development that identifies the unique character of globalization and makes it different from the traditional international relations based on the state system. These transnational structures are not just another set of networks that replaced interstate structures. They are qualitatively different from traditional networks that connect the state system at the level of international society. The main difference between the two structures is that while international relations recognize the state authority and draw their authority from the state, transnational relations are partially disengaged from the state and have an authority and legitimacy of their own. The emergence of transnational structures implies the existence of players that are gaining independence from the state system but also downgrades state authority.[4] The state under the new circumstances is not the final arbitrator of action, either national or international. It is this development that is the defining character of contemporary globalization.

The agencies of the interstate system, such as the United Nations, the World Bank and others, are gradually expanding their roles. There are other new agencies such as the World Trade Organization and the World Court. Though they are part of the interstate system, in that they deal through the state, their role is more proactive today, something that was not part of the interstate system earlier. Further, they are no longer mere facilitators of international relations based on the state system. The United

Nations is now intervening in the internal affairs of nations. The World Bank has become a regulator and decision maker of economic affairs of the state and lays down conditions before approving funds. This is bypassing the state and is something that is questionably acceptable under conventional international relations.

There are two other players who are playing an increasing role on the global scene as influential transnational actors—non-governmental organizations (NGOs) and the media. The international NGOs are engaged in a wide range of activities from human rights, poverty alleviation and empowerment to peace making and the conservation of the environment. They are continuously building their local networks to cover the globe. Today it is common for agencies like the World Bank to consult with NGOs about policies to be implemented within Sri Lanka. (The earlier chapter by Caspersz provides examples—Eds). The media on the other hand, with the developments in communication technology have been able to connect the world together more directly through TV and the Internet. News from different corners of the world is brought to the living rooms of individuals, making the global village a reality. The result of this is increasing awareness and sensitivity across the world. These two newer players, NGOs and the media, are particularly important in understanding claims to legitimacy by governments and of non-state actors. Now governments are being held to higher standards for the performance of their justice system, protection of their citizens and the distribution of benefits. Local NGOs with international linkages and the media carrying information about the standards of living and values elsewhere in the world are combining to raise expectations about what constitutes good and fair government.

The Spread of Violence in Sri Lankan Society

Organized violence in Sri Lanka is a recent development. The first two decades of independent Sri Lanka (1948–68), were free of organized violence except for three incidents. Of the three incidents, two were ethnic riots that took the form of short-lived mob violence. The other one was an organized anti-government protest that was led by the left movement and the trade unions in 1953. Though some leaders of the government were alarmed by the protest, in the end it was easily controlled. The lives lost in this protest were 11, which was a very high casualty rate for that period. The first election-related violence occurred in 1970 when the supporters of the party that came into power in the elections began attacking the supporters of the party that had previously formed the government. These attacks, however, were not organized and did not have the backing of the leaders except for approval from some local politicians. In the year following this incident, Sri Lanka witnessed the first insurrection by a left wing youth movement called the Janatha Vimukhti Peramuna (Peoples' Liberation Front), which was the first organized violent confrontation between the state and a political movement. This insurrection was put down relatively easily with minimum loss of life to the security forces but there were many deaths among the insurgents. The JVP regrouped again after a lapse of almost two decades and staged its second insurrection during 1987–90, which resulted in a bloody confrontation between the state and the rebels, inflicting heavy losses on the both sides. The total number of lives lost in the insurrection is conservatively estimated to be around 25,000 though some quote figures exceeding 60,000.[5] This insurgency brought to the south of the country two important features that had already become an integral part of organized violence in the ethnic conflict in the north. These two are the attacks on civilians by the combatants and the use of paramilitary forces by the government.

The 1970s also saw the emergence of the most destructive violent phase of Sri Lankan politics with the emergence of the Tamil militant movement. The Tamil militancy which began in the mid-1970s with several radical groups staging hit-and-run guerilla attacks on the government is today one of the most violent and highly successful guerilla movements in the world. The dominant player of the movement today is the Liberation Tigers of Tamil Eelam (LTTE) that has managed to establish its hegemony over other groups by gradually eliminating them through internecine killings. Use of violence by Tamil militants brought into the country a new brand of organized violence. They were the first to use attacks on civilians as a tactical means of achieving the objectives of the struggle. These attacks, that were directed only against the Sinhalese in the early days of the struggle, were later used against Tamil civilians as well. This was mainly during the period when the LTTE was establishing its hegemony over the other militant groups by eliminating them. The civilians who supported the rivals always became targets in these internecine fights during the mid-1980s and 1990s. The government also, in their counter-insurgency measures, began using unconventional methods in the north leading to a new era of organized violence. It was in the fight against the Tamil militants that the government first started using paramilitary forces. In the early phase of the Eelam war there was only one group of paramilitaries—known as home guards—whose formal role was to protect the civilians in border villages. Later these paramilitary groups were added to through the recruitment of members of rival militant groups that were under attack from the LTTE. The anti-state struggle in the north so far has resulted in civilian and combatant deaths of between 20,000 and 30,000.[6] Added to this are the civilian deaths and the deaths of members of the militant groups killed by the LTTE or through intra-group fighting which are estimated to be around 30,000 up to 1998.[7] A similar number is estimated to have disappeared during the period. In addition to that the war has created around one million refugees/migrants of whom over 400,000 are overseas.

In addition to the fighting between the state forces and the Tamil militants, ethnic riots that were spontaneous mob attacks in the early days have become part of organized violence in the later stages of the ethnic war. The so-called 'ethnic riots' in 1983 are well known for their organized character and the involvement of the ruling party politicians in planning, organizing and carrying out attacks against the Tamils. The riots in 1983 were unprecedented in the numbers killed: 367 Tamils according to official estimates but according to unofficial estimates over 3,000. But they were also unprecedented in the manner in which the pre-riot situation was created—the way the Tamils were hunted down by the attackers and the selection of targets, which were mainly businesses. The involvement of a minister of the government, who was known for his use of violence in attacking trade unions and for his strong anti-Tamil views, shows that political organization was behind the attacks. The recent violence in 2001 in Mawanella against the Muslims is another example of ethnic riots going beyond mere mob violence. Though the incident was triggered by a regular trader–client dispute, the background was Sinhala–Muslim business conflicts and supporters of local politicians who were engaged in collecting protection money. There is general agreement that the post-1977 period was the period that saw institutionalization of violence in Sri Lanka.[8]

THE RESPONSIBILITY OF POLITICIANS FOR THE RISE OF VIOLENCE

A major factor in the growth of violence has been the willingness of the political leadership to condone electoral intimidation and violence by their followers. The actual agents of violence were sheltered from investigation and prosecution by the influence of their patrons.

The election-related violence of 1970 was in the form of mob attacks and did not have any organization/plan or the support of the national leadership. The situation began to change when in 1977, Sri Lanka saw the first major outbreak of pre-election violence that killed over 60 people. Since then, election-related violence has became the norm of Sri Lankan politics. Politically organized violence expanded with the rise of the ethnic struggle. Tamil militants began to attack the government forces in the early 1980s and the intensity of the attacks increased after the 1983 ethnic riots. Today political violence is not limited to conducting elections but pervades the whole political process. This is the new development in organized violence facing the country since 1977. Increasingly, the exercise of political power is conducted through violence today. Table 13.2 outlines the violence involved in the conduct of elections in Sri Lanka since 1977.

It was widely reported in the pro-government media during the run-up to the 1977 election that the then opposition leader Mr. J.R. Jayewardene, who was widely tipped to win by a landslide, would give leave to the police for seven days after he came to power. Ostensibly, the leave was to reward them for extra duty during the electioneering. But it was widely understood that this was a signal and a sanctioning to attack the followers of the defeated political party and the carnage that followed the elections gave credence to the above claim. This pattern continued with increasing regime involvement in violence against the opposition. The District Development Councils' election in Jaffna in 1981 was marked by violence and this time a powerful minister who was to contest the presidential election later was cited by the press as

TABLE 13.2
Incidents of Election Violence since 1970

Year	*Election*	*Murders*	*Other Incidents*	*General Characteristics of Violence*
1970	General Election			First post-election violence.
1977	General Election	62	7,817	Open support for violence by regime.
1982	Referendum			Regime actively participates in violence.
1981	DDC Elections	4		A Minister is named for involvement in the hijacking of ballot boxes.
1989	General Election	669		Majority of killings by the JVP and paramilitaries of the regime.
1994	General Election	12	45 serious incidents	Regime violence is countered by the opposition for the first time. Non-state actors come in to monitor election violence.
1997	Provincial Council	7		Regime attacks on the opposition.
1999	Presidential Election	8	320 serious incidents	Regime attacks on the opposition. LTTE for the first time enters in to election violence in the south.
2000	General Election			
2001	General Election	56	1,514 serious incidents	Opposition violence becomes intensified. Post-election, it causes 11 deaths.

Source: Administrative Reports of the IGP, Colombo and PAFFREL Reports.

the main culprit. In the 1982 referendum the government used false charges to get the opposition members arrested and in 1983 the JVP was banned for instigating anti-Tamil violence though the real culprits were government politicians. This was done mainly to get the JVP out of mainstream politics, as it was by then becoming popular as an alternative political voice.

In addition to election violence, violence against opponents also became a regular feature since 1977. The government party politicians started using violence to establish a hegemony of the regime in all activities. The government particularly directed its attention to the trade unions that were considered the main threat as the opposition in the parliamentary chamber had been reduced to an ineffective voice due to the landslide victory the government achieved in 1977. The government began to use the judiciary, the public service and the security forces, as well as the underworld, in an unprecedented manner. Though it is true that it was during the 1960s, under the previous left-of-centre government, that the judiciary and the public service came to be under the Cabinet Executive. Political interference in these institutions was of very limited extent in the pre-1977 period. The previous regime's interference in the state system was mainly limited to gaining personal favours rather than harassing oppositional groups, so there was still a rule of law. In the 1980s the domination of the regime over the state apparatus became institutionalized and it became an extension of the regime.[9] Politicians of the ruling party used the state machinery not only to help their followers but also to silence their opponents.

Analysts see the 1980s as the period marked by the rapid breakdown of civil political order.[10] The state was going through a crisis of its own creation, facing violent attacks from the southern insurgents and the northern Tamil militants. Organized violence by the regime, using state power, also came to be established as the normal way of conducting political activities during the period. The use of extra-judicial forces by the regime became a normal part of political process. There were two forces that the regime mobilized to achieve their political objectives, the state security forces and the underworld. The underworld became an integral part of political action during this period with politicians depending on its support to intimidate the opposition. One such noted criminal supporting the UNP was Gonawala Sunil who according to some had very close connections with ruling party politicians including the then President J.R. Jayawardene. Another character was Sothi Upali, a notorious underworld boss who was on the Working Committee of the UNP and a close associate of Premadasa, who was elected President after Jayawardene.[11]

After 1982, the government started using the security forces to break protests and attack unions. Security forces were rewarded for serving the regime. When an officer of the police was found guilty by the Supreme Court of violating civil rights by seizing leaflets of an opposition political party, his fine was paid by the government. Another officer who was found guilty of violating one of the prominent lady politicians of the left was promoted on the same day he was found guilty. Government-owned buses were used to take thugs to attack opponents. Politicians in power abused their power by using state agencies and state resources. But worse, they were not ashamed to do that. During this period organized violence not only came to be institutionalized but also became a self-perpetuating process. It is therefore correct to say that the 1980s were the watershed of organized violence in the country, which continues today.

GLOBALIZATION AND VIOLENCE IN SRI LANKA

It is not possible to argue that global actors, either economic or otherwise, have caused the crisis of violence in Sri Lanka. Neither the two southern insurrections nor the ethnic war were caused by global economic forces. In fact, the period that saw their emergence was a period of economic growth, though the growth was uneven and increased the gap between the poor and the rich. Though it is true that increasing exposure to violence through television has an overall impact on the population in the way they view violence and its uses, it would be a simplification to argue that it has also had a significant impact in increasing violence in Sri Lanka. As we saw in the previous section, the violence in the country is more associated with local process such as the crisis of the state. However, this does not mean that Sri Lanka's organized violence can be understood without situating the local in the global context. Though there is no direct connection between global forces and local violence in Sri Lanka in terms of the global being the cause of the local process, the local violence is connected to globalization. Globalization is connected to local organized violence through several transnational actors. The transnational actors that are important in this connection are the ethnic diasporas, the non-governmental organizations and the media. Each has existed long before the recent onset of globalization but each has grown in importance during the last decades of accelerating linkage of the peoples of the world.

THE SRI LANKAN DIASPORA

Diasporas have become important players in the politics of both the receiving country and the country of origin. For instance, we know that the Irish in America always supported the Irish struggle.

With globalization the involvement and importance of the diaspora as a transnational actor have increased. They have undergone changes in both operation and organization. They have become a force that is involved in promoting home-country politics in the host country. In that exercise they bring the home-country violence to host countries in two ways. First they become perpetrators of violence in the host country against their home-country enemies. Second, and more important, they use the power of their diaspora to canvass support of the host country's government for their cause. As most of these are violent conflicts, as in the case of the ethnic war in Sri Lanka, the result of these brings violence, both physical and political, to the host country. In terms of organization, diasporas have changed. They are no longer country-based operations but global networks. Globalization has allowed this development through the advancements and expansion in communication. The Internet is a very important vehicle for this transformation of diasporas into global networks. In the case of the Sri Lankan diaspora there is a well-organized network connecting diaspora groups in many countries and operations are carried out mainly through the Internet.[12]

The Sri Lankan diaspora consists of three distinct groups of people, namely, professionals, contract workers and refugees, coming from all three major ethnic communities (Sinhalese, Tamils and Muslims). They are present in almost all parts of the world with concentrations in Europe, North America, Australasia and the Middle East. The Sri Lankan diaspora in the Middle East are mainly contract workers who are in the lower and middle occupational categories. About 70 per cent of these workers are women working as housemaids. Refugees in the diaspora are, except for very few, members of the minority Tamil community and are present in the West and in India. It is estimated that there are about 125,000 Tamil refugees in India and half-a-million in the West. The third group, which includes professional members of the diaspora, come from both the Sinhala and Tamil communities and are concentrated in the West and in Australasia. The fact that the members of the Tamil community have left the country due to social injustice such as discrimination in employment and education (professionals) and also as a result of the ethnic war (refugees) is important to understand the dynamics of the Sri Lankan diaspora and their involvement in the ethnic conflict. The very strong identification with the Tamil struggle is mainly due to this. Though the Sinhalese do not have the same emotional attachment to the political struggle in their home country, they are also an important diaspora player in the home country politics. They are becoming part of the ethnic conflict in Sri Lanka as a reaction to the activities of the Tamil diaspora. During the height of the JVP violence there was a section of the Sinhala diaspora supporting the cause of the JVP as well.

The diaspora activities, mainly the activities of the Tamil diaspora, have brought the organized violence of Sri Lanka into the wider world. The activities of the diaspora connect home and host countries in two ways. First is by lobbying for support. This involves lobbying for the support of the host governments, NGOs and international organizations to bring pressure on the Sri Lankan government. In addition to lobbying, activists organize demonstrations and other political activities on behalf of the struggle. The activities here are not directly aimed at the promotion of violence but the final result of these is continuation of violence. Political activities by the Tamil diaspora, supporting the conflict in Sri Lanka, are helping to legitimize the anti-state violence and projecting the state as the culprit. Tamil activists arouse the sympathy and support of both migrant Tamils and members of the public in the host country. They collect donations to support the struggle for Tamil Eelam. Less visible is the systematic collection of money from the migrant communities—sometimes by methods resembling those of the Mafia, which are illegal in the host country. They not only collect funds but also invest them, making the diaspora part of the global economic actors, i.e., becoming a transnational economic force. The LTTE for example recently established its Chamber of Commerce in London. These economic agencies are working with the arms dealers to buy arms and other war equipment with the funds they collect. The LTTE is said to be operating a shipping service with funds and the shipping network is used to transport arms to Sri Lanka. It is also known that the underground economy, mainly drug trafficking, is also part of their work.

The Non-Governmental Organizations

One of the identifying features of contemporary globalization has been the rapid growth of the NGOs. Sri Lankan and foreign NGOs interact with each other, reinforce each other and develop some overlapping missions. Among these is a growing concern for individual and group rights. The emphasis on group rights and human rights challenges the rights of the state and its sovereignty. Individual and group rights are becoming a factor in international relations. Today NGOs have extensive networks connecting the global with the local. They are beginning to play three main roles in the global village. They are recognized as watch dogs over governmental actions, as informal defenders and advocates for rights and politically correct conduct, and as agencies for relief and rehabilitation. Each of these roles is being played by groups in Sri Lanka, particularly in the areas in the north and east. NGOs are providing humanitarian aid and development aid in the north. These include organizations such as the International Committee of the Red Cross (ICRC) and the Doctors without Borders. NGOs dealing with human rights such as Amnesty International and the Human Rights Watch have also been active in the country, especially since the escalation of the ethnic violence.

The presence of the NGOs is related to the reality of violence in the country. First, both the human and material damages of organized violence open the way for service NGOs to provide assistance and support to affected communities. They are particularly helpful in providing or assisting in organizing logistics in providing essential services such as health facilities in areas affected by violence. They run refugee camps. They also coordinate activities between the government forces and the militants, which is essential for the people who live in areas under the control of the militants. This is done by NGOs such as the ICRC. NGOs concerned with human rights are also active. Their attention is on the excesses of the conflicting parties and is in most cases limited to observation and reporting.

It is possible to argue that violence in the country is influenced and even encouraged by the actions of these organizations. NGOs, especially the human rights NGOs such as Amnesty International, help bringing the attention of the world to what is happening on the ground. The reports of the Human Rights Watch and Amnesty International influence the decisions of funding by donor agencies and countries and the government is therefore concerned about their comments. The militants are similarly concerned as their struggle depends on the sympathy of the diasporic community and foreign governments. Thus, the NGOs work as local and international pressure groups. Their presence is important as monitors of violence and also serves as a constraint on the actors who are involved in violence. Beyond the NGOs' role as monitors and service providers, however, there is a further, unintended function. By carrying out these two functions they also indirectly help continue the violence. The moral condemnation of government violence provides support for the militants' cause and the excesses of the militants is taken as justification by the government to continue the struggle to defeat the militants. By calling attention to the violent behaviour of each party, the other party gains a justification for continued violence. Moreover, relief services provided by NGOs make violence tolerable for those who live with it. They try to make sure that basic services do not completely breakdown. They become safety valves of social life in a violence-dominated society. Their presence makes sure that violence does not totally destroy the social organization. In the past people fled areas of violence because, among other problems, there were no basic services. Today NGOs provide basic services or provide logistics and co-ordination and by providing them enable the fighting to continue.

THE MEDIA

The third transnational actor that plays a role is the media. The media is the opinion maker of global society and plays a very important role in creating awareness. It connects organized violence into a global distribution of images and ideas raising the consciousness and conscience of the global village. The impact of television is important as it portrays a strong visual of the results of violence. Similar to the role of the NGOs that unconsciously perpetuate violence, the media plays a similar role in global society. It keeps the violence going by raising issues of conscience that could endorse the actions of one party. But the flow of information and images is two-way—from Sri Lanka to the world and the world to Sri Lanka. The globalization of the media has enabled the international media to enter homes as an alternative to the locally produced news reports. The international media is easily accessible in most parts of Sri Lanka. This distribution of foreign and international programmes is an alternative source of information to that of the government in the country. These external sources of news have given the locals a reliable source of information that does not repeat the government's bias. The impact of these external sources is raising questions about the credibility of the locally provided news reports. Like the NGOs, the presence of the international media is a constraint on the perpetrators of organized violence as judged by the reactions of the government apologists.

The growth of the above three transnational actors—the diaspora, the NGOs, and the media—has helped reduce the role of the state. The decline in the state's freedom of action is often described as the state losing sovereignty as a result of either international organizations: such as the Bretton Woods institutions taking over decision making power in the economy or due to the ever-increasing role of transnational actors under globalization.[13] As a result, the state has local responsibility with reduced powers and the supranationals exercise more power without responsibility. As a result, the role of the state has been curtailed in several important areas. This has resulted in the state losing its prerogative to be the sole originator of political action. This is true of its sovereign right to exercise force in the territory. The limitations on the state as the originator of force creates a partial power vacuum that is filled by various regime actors who perform the role on behalf of the state, resulting in uncontrolled organized violence. One of the regime actors recruited and encouraged in these situations are the paramilitaries.

The regime actors who can use violence on behalf of the state become an essential part of the state's survival strategy under these circumstances. As the state is answerable to transnational actors and interstate agencies, it cannot use force of the same kind or in the same way as the militants. This is mainly because anti-state forces use unconventional methods in their violence but the legitimate state cannot use the same methods. If they do, they will bring down on themselves the disapproval of the international community. This would have an impact on the flow of aid and investment as well as in other ways. No legitimate state wants to be an international pariah state in this age of globalization. So for the sake of its own survival, at least, the state has to abide by the rules of the game. This is the dilemma the state faces under globalization, when it must counter organized violence by actors who do not play by the rules. When the state becomes ineffective, i.e., when this power vacuum is created there is space for alternative, irregular actors to move in. In Sri Lanka this has been the case during the 1987–90 insurrection and also in fighting the ethnic war. During the 1987–90 insurrection when the JVP was riding high there emerged numerous paramilitaries, apparently with government blessings, to support the security forces. They engaged in indiscriminate killings that immensely helped the forces put down the insurrection. These paramilitaries who support the regime do not emerge by themselves. They may be covertly organized by the state so that the state has a force to do its dirty work. It was an open secret that the numerous paramilitary organizations that emerged in 1987–90 were actually formed with the blessings of the government. Some of the paramilitaries who cooperated with the government forces in the ethnic war received their training and logistic support from the forces. One of the most important things about the paramilitaries, whether organized covertly by the state or not, is that the government can engage in a dirty war without getting blamed for it. So they are a blessing in disguise to the state though their existence is dangerous for the survival of the state in the long run.

Transnational Actors and Their Role in Lowering the Level of Violence

The rise of organized violence in politics is the most important political development in independent Sri Lanka. The damage it has caused to Sri Lankan society is visible at all levels of social organization and in all sectors of society. Loss of life, livelihood and property apart, the high cost of the psychological damage cannot be calculated. The economic activities of the country have been severely disrupted, retarding growth and development. Sri Lanka for the first time in its post-independence history experienced negative economic growth. Though it could be argued that the economic slowdown of the country has multiple causes ranging from domestic to international, it cannot be denied that the single most important contributor to the slow growth of the economy during the last decade was the violent conflicts the county was experiencing. The Sri Lankan state is also on the verge of collapse, unable to establish its authority over the perpetrators of organized violence. A political class, which freely resorts to violence as a political tactic, has gradually taken over the state on the one hand while anti-state challengers have been taking away both territory and authority on the other. The Sri Lankan polity is being fragmented both spatially and organizationally. In this context the most important task before the country is finding ways to control the ever-escalating organized violence.

Ending organized violence in society is a complex issue. Finding solutions means addressing the whole range of socio-economic issues that have led to the situation, which requires extensive evaluation of possible political measures and structural changes. The discussion here is limited to the short-term rolling back of the level of organized violence and to the examination of the potential role of some international actors in limiting organized violence in the country. It is argued here that de-escalation of organized violence in Sri Lanka is primarily a role of the actors of globalization for they occupy a special place in both global and local contexts.

In an earlier discussion it was noted that one important development of globalization is the emergence of transnational actors and structures. Transnational relations, as distinct from international relations, connect societies and not just states for transnational actors do not have to work on the basis of state structures. They do not derive power and authority from the state as in the case of traditional interstate actors such as the United Nations. As they do not rely on the state to reach into societies, they are not perceived as representing state interests at either local or global levels.

The interstate actors have also changed their modes of operation under globalization. Both transnational actors and interstate agencies are actively involved in reducing organized violence. Their involvement needs to be seen in the context of changing views of control of violence under globalization. Today control of violence is seen as a process that requires negotiation and not an act that requires force. Control of organized violence is no longer the sole responsibility of the state under globalization. These developments in violence control are particularly evident in Sri Lanka's attempt to end the ethnic violence.

Globalization, as we have argued, has resulted in changing our perception of violence and thus redefining what organized violence is. Today the use of force is not the legitimate right of only the state. Other actors also have the right to use force. This development is a direct result of the changing views of the legitimacy of violence for which globalization has been responsible. The result of changing views of the legitimacy of violence has led to the adoption of new rules and methods in dealing with violence. Unlike the past, control of violence today is not the sole responsibility of the state because it no longer has the sole legitimate right to use force. If the governing regime is not representative of society, it has no right to use force to control challenging violence because its own violence is used to benefit only one group. Then the state would be seen as engaging in organized violence against its citizens and this is the situation in Sri Lanka. So the control of violence in Sri Lanka has become a complex issue under globalization. Today it is a dual affair undertaken by both the Sri Lankan state and the transnational actors. Efforts to control organized violence in Sri Lanka today are part of a process that takes place as a dialogue between the conflicting parties with the involvement of the transnational actors and interstate organizations.

The acceptance or, at least, recognition that the control of violence should be through dialogue and not by force has brought new issues and concerns onto the agenda. First, it has brought in both transnational actors and interstate organizations as partners in controlling organized violence in the country. Second, today there is a growing equality between the conflicting parties. The state does not hold an exclusive, dominant position in the dialogue to control violence. This equality may be viewed as a direct result of non-state groups getting new recognition under globalization that places special value on group rights. This has now happened in Sri Lanka and it is reflected in the mediated negotiations between the state and the LTTE. To a lesser extent it is seen in contacts between the state (regime actors) and opposition groups in mainstream politics. As the state is no longer above its adversary it cannot dictate terms. Both have to observe the terms and conditions agreed upon in the dialogue. The result of this is that monitoring and mediation become essential parts of violence control. The present attempts to control organized violence in Sri Lanka follow the above violence-control paradigm of globalization.

There are a number of transnational and interstate actors who are involved in the control of violence in Sri Lanka and their involvement varies depending on the actor and the context. Some are general observers of the events like Amnesty International and the Human Rights Watch. They make reports and recommendations that are meant for the potential mediators and activists. There are other monitors who work in Sri Lanka either by the invitation of the government or some other agency such as an NGO. They have a specific area or event to monitor such as fairness and intimidation during the elections. Their task is specific and their recommendations are also directed to a specific client or clients. Neither of these groups of monitors are received by the government, therefore no action is taken. NGO groups cannot act on these recommendations as they have no power. There is a third type of violence-monitoring in Sri Lanka which has clear-cut objectives and well-defined areas of authority. Norway's involvement in mediation between the state and the LTTE belongs to this type. However, this monitoring involvement is fundamentally different from traditional third-party mediation by state actors.

Earlier cases of third party intervention and mediation followed the pattern of state-to-state agreement. In 1971, the first southern insurrection was put down with outside assistance. Both India and Russia provided military hardware to the then government. In 1987, India came into Sri Lanka to mediate between the Tamil militants and the government. Both these cases followed the norms of conduct of interstate relations. Russia and India came to Sri Lanka with the stated objective of helping the Sri Lankan state on an invitation by the government.[14] In 1987, the norms of interstate relations were reinforced when the two countries signed the Indo–Sri Lanka agreement before India formally sent their forces to the country. The sending of forces to keep peace also signifies another aspect of traditional interstate norms for involvement. The Norwegian involvement in the management of conflict in Sri Lanka does not adhere to the above norms. First, the Norwegian involvement is not on behalf of the government though the invitation was formally extended to them by the government. Norwegians had been in consultation with the LTTE and the government informally long before the government took the formal decision to invite them. Second, the process that has been established as a result of Norwegian mediation treats both parties as equals. Norwegians only facilitate the dialogue and monitor the implementation of the agreement between the two parties. This process of violence-control is therefore following a paradigm that is based on the norms and values which have spread with globalization.

The spread of organized violence has a close association with the deterioration of state structures and the weakening of civil society institutions. This has led to a crisis of the state where partisan political actors took over the control of the state. There is, therefore, a need to rebuild structures that have been destroyed as a result of the crises that the country has been going through. This means depoliticization of the public service and the police force, the two state structures that have been misused by politicians. It means restoring a measure of civility and cooperation among the political parties rather than treating each other as enemies. It also means creating an environment in which civil society organizations can be created and function without harassment by regime actors. These and similar measures are accepted as part of the process of addressing the problem of organized violence. They come together under the umbrella term of 'good governance'.

Rebuilding efforts should concentrate on capacity building and empowerment of both civil society structures and state institutions. The principal actors are the NGOs.[15] They have the skills and resource base necessary for rebuilding civil society and state structures. They also have well-established networks connecting the local resources and actors with those at the global level. These networks help them to draw on international expertise on the one hand and, on the other, they can use the local networks in the delivery of services. No other agency operating at the local level possesses such a capacity. In addition, the globalization process has gained for the NGOs recognition from the interstate actors. They are considered to be less prone to political interference and less bureaucratic in their operations. Thus they are more trusted by foreign governments and interstate agencies. The international connection that they have and confidence they command from other relevant actors mean that they are in a better position to secure some kinds of funds and resources than the Sri Lankan state.

The attention paid to violence in different regions of the country is different both in quantity and quality. International attention is focused on the ethnic conflict in the north and east. It is the major social crisis in the country. It has both political and moral considerations that attract the attention of international agencies. Further, the northern problem has other international repercussions such as refugees, that directly affect India and the West. The organized violence in the south, which largely originates from the regime in power, is seen as a governance issue and therefore an internal national concern. It does not receive the same attention from international agencies as the conflict in the north. Also, there is the reluctance of the government to have foreign agencies involved in the south, though they are keen on getting their help to work for a solution in the north. The principal reason for these seemingly double standards is clearly a question of survival. The regime actors in the south use violence for their own benefit and their continuation in power is thought to be dependent on violence. Therefore they do not want anything to happen to their principal means of remaining in power. On the other hand such continued violence directly affects the state and serious damage to the state will mean that it will threaten their own political future as they use the state apparatus to protect themselves and their interests. This does not mean that there are no violence-control activities in the south. There are a few but they are not carried through in a coordinated manner. Further, they receive only lukewarm support from the regime in power. It is only the political opposition that wants improved control of organized violence in the south. This situation seriously hampers violence control in the south.

FINAL THOUGHT

Organized violence in contemporary Sri Lankan society can be very broadly divided into two types, anti-state violence and violence sponsored by state actors. The anti-state violence in Sri Lankan society today is mainly part of the ethnic war but extremist left-wing revolutionaries have also been active until recently. The second type, which is violence in the conduct of mainstream political activities, is sponsored by regime actors who use violence as the principal means of power. Election violence is the main activity of these actors and it has dominated the Sri Lankan electoral process since the late 1970s. In this the violence is directed not against the state but by the regime in power against their opponents, i.e., political groups that seek to form the government.

This situation is somewhat different from the violence associated with elections in many other parts of the world where election-related violence is the norm, as in Latin America. In those countries election violence is, on the whole, anti-state violence as seen in the work of left-wing revolutionary groups like the FARC (Fuerzas Armadas Revolucionarios de Colombia) and Zapatista. Political violence organized by the mainstream political actors is a new phenomenon, that is so far limited to Sri Lanka, Pakistan and, to some extent, India.

Organized violence in Sri Lanka is the culmination of a series of events since independence. An interconnected series of political decisions, both in handling the demands by minority ethnic communities and the general handling of the economic and social issues, have contributed to the present crisis. The crisis therefore could be described as a direct result of political mismanagement by short-sighted political leadership whose prime objective was holding on to state power. Though there is no causal connection between globalization and organized violence in Sri Lanka there is a close association between transnational actors (who have acquired a new role under globalization) and violence in the country. For example, the ethnic diaspora and the international NGOs have been playing an important role in the ethnic conflict since the middle 1980s. They have also started mediating in the mainstream violence as seen from the involvement of election observers and regular contacts between international Human Rights groups and the Sri Lankan government and the opposition groups. Today, organized violence in Sri Lanka is gradually becoming more than a national problem, with transnational actors asserting their role as both mediators and regulators.

Though civilians bear the brunt of the violence, the state is the principal victim of violence in Sri Lanka. The state condones violence and all state power and machinery is used against the opponents of the regime in power as the regime cannot survive without violence. The Sri Lankan state has lost its legitimacy as a result of becoming the instrument of a particular regime. The Sri Lankan state has lost both politico-legal legitimacy and moral legitimacy and cannot therefore play an effective role in establishing law and order. The outcome of this is that the state is losing its role as the controller of violence necessitating external involvement. The vacuum that has been created in the state–civil society interface has enabled transnational actors who are part of the globalization process to intervene in this context.

This brings us to the question of what the formal role of transnational actors is in this situation. As we have already discussed, the transnational involvement is a legitimate action under the emerging new rules of globalization. The state is not the prime mover of national affairs in the new globalized world society. Though there are some emerging networks uniting the global action with local action, for example, strong collaboration between local NGOs and international NGOs, there are still no permanent and formally recognized structures to co-ordinate the actions of transnational actors at the national level. Establishment of such structures, further, is not within the purview of one nation or one government as it needs international sanctioning of any such activity. Therefore the role of these actors in the Sri Lankan context is not yet fully developed. The way things are moving in the two main areas of violence in Sri Lanka, namely, in relation to the highly visible Norway-sponsored mediation in the ethnic conflict and also low-level involvement of NGOs and formal state actors in the control of election violence in the south of the country is evidence that such structures are slowly getting into place.

NOTES

1. University Teachers for Human Rights, 'Children in the North-East War 1985–1995', in J. Uyangoda and J. Biyanwila (Eds), *Matters of Violence; Reflections on Political Violence in Sri Lanka,* Colombo: Social Scientists Association, 1997, pp. 44–51.
2. J. Uyangoda, 'Local Bodies and Domains of Localized Power', in *Matters of Violence,* pp. 56–73. See n. 1.
3. C.A. Chandraprema, *Sri Lanka: The Years of Terror; The JVP Insurrection 1987–1980,* Colombo: Lake House, 1991.
4. P.J. Taylor, 'The Modern Multiplicity of State', in E. Kofman and G. Young, (Eds), *Globalization: Theory and Practice,* London: Pinter, 1996.
5. See Chandraprema, no. 3.
6. J. Uyangoda, 'Sri Lanka's Political Violence: Fifty Years of its Making', in *Sri Lanka: Fifty Years of Independence,* Colombo: A Ravaya Publication, 1998, pp. 91–111.
7. H. Goonathilake, 'Dimensions for National Security', in *Sri Lanka: Fifty Years of Independence,* pp. 83–90. See n. 6.

8. Y.R. Amarasinghe, 'Aspects of the State Crisis in Sri Lanka', in P.V.J. Jayasekera (Ed.), *Security Dilemma of a Small State*, New Delhi: South Asian Publishers, 1995, pp. 69–90. And S.G. Liyanage, 'Three Models of Democracy: Some Reflections of Sri Lankan Post Independence Experience', *Sri Lanka: Fifty Years of Independence*, pp. 113–17. See n. 6.
9. G. Keerawella, 'Political Anatomy of Southern Militancy: The Insurrection of the Janatha Vimukthi Peramuna 1983–1990', in *Security Dilemma of a Small State*, pp. 69–90. See n. 8. Also Amarasinghe, n. 8.
10. Keerawella, n. 9.
11. Gonawala Sunil was killed by the JVP during the 1987–90 insurrection while Sothi Upali was gunned down after the PA government came to power in 1994. One characteristic of the association between the underworld and the politicians is that they often changed their political loyalties with the change in government.
12. S.K. Pinnawala, *Nation Building in Cyberspace: Sri Lanka's Civil War, Tamil Diaspora and the Internet*, Unpublished paper presented at the Institute of Asian Research, The University of British Columbia, 2000, p. 17.
13. J. Peck and A. Tickell, 'Jungle Law Breaks Out: Neo Liberalism and Global-Local Disorder', *Area*, Vol. 24, No. 4, 1994, pp. 317–26.
14. This involvement has another dimension to it. Sri Lanka was forced to ask India to help because India was planning to intervene anyway. Shortly before India was asked to help, India violated Sri Lankan air space by dropping food parcels in Jaffna, claiming that Sri Lankan military action was leading to starvation among Tamil civilians.
15. There are debates on the question of who represents civil society and who works for these representatives. The question often asked by those who criticize the work of the NGOs is whether they are the real representatives of the people in the country. These critics say that the NGOs are mainly organized by Colombo-based, English-speaking, middle-class activists who are out of touch with reality. Therefore, they do not represent Sri Lankan civil society as they claim. See S. Goonatilake, 'The Peace Process: Picking Up the Alternatives', *The Sunday Times* (Colombo), 26 May 2002, p. 10.

Conclusion

Reflections on Globalization and Social Cohesion in Sri Lanka

S.H. HASBULLAH AND BARRIE M. MORRISON

The mandate of our project was to assess the interaction of globalization and social cohesion in five countries in Asia—Sri Lanka, Indonesia, China, Korea and Japan. As we began to think through the issues for our book on Sri Lanka our expectation that the concepts 'globalization' and 'social cohesion' would be useful in understanding the changes and tensions in the country have been displaced by the nationally important process of 'rebuilding society'.

With visits back and forth among contributors, email exchanges, and a workshop in Shanghai, which included colleagues writing about other countries, we shifted the focus of our concern to the issue of building an inclusive, forward-looking society. The statement by President Chandrika Kumaratunga that '... We have faltered in the essential task of nation building since independence ... we have failed to address the issue of building a truly pluralist nation state.' (April 2002) succinctly summed up our redefined concern. What was and is true for the state, was and is true for the encompassing society.

From this perspective, 'social cohesion' is the concept to be tested. How much social cohesion is needed in a society experiencing fundamental changes and unprecedented problems? And then, what have we come to understand by the term 'social cohesion'? The societal unit being tested for cohesion needs to be specified—a residential community, a cultural minority, a voluntary grouping, an ethno-nationalistic solidarity, all citizens of Sri Lanka, or something else. And as soon as such a listing is written down it is apparent that there are multiple levels and forms of cohesion. The same individual may be a resident of Mannar town relating to her neighbours; a member of a Tamil-speaking minority supportive of claims for equal rights for her cultural group; an ardent feminist connecting to women in Mannar, in Colombo and the Third World, and an outspoken Sri Lankan nationalist critical of the presence of the Indian Peace Keeping Force on the island. So cohesion is the empathetic identification with the interests of others and the willingness to commit personal time, energy and resources to support the group and its goals. We suspect that most people have such empathetic identifications with many different groups.

As we have argued earlier, the social units are changing. At the most intimate level, families are smaller with fewer children and the generations are more dispersed away from the natal community and even out of the country. Families' involvement in marriage arrangements, childcare and elder care have become attenuated. With the decline in mutual support the traditional duties of the generations to one another have surely weakened. Much the same is true for the home communities where the migration of the able-bodied adults, temporarily or permanently, reduces the pool of those able to cooperate in cultivation, in credit circles, in funeral societies and in providing neighbourly support. As functional interactions decline so does the social cohesion of the community. Movement into the rapidly growing towns and cities brings strangers of different castes, religions and languages together. Young women working in the suburban garment factories move into dormitories with strangers. They have to start afresh in building relationships, testing trustworthiness and then find that friends move on and a new set of strangers moves in. In less transient urban neighbourhoods, stable relations with neighbours, fellow workers and co-religionists exist or are created and so form the bases for social cohesion and collective action. But a fraction of the urban population are recent migrants faced with building new relationships.

At the other extreme of the size range of social units is the state. The Sri Lankan state after independence undertook too many functions and awakened too many expectations. When it began to narrow the beneficiaries to the Sinhala-speaking Buddhists, the marginalized minorities challenged the legitimacy and, subsequently, the very existence of the state. Up until the recent ceasefire agreement between the government and the LTTE, it was possible that the state would lose as much as 20 per cent of its territory and many citizens. Further limiting the capacity of the state was the large foreign debt and continued dependency on foreign aid which constrained the policy alternatives of the government. Also, as foreign direct investment had helped generate jobs and tax revenues it had become a critical concern for officials. If the government altered its investment, trade or fiscal policies, much of that investment could rapidly drain out of the country. And as has been argued earlier, the combination of increasing international media coverage, the capacity of the diasporic activists to influence their host-country governments, and the attention of international NGOs have further narrowed the freedom of action of the government. People in the aid-providing countries with their hands close to the levers of power are watching much more closely what the Sri Lankan government does. In short, the idea of a state as an independent sovereign entity justified by and promoting the ideology of nationalism is losing its force. Perhaps the time has come to move on past the ideology of ethno-nationalism to a new set of ideas supportive of 'a truly pluralist nation state'.

Lying between the largest territorial unit of organization, the state, and the smallest social units of family and community, is a large and amorphous body of organizations. (Some of our contributors select some fraction of these and label it 'civil society'.) We think that it is here, in the midst of a sea of groupings, associations, corporations, parties and organizations, that the support for particular governmental policies and actions will be generated. The individual's voluntary commitment to this group and to that cause can be used to mobilize many individuals through their affiliations. On 25 October 2002 this was reported:

> More than ten thousand people representing workers, farmers, fisherfolk and [others]...held a massive march in Colombo ... insisting that the Government had no right or power to sell the people's resources to transnational corporations .... Spokesman for the Organizers—the Movement for the Protection of National Resources and Human Rights—which brought together some 130 groups for yesterday's demonstration said that national resources did not belong to the government but to the people. The Government had been

given a mandate by the people to develop those resources but not to sell them to global corporations for exploitation. (*Daily Mirror*, Friday, 25 October 2002. Quoted on LacNet, 26 October 2002.)

Examples, more numerous than can be reported, demonstrate the capacity of the leaders of parties, corporations, religious organizations, trade unions, and activists in the NGOs to identify critical issues, mobilize their members and adherents, build alliances and campaign for favoured policies. Such campaigns are conducted in many different settings—from boardrooms and prayer halls to the streets. It is in such collective actions that we find many social cohesions, not just a single dominant one. On certain issues, such as opposing the presence of the Indian Peace Keeping Force or supporting the Peace Movement, millions of Sri Lankans have been united. On other issues, such as the condition of the Tamil estate workers addressed by the Coordinating Secretariat for Plantation Areas, fewer have been united. Social cohesion is group- and issue-specific.

Even though we believe that there has been a shift in power away from the state towards foreign and international agencies and towards intermediate organizations within the country, a state remains important. It is obviously important as the paramount institution to protect the interests of the people of Sri Lanka. The earlier example of the rally to influence government decisions that might lead to global corporate exploitation makes the point. Also important is the function of the state as the keeper of the ground rules for the participation of the multiple intermediate organizations in the public dialogue about future policies. It is mainly through the uncoerced give and take among such organizations that support can be rallied for difficult policy decisions of the future. And it is clearly important that this most inclusive institution urgently addresses the distorting electoral violence. The conditions for governmental renewal must be fair. This is an obvious basic condition for democracy.

Is there some utility for our study in the second initial concept, 'globalization'? We understand globalization to be a cover term for the present effects of a number of largely independent initiatives taken by governments, corporations and other agencies. These initiatives created the technology, the physical and institutional infrastructure and other facilitating innovations, which people and organizations took advantage of for their own purposes. There has been no grand design for globalization but rather a convergence, sometimes with unexpected consequences such as the spread of AIDS, of the uses to which the new structures have been put.

Of the many changes in Sri Lanka, the three that the structures of globalization contributed to most obviously are easing the movement of people, the growth of export manufacturing and the networking of intermediate organizations. These have not been caused by globalization but are the result of people gaining new options and seizing new opportunities. The circumstances—local, national and international—which the individual learns about, provide the grounds for deciding to take advantage of the new options. Approached from this perspective, globalization has increased choices and added to the fluidity of Sri Lankan society. And it also suggests an explanation as to why there has been such a growth of intermediate voluntary organizations. Coming together to share experiences, to offer advice or consolation, to seize new opportunities are part of the individual's means of coping with an increasingly unpredictable environment.

It is here that globalization and social cohesion interact. The options created by the new structures of globalization help to both dissolve prior authority relations and to stimulate the formation of new voluntary organizations. In turn, these organizations are empowering people to question some of the actions of those exploiting the new opportunities for private advantage and potential public risk. And where globalization has created the opportunity for international actors to gain influence over policy making within Sri Lanka, we doubt that it helps in the building of a new, forward-looking society. We have argued that this is the task of Sri Lankans, all of them, in a public and democratic dialogue.

About the Editors and Contributors

The Editors

S.H. HASBULLAH is Senior Lecturer in Geography at the University of Peradeniya, Sri Lanka, and participated as a Resource Person in the Sri Lanka Peace Talks of 2003. He also served as a member of the sub-committee on Immediate and Humanitarian Needs of the War-torn Areas of Sri Lanka. Dr Hasbullah has been Fulbright Research Associate at the Institute for the Study of International Migration, Georgetown University, Washington, D.C. Actively engaged in teaching, research and writing in the areas of demography, employment and migration, he has a special interest in refugees and internally displaced persons. He has written various reports while his articles have been published in edited volumes and journals.

BARRIE M. MORRISON is Professor Emeritus at the Department of Asian Studies and Honorary Professor at the Institute of Asian Studies, University of British Columbia, Vancouver, Canada. He has been a Consultant to the Canadian Ministry of Foreign Affairs and the International Centre for Development Research. His recent research has been on rural social change and agricultural development in Sri Lanka and India. He has published articles on social change in Sri Lanka and development policies in Asia. He has written on the history of Bengal and co-authored books on Kerala and Sri Lanka.

The Contributors

KARUNATISSA ATUKORALA, a Senior Lecturer in Sociology at the University of Peradeniya, has been teaching and researching in the fields of the sociology of development, suicide, youth and children. He has undertaken a number of monitoring and evaluation projects on behalf of national and international organizations and has developed participatory monitoring and evaluation tools. He has participated in a national-level research for the government on the status and options for the handicapped, the elderly, and for households headed by women.

PAUL CASPERSZ, a Sri Lankan Jesuit, founded the Satyodaya Centre for Social Research and Encounter in 1972, which gave birth to the Coordinating Secretariat for the Plantation Areas (CSPA) in 1974. This in turn led to the formation, in 1979, of the Movement for Inter-Racial Justice and Equality. He is the author of several journal and newspaper articles and of *Development, A Third World View*.

DAGMAR HELLMANN-RAJANAYAGAM, currently Privatdozentin at South Asia Institute, University of Heidelberg, commenced her studies at the University of Hamburg and completed her D. Phil and, subsequently, Dr. Habil (D.Litt) at the University of Heidelberg with concentrations in History, Tamil Philology and Comparative Religion. She has taught at universities in India, Sri Lanka and Malaysia. Her research interests are South Indian history, cultural nationalism in India and Sri Lanka, and Indian minorities in Southeast Asia.

BRUCE MATTHEWS is the Dean of Arts and C.B. Lumsden Chair of Comparative Religion at Acadia University, Nova Scotia. He initially went to the University of Ceylon at Peradeniya as a Commonwealth Fellow in Pali and Buddhist Civilization in 1970–71, and has retained an active interest in the peoples, cultures and political affairs of the country for over two decades. He has written extensively about religious issues in Sri Lanka.

SISIRA PINNAWALA, presently Professor in the Department of Sociology at the University of Peradeniya, graduated in Sociology from the University of Ceylon, completed a Masters in Settlement Planning at the Asian Institute of Technology in Bangkok, and read for his doctorate at the Australian National University. In 1992 he served as a Senior Fulbright Fellow in the Peace Studies Program of the Cornell University. Dr Pinnawala's research interests include ethnic studies, study of conflict and violence, and development studies. In addition to his teaching and research he has also provided consultancy services both to the government of Sri Lanka and to several international agencies.

SRI RANJITH, a Senior Lecturer in Economics at the University of Peradeniya, graduated from the University of Peradeniya and obtained an M.A. from the School of Community and Regional Planning at the University of British Columbia. His research interests are presently focused on slum upgrading projects and community participatory development projects at a regional level.

M. SINNATHAMBY, Professor of Economics at the University of Peradeniya, has had long years of close involvement with the Tamil estate workers both as a researcher and as an activist. He is presently participating in studies of the garment industry and the condition of the workers.

SIVAMOHAN SUMATHY, teaches in the English Department, University of Peradeniya. She studied in Sri Lanka and took her Ph.D. from Washington State University. Her interests are critical theory, including Marxism and Feminism, performance studies and film and film theory. At present she is engaged in studying representations of the ethnic conflict in Sri Lankan film.

NANCY WAXLER-MORRISON, Professor Emeritus in Sociology at the University of British Columbia, studied at the University of Illinois and took her Ph.D. from Radcliffe/Harvard. Her special interest is in medical sociology and she has conducted research on psychiatric treatment regimes in Boston and Sri Lanka. She has conducted research on the health of households in Sri Lanka since 1971 and more recently in Kerala, India. She has taught sociology at the University of Peradeniya. She is presently revising a book on cross-cultural health care in Canada.

Index